In Defense of German Colonialism

IN DEFENSE OF
GERMAN
COLONIALISM

And How Its Critics Empowered Nazis, Communists, and the Enemies of the West

BRUCE GILLEY

Author of *The Last Imperialist*

REGNERY GATEWAY
Washington, D.C.

Regnery Gateway™ is a trademark of Salem Communications Holding Corporation
Regnery® is a registered trademark and its colophon is a trademark of Salem Communications Holding Corporation

Cataloging-in-Publication data on file with the Library of Congress

ISBN: 978-1-68451-237-9
eISBN: 978-1-68451-324-6

Published in the United States by
Regnery Gateway, an Imprint of
Regnery Publishing
A Division of Salem Media Group
Washington, D.C.
www.RegneryGateway.com

Manufactured in the United States of America

10 9 8 7 6 5 4 3 2 1

Books are available in quantity for promotional or premium use. For information on discounts and terms, please visit our website: www.Regnery.com.

CONTENTS

Black Berliners and Their White Supporters

I became interested in German colonialism while writing *The Last Imperialist*, a biography of the British colonial governor Sir Alan Burns published in 2021. As a young administrator in West Africa, Burns was sent into combat against neighboring German colonies when the Great War began in 1914. Despite being vastly outnumbered, the African natives fighting for Germany were tenacious and loyal. Native support for the Germans was so vigorous that the young Burns was taken out of the field and sent to British Lagos to recruit more soldiers. All this seemed puzzling to me because, having read what passes for scholarship on German colonialism, I believed that Africans (as well as the Arabs, Chinese, and Samoans) hated the Germans. But if that were so, then why did these peoples rally behind their German governors during the war? In East Africa, the natives did not lay down arms until word came that the fighting had ended in Europe. In West Africa, they followed their colonial masters into exile in neighboring Spanish territory and petitioned world leaders to restore Berlin's authority. Such stubborn facts are incomprehensible to the modern mind, trained as it is to think of European colonial rule as loathsome and unwelcome.

My interest in this footnote to history caught the attention of colleagues in Germany, where calls to "decolonize" the country's understanding of its brief colonial era were running wild. In 2019, I offered an alternative account of this era to legislators and staff of the aptly named Alternative for Germany (AfD), the largest opposition party in the Bundestag. Despite diligent efforts to paint it as a reincarnation of Germany's evil past, the AfD is the only political party in Germany that still believes in the Western tradition. (It is also Israel's most staunch and outspoken defender.) The response to my talk revealed the suppurating sore of anti-colonial activism in Germany. Woke warriors in the city organized a protest outside the Reichstag building for "black Berliners and their white supporters."

About fifty white Germans and perhaps two black people (who may have been tourists) took part in the ritual. The usual mesh of slogans about unrelated issues appeared. One had to notice the "colonialism kills" signboard to guess the focus of the evening's chanting.

Activists protest the author's talk on colonialism inside the Reichstag Building in 2019. The sign on the right reads: "Colonialism Is Murder." *Author's collection*

"There is no such thing as good colonialism!" a young woman wailed into a bullhorn, demanding that my talk be cancelled. I might have joined the protest to partake of the Christmas spiced cookies but feared that I might be "decolonized" in the resulting melee.

In the media, meanwhile, prominent anti-colonial scholars in Germany denounced the talk and insisted that its contents be censored lest any new ideas percolate into the public mind. "This is a conscious provocation!" declared one prominent scholar. "It shows that the federal government has failed to make progress on this important issue of historical guilt and instead allowed it to become a partisan issue up for debate."[1] The *Frankfurter Allgemeine Zeitung* ran an article entitled: "The AfD and German colonial era: Thanks for the oppression!" German colonialism in Africa, the newspaper declaimed, "is a story of cruelty, racism and ruthless humiliation." This conclusion was "beyond dispute," and any dissenting views were "not to be taken seriously."[2]

Inside the building, we had a civilized, dare I say "colonial," discussion. One AfD staffer who is a native of Benin rebuked the Woke white youth outside the building for their arrogance in telling black and brown people what to think about colonial history. "All people in Africa know that what you say is true," the African man said to me at the gathering. "Germany has done a lot of good in Africa. So I want to thank you for your honest words." The talk cost me the friendship of a dear Jewish colleague in the United States who, despite his vast learning, fell easily for the charges that I was consorting with neo-Nazis and promoting Prussian militarism. Fortunately, the AfD had invited members of the press to the gathering, and their coverage suggested a growing fatigue with such nonsense.

My talk was well received by the German public and became the basis for a German-language book, *Verteidigung des deutschen Kolonialismus* (*In Defense of German Colonialism*) published in 2021. In Germany, as elsewhere in the West, the educated public is broadly liberal, tolerant of competing views, and determined to uphold the Western heritage. It is rightly suspicious of the drivel that passes for academic history. As a result, my book is now used widely in independent high schools in Germany by teachers who engage in the daring feat of exposing their charges to more than one point of view.

This revised and expanded English edition takes into account further research as well as critical responses to the German book. It is twice as long as the German version and significantly expands on the thesis that the termination of German colonialism was a major contributing factor to the rise of the Nazi horror in that country and more generally laid the foundations for the series of illiberal movements in Germany that followed, first in the communist-inspired movements of the Cold War and then in the debilitating Woke activism of our days. All this, I argue, is critical to understanding the great hole that now stands at the center of Europe. Rebuilding Western civilization requires many hands. One of the most important of these will seize back an objective understanding of Germany's brief colonial era.

I am grateful to Regnery and to Harry Crocker III, author of *The Politically Incorrect Guide to the British Empire*, for bringing this politically incorrect guide to German colonialism to English language readers.

Bruce Gilley
Portland, Oregon
September 15, 2021

CHAPTER 1

Laying the Prussian Lash on German Colonial History

I n 2019, anti-colonial activists in Berlin erected a plaque outside the former headquarters of Germany's colonial office. The plaque honored the life of the black African Martin Dibobe, who at the age of twenty in 1896 was sent from the colony of German Cameroon to participate in the Berlin Trade Fair. The activists considered Dibobe one of the colonial project's victims, but he was in fact one of its most avid supporters. Seeing that life was better in Germany than in Africa, Dibobe remained after the fair. He was offered a job with the Berlin train system, in which he worked his way up to the position of senior driver, becoming something of a local celebrity. In May 1919, when Germany was about to be formally stripped of its colonies during negotiations at Versailles, Dibobe wrote to the last German colonial minister Johannes Bell hoping for a miracle:

> The people cling to Germany with all their energy and firm conviction. The only wish of the natives is to stay German. The Socialist [Party] represents their interests in the Reichstag and the natives have been recognized as citizens by the former imperial government. . . . The natives cannot wish

1

for a better lot than the [1919 Weimar Constitution] has brought them.... We reaffirm to the government all of our dedication as well as our unbreakable, firm loyalty.... With this appeal we assure the government that we want to remain German.[1]

The following month, Dibobe and seventeen other Africans from German colonies wrote another letter, adding a thirty-two-point list of priorities. Only with continued German rule in Cameroon, they wrote, could the successful political and economic development of the area continue. "We protest against the rape of the colonies" by the Allied powers and "swear our unswerving allegiance" to Germany, they began. Under the new Weimar Constitution, Germany would live up to ever-higher standards of colonial rule, bringing untold advances to peoples who just a generation before lived in

The Cameroonian Martin Dibobe (center) with Berlin train system colleagues, 1902.
Berliner Verkehrsbetriebe Archive

jungles: equality before the law, an independent legal system, an end to discrimination, permanent representation for Africans in the German legislature, German education, Christian religious instruction, and the establishment of a regular colonial police force.[2] It was a stirring appeal for colonial rule and progress.

Dibobe's letter and petition were cited at the time as evidence of the success and legitimacy of German colonialism. Unfortunately, his arguments fell on deaf ears at Versailles. Refused re-entry to Cameroon by the new French administration in 1921, Dibobe disappeared from history.

Dibobe's story encapsulates the German colonial story—its success in extending the benefits of liberal civilization, its legitimacy and support among natives, and the tragedy of its premature termination by the Allied powers after 1919. It is odd then that the plaque erected by anti-colonial activists in 2019 told a wholly different story: that Dibobe was a "victim" of colonialism, that he "resisted" German rule, and that his unexpected and voluminous statements in support of German rule were just clever forms of deceit that concealed "implicit" anti-colonial messages. Rather than communicate how Dibobe represents the mutual benefits and enrichment of the German-African encounter, the plaque tells a distortionary story of German guilt and African victimization. The same year the city government of Berlin voted to erect a memorial to "all victims of German colonialism." It is high time to challenge the unfounded and mischievous abuse of German colonial history, which reflects a more general assault on Western or European colonial history that began in the 1960s.

In recent years there has been a growing interest in resurrecting a more balanced account of European colonialism, including German colonialism. A large amount of research has emerged to show that colonialism was both objectively beneficial and subjectively legitimate.[3] Countries that were colonized more intensely and for longer periods had faster economic growth, higher standards of living, more democratic politics, better health, better education, better safeguarding of human rights, and better legal systems. Countries that threw off colonialism too soon, or that were never colonized, did worse. Moreover, countries whose post-colonial leaders clung more closely to the colonial inheritance did better as independent states. The countries seized by anti-colonial radicals collapsed into famine, civil war, and tyranny. It is a cruel irony that the most virulent anti-colonial critics from the Third World all prefer living in the West rather than in their "liberated" homelands.

Today, anti-colonialism is synonymous with all sorts of contemporary "social justice" movements. The African activist Arlette-Louise Ndakoze, for instance (who prefers living in Germany to her native Burundi), wrote for the features section of taxpayer-funded German radio in 2018: "German colonialism was a crime against humanity. . . . Its imperialism finds expression today in globalization, in neoliberalism, in racism." To be anti-colonial today, she averred, means to oppose "Germany's political, economic and cultural position."[4] Nothing could better summarize the sweeping condemnations and contemporary radical agendas of anti-colonial dogma. Anti-colonial activists will not cease their efforts until Germany and other former colonial powers, as well as Anglo settlement countries, are reduced to ashes.

The debate on European colonialism is thus strongly relevant to the present. It bears on the future not just of Germany but of other former colonial powers of the West—especially Britain, France, Belgium, the Netherlands, and Portugal—as well as the major Anglo-settlement colonies of the United States, Canada, Australia, and New Zealand. It plays a direct role in shaping contemporary policies relating to foreign aid, immigration, domestic cultural policy, and international relations. Where those policies are informed by a misplaced sense of guilt, they not only impose unjust penalties on the citizens of Western countries but they also do grave harms to the supposed beneficiaries in the Third World. Anti-colonial dogmas strike at the very heart of concepts like civilization, modernity, and human welfare. Everything from urban planning to the internal combustion engine have been assailed as "colonial," leading to the necessary conclusion that decolonization requires a great leap backwards in human progress. When applied to Western countries, the "decolonize" agenda has been used to advocate a ghettoization of non-white communities and a government takeover of a free society. There is much at stake in getting the colonial record straight. The study of Germany's fleeting colonial era opens a window to a much larger debate on the West itself.

• • •

Until World War I, German colonialism was widely praised in Europe, especially in Britain. There was wide admiration for what this relative latecomer had achieved in its colonies. Despite, or perhaps because of, the constant eruption of "colonial scandals" invented by Socialists in the Reichstag, Germany was seen as an advanced colonial trustee. As an eminent American historian wrote, "If an opinion poll had been taken in England before August 1914, the result probably would have been that the Germans were regarded as better colonial rulers than any others except the British."[5] After the Great War, everything changed. The Allies rewrote German colonial history as a tale of woe and oppression. They needed to justify their seizure of German colonies at Versailles. A British Colonial Office mandarin, writing under the pseudonym Africanus, published *The Prussian Lash in Africa* in 1918, an early entry into a genre that described German colonialism as "a system resting on force and cruelty, a system based on slavery, a system of naked exploitation."[6] In the inter-war period, first the Stalinists in Russia and then the Nazis in Germany poured scorn on the German colonial record. Both Stalin and Hitler styled themselves "liberators" of black and brown people from decadent Western-liberal civilization. After World War II, things got worse for the German colonial reputation. The colonial archives were marooned in East Germany, where propagandists were put to work churning out Leninist critiques about "the proletariat" in the jungles of Cameroon. After the Cold War, Woke progressives took up the harness, carrying on the grand tradition of historical distortion.

But from the time of the Treaty of Versailles to the present, some free-spirited scholars have challenged anti-colonial orthodoxies. William Harbutt Dawson, a member of the British delegation at Versailles, was an early example of an independent-minded scholar who broke with his country's official position and declared that German colonialism had been a success. In 1926, Dawson wrote a lengthy foreword to a book on the German colonial achievement of the last governor of German East Africa, Heinrich Schnee. The "shabby annexations" at Versailles, Dawson warned, were a major sore point that undermined mainstream support for democracy in Germany.[7] In 1938, a Yale historian, Harry Rudin, published the results of his fieldwork in the 1920s in the former German Cameroon, noting that "wherever I went, I heard natives praise the excellent German administration."[8] The last time anyone had anything positive to say about German colonialism was in 1977, when two Stanford economists published a book on the excellence of German colonial administration.[9]

The dominant approach today to the study of Germany's colonial era is a sneering, judgmental trial of alleged crimes. It is not scholarship so much as ideological vivisection. Very little meets the most basic standards of scientific research. It begins with conclusions and then selects and interprets evidence to fit the desired narrative. Those conclusions are held ever more tenaciously as contemporary political agendas are added to scholarly considerations. Academics today see their role as bringing the German people to trial for the blood debt of colonialism. As two leading exponents of this prosecutorial history wrote in a 2010 book: "Germans believed that they had nothing to do with the colonial exploitation of large parts of Africa, Asia or South America. They were innocent—so many believed—of the devastations brought about by European colonialism and could therefore engage with the new post-colonial world without the dark shadow of a colonial past."[10] According to such claims, the "exploitation" and "devastations" did not need to be proved, only asserted, to carry out the revolutionary war on the German past and present. In a typical classroom in Germany today, the unsuspecting students are perp-walked through colonial history, unless they are the children of migrants, in which case they are used as victimized stage props.

Today, most that is published about German colonialism (as with other Western colonial episodes) is nonsense, as I showed in responding to critics of my 2017 article "The Case for Colonialism."[11] Very little meets the most basic standards of social scientific research. The overwhelming majority of work is ideological, biased, and often self-contradictory. History as a field today often reads like free-form flights of literary fancy that combine with strong normative agendas, turning the historical past into a plaything for modern intellectuals. German colonialism in particular seems to bring out the very worst of this tendency thanks to the license the Nazi era grants intellectuals to pummel German history.

The de facto mandate for scholars to take an anti-colonial stance at the very least presents a problem for our understanding of the past. Since only one viewpoint is permitted, the knowledge researchers generate is defective. In this sense, the received scholarly wisdom on German colonialism suffers from the same acute problems as scholarship on Western colonialism more broadly. In a nutshell, anti-colonial conclusions are so deeply entrenched as the nonnegotiable starting point for all research (young scholars will quickly find themselves out of a job if they dissent) that there is *no possibility* that valid findings could *ever* emerge, except by fluke or by some fool purposively stepping outside of the groupthink consensus. So long as anyone who challenges anti-colonial conclusions is branded a racist and subjected to mob attacks, the conditions for scientific research into colonialism will not exist. Most scholarship on German colonialism for the last half century fails to meet these criteria. It is as untrustworthy as a pharmaceutical drug produced in a laboratory filled with viruses and bacteria.

To make your mark as an "expert" on German colonialism today requires following a few simple steps: find something you do not like in the contemporary world; find any link, no matter how tenuous, to the German colonial era; and finally, attribute the former to the latter. Presto! We have an all-purpose explanation for everything that ever went wrong in the Third World and, for good measure, an all-purpose explanation for the wealth, freedom, and civilization of the West. According to this dogma, the factors normally used to explain the rise of the West—the Greco-Roman and Judeo-Christian heritage, the medieval inheritance, the Reformation, the Enlightenment, the Industrial Revolution—are all self-serving myths. Rather, Germany owes its position in the world today to the unpaid labor it used to build railways in Togo! By that logic, contemporary Libya and Somalia, where slavery and forced labor persist, should be emerging giants of the global economy.

To triumphantly ascend to the top of the ladder, young scholars must learn obscure jargon and fragile moral posturing: the wicked German colonialists were "Eurocentric"; they "othered" their subjects; their knowledge was "epistemic violence"; the motivation was "desire"; the jobs they offered were "exploitation"; every instance of the use of force was "genocidal"; everyday government was "structural genocide"; and so on. Anti-colonial dogma has become the magical lantern of an entire intellectual cohort. It seems fitting therefore that scholars who specialize in fairy tales and children's fiction have recently taken up prominent positions in the field of research on German colonialism.[12] As one scholar wrote approvingly of this new trend, "Scholars of (post)colonialism have long asserted that the significance of colonialism in the metropole needs to be analyzed within the realm of fantasy and the imagination."[13]

A summary of this "scientific" approach can be seen at the Frankfurt Research Center for Postcolonial Studies. It promises that German taxpayer monies will be used to combat the "normative violence" of colonialism that the center defines as "rationality, progress,

Germany's chief anti-colonial professor, Jürgen Zimmerer, virtue signaling his decolonizing *bona fides* by posing with a Herero "victim" in Namibia. *Author's collection*

and development." Not surprisingly, the center is headed by Nikita Dhawan, a native of India, a country that has exported more anti-colonial bombast to the West (its chief export as the joke goes) than any other. Dhawan's other projects have included efforts at "decolonizing the Enlightenment" and espousing "the erotics of resistance."

Few better encapsulate such utter detachment from historical reality than the foreman of this medieval torture chamber, Hamburg University's Jürgen Zimmerer. Zimmerer rose to the peaks of the historical profession by making the bizarre argument as early as 2003 that German colonialism caused the Holocaust. Here, for instance, is Zimmerer offering up to *Der Spiegel* what he means by colonialism: "If you understand colonialism more broadly, even as the self-imposed right to change regimes somewhere; if you see it as a system of unequal relationships, then you can say that we are still living in a colonial world."[14] Zimmerer is a theorist of "unequal relationships," which he believes are always bad. The stuff of colonialism is therefore merely a plaything for his tantrum against a grown-up world filled with "unequal relationships" and inequality.

There are of course some exceptions. A 2017 book in German titled *Die Deutschen und ihre Kolonien: Ein Überblick* (The Germans and Their Colonies: An Overview) steered clear of sweeping condemnations in favor of the "everyday experiences" of people who lived under German colonial rule.[15] It was immediately condemned. The Congolese activist George Kibala Bauer, who prefers to live in Germany, charged that the book "falls short of critically examining the legacy of German colonialism."[16] Despite its many critical chapters and sections, the problem for Kibala was that *any* open-minded inquiry about the colonial record was unacceptable. Works that did not begin with the premise of colonial evil and then torture the evidence to confess were to be scorned. Unbiased data selection, logic, and testing (the critical and precious legacies of

Western civilization) were part of the "problem"—the "normative violence"—to be eliminated by anti-colonial activists like Kibala Bauer, Zimmerer, and Dhawan.

One of the coeditors of that 2017 book, the German academic Horst Gründer, is no stranger to the virulence of anti-colonial rage in the German academy. He has been called the dean of German colonial history. He earned his credentials through careful and unbiassed research rather than political activism and social-justice grandstanding. As part of a television series and accompanying book in 2005, Gründer was charged by Zimmerer with the unforgiveable sin of saying that there were *some* positive values in Germany's colonial past.[17] Gründer's failure to conform to the rigid ideology of anti-colonialism, another professor decried with a straight face, "shows that extensive factual knowledge does not protect against equally problematic interpretations."[18] Gründer responded that these anti-colonial activists were ignorant of how historical processes unfold and held a romanticized view of what would have happened in the colonial areas absent German rule. One thing is clear: the anti-colonial establishment in Germany will ensure that no scholar of Gründer's caliber ever emerges again.

• • •

Before leaping into the particular experiences of German colonialism, it is worth making a few general points about European colonialism. By European colonialism, I am referring to what the American scholar David Abernathy defined as the period of European expansion from the early 1800s to the mid-1900s. This epoch should be distinguished from the earlier waves of European exploration, trade, and settlement because it was the first time, according to Abernathy, that empires were seen as places where the governance model of the home state would be replicated.

Brazil became independent from Portugal in 1822, marking the end of the first era of mainly Spanish, Dutch, and Portuguese expansion. Two years later, in 1824, the British began a major expansion of their South Asian territory by pushing into what would become Burma or Myanmar, marking the beginning of the second era. What distinguishes these two eras is not just the different European powers involved (Spain, for instance, largely disappeared as a serious colonial player) but more importantly the different ideas and institutions that came with modern European colonialism. While the word initially connoted the settlement of people, often with little or no control over events by the colonial power, in the course of the nineteenth century it came to connote more the orderly settlement of ideas and institutions—in particular liberal toleration, political representation, the rule of law, property rights, and the security of borders. This "sane imperialism" as the English liberal politician Lord Rosebery described it in 1899, was distinct from the "wild-cat imperialism" of the past and as such was "nothing but this: a larger patriotism."[19]

It was these Enlightenment ideas and institutions, far more than soldiers and administrators, that colonized the world. Sending settlers, building a fort, or establishing a silver mine was now disparaged as "mere" or "wild-cat" imperialism. The new patriotic vocation of European nations like Britain, France, and Germany was to share their liberal institutions with the world for the betterment of all. "Colonialism" represented a more elevated vocation in which improving the lives of subject peoples through a transfer of liberal norms and impersonal-governance institutions was the goal.

In terms of dimensions, by 1913, European colonialism consisted of British India (about 63 percent of all colonial peoples) and the rest. The rest was made up of three more or less equally sized pieces with about 10 percent of the global colonial population each: the rest of the British Empire, French colonies, and Dutch colonies. The leftover

7 percent was about 2 percent each of German, Belgian, and Portuguese colonies, and a small Italian remainder.[20] This is why debates on the British Empire, and India in particular, loom so large in the overall debate on European colonialism. Still, each of the roughly eighty European colonies in 1913 has its own value in reaching conclusions irrespective of its size. German colonialism, because it was limited to just seven colonies and lasted only thirty years, provides a powerful lesson in rapid results.

Much of the debate on colonialism involves complex empirical arguments about what happened, why it happened, what would have happened otherwise, and what the locals thought about the whole thing. But we can briefly step back and ask a simpler question: If a people in a subsistence condition had an opportunity to be governed by a state with a political and economic system that patently made lives better (children surviving childhood, diseases held at bay, violent death controlled, food supply plentiful, and a far more liberal regime than anything locally available, et cetera) how would they respond and what would be the results? Obviously, some native powerholders would be wary. They would accept European colonization if it would boost their status and oppose it if not. The people, meanwhile, would mainly support the takeover: the proportion of the local population rallying in support would far outnumber those who rallied behind resistant elites. The "pull" factors from native populations would be as strong as the "push" factors that brought Europeans to their shores. European rulers would be reluctant to get involved unless there were economic, military, or diplomatic gains. Where they did get involved, all parties had a stake in making the encounter mutually beneficial.

Inevitably, the European rulers would be fatigued by colonial rule because of the net economic and fiscal costs of providing public goods to strangers. There would also be growing criticism from liberals on the home front as well as from the newly educated and growing native population that colonialism itself had nurtured. Attempts to fully incorporate those colonies into the home state would be infeasible. Once it became apparent that the European will to govern was flagging, local opportunists styling themselves "liberators," "nationalists," and "anti-colonial resisters" would step into the political vacuum demanding self-government and independence. Their "success" would be a fiction: they were pushing on an open door and had little idea what they wanted or why. Generations of adulatory biographies would be written about these "nationalists": but the real nationalists or national heroes were the late colonial administrators who took an enlightened interest in preparations for self-government and created the conditions for its attainment.

If colonialism had not lasted long enough or gone deeply enough with the new elites, their post-colonial rule would be disastrous. Within months or years, the states would be in crisis, thrown back into the primitive conditions of their pre-colonial worlds. Civil war, famine, and tyranny would quickly return. Critics would blame the colonial rulers. But blame would lie locally. The few native leaders who insisted on continuity with colonial rule—constitutional government, a free market economy, an independent rule of law—would avert the nightmare of decolonization. Just as the catastrophes would be blamed on colonialism, these few success stories would be attributed to indigenous brilliance. The gift of colonial rule would be forgotten.

• • •

That is, in a nutshell, the logical argument for European colonialism. The empirical evidence in its favor is strong.[21] The reason that little of this is known is that scholars prefer to comb through the colonial archives and cherry-pick evidence that they find objectionable—racist comments

by settlers, abusive behavior by administrators, and unfair business practices by white traders. Yet this tells us nothing about
whether colonialism was good or bad overall, a judgement that
depends both on a consideration of the conditions under which
it operated and a consideration of what would have befallen these
places otherwise.

To take a "germane" example, much has been made of the case
of Heinrich Leist, acting governor of German Cameroon. In 1893,
Leist came into conflict with native soldiers from the region of
Dahomey over pay and work conditions. After they tried to kill him,
Leist whipped their wives and arrested the conspirators, hanging
several of them. After an official investigation, he was charged with
brutality for the whippings. He was tried in Potsdam, found guilty,
and removed from his position. Legislators debated the case in the
Reichstag and introduced a new legal code to manage labor relations
in the colonies.

What should an intelligent person make of this case? Certainly,
they should not take their cue from German academics, who fly into
a rage with cries of misogyny, racism, and exploitation. These great
minds make no effort to imagine what it was like for a lone German
official in a remote station to bring security and development to a
region long plagued by tribal warfare and human carnage. In addition to his governing duties, Leist was patron of the local nursing
association that cared for rescued black slave children. He also,
unusually, offered free medical services to all black staff lucky enough
to work for the German authorities.[22] More pointedly, the Dahomey
soldiers who rebelled had been purchased by a German explorer from
a local chief who planned to use them in a human sacrifice ritual.
Their fate under German colonialism was far better than under tribal
rule.[23] How many Dahomey women and slave children would have
been beaten, whipped, and left to die by fellow Africans absent

German colonial rule? Was the overall trend of justice under the Germans improving or getting worse?

During the Leist trial, one Reichstag critic brandished the hippo-leather whip that Leist had borrowed from the natives to flog the women. Why did the natives have hippo-leather whips? Because corporal punishment was widely practiced in West African society for theft, infidelity, and unpaid debts. The use of flogging, as in Europe not long before, was considered more humane and effective than other forms of punishment. Most criminals could not pay fines while prison was considered a luxury because of the food and bedding. Flogging as a form of punishment had been abolished in Germany itself only in 1871. In fact, everything about the Leist case sounds a ringing endorsement of German dominion. If this is the "dark side," then there is clearly a marvel awaiting discovery.

Moreover, a quirk of German politics at the time was that the Reichstag had very little to occupy its time except making grand speeches on colonial affairs. It controlled the colonial budget and used this power to enhance its authority. "Participation in colonial debates and in the establishment of the colonial budget became the means to legitimize the delegates' presence in the legislative building," noted two German scholars.[24] Legislative critics, like contemporary Woke warriors in the academy, swung freely from criticism that there was too much German colonialism to criticism that there was too little. One legislator, who had freely criticized the disruption, exploitation, cultural imperialism, and coercion of the German colonial endeavor, did an about face in 1895 and assailed the authorities for their failure to engage adequately in "road construction, the development of natural resources, raising the material and moral condition of the population," and "protection for security and justice."[25] The skepticism with which anti-colonial historians normally treat official records on colonialism is thrown to the

wind when it comes to the moralizing speeches of Reichstag legislators on "colonial scandals" and "colonial failings" (too little or too
much). They rush to judgement, citing such debates as irrefutable
evidence of colonial misrule.[26] These debates are better seen as
evidence of the robust liberal institutions through which German
worked its colonial miracle. If this is the "dark side," then the critics
must be at a loss for good evidence.

● ● ●

I will highlight three rigorous pieces of scientific research showing
the benefits of European colonial rule—one concerning economics,
one concerning politics, and one concerning social legitimacy.

Islands offer an almost perfect natural experiment in colonialism's economic effects because their discovery by Europeans was
sufficiently random. As a result, they should not have been affected
by the "pull" factors that made some places easier to colonize than
others. In a 2009 study of the effects of colonialism on the income
levels of people on eighty-one islands, two Dartmouth College economists found "a robust positive relationship between colonial tenure
and modern outcomes."[27] Bermuda and Guam are better off than
Papua New Guinea and Fiji because they were colonized for longer.
That helps explain why the biggest countries with limited or no
formal colonial periods (especially China, Ethiopia, Egypt, Iran,
Thailand, and Nepal) or whose colonial experiences ended before the
modern colonial era (Brazil, Mexico, Guatemala, and Haiti) are
hardly compelling as evidence that not being colonized was a boon.
The people of "liberated" Haiti began fleeing to the colonial Bahamas
or to the slave-owning and later-segregated American South almost
as soon as they were "free" from the white man. One can applaud
their sense of irony.

Of course, colonialism often (not always) made the colonizers better off as well. But if our concern is with the absolute well-being of the colonized compared to their situation before colonialism, or absent colonialism, the economic advantages of being colonized are clear. As the English economist Joan Robinson once quipped, "the misery of being exploited by capitalists is nothing compared to the misery of not being exploited all."[28] A piece of native doggerel from the German period in East Africa put it nicely:

> Police and houseboys
> All are at work
> At the end of the day
> Gathered around a table
> They get a lot of money
> Money pleases their hearts
> And removes doubts
> We praise Germany![29]

Colonialism also enhanced later political freedoms. To be colonized in the nineteenth–twentieth-century era was to have much better prospects for democratic government, according to a statistical study of 143 colonial episodes by the Swedish economist Ola Olsson in 2009.[30] Since Germany's colonies were short-lived, sparse in number, and later folded into British and French colonies, Olsson's research could not identify the precise democratic contribution of German colonialism. However, what explained the democratic legacies of colonialism, he argued, was not particular national strategies but the more common European principles of free trade, humanitarianism, property rights, the rule of law, native uplift, and constraints on political executives, factors certainly present in the German colonies: "All this strongly suggests to us that colonization during the imperialist era, regardless of the nationality of the colonizer or the particular circumstances in the colonies, should be more conducive to current levels of democracy than colonialism under mercantilism."[31] The Danish political scientist Jacob Hariri, meanwhile, found in a study of 111 countries that those not colonized because of the existence of strong premodern state, or only symbolically ruled by Europeans piggybacking on traditional institutions, were more likely to be saddled with a dysfunctional state and political system later on.[32]

These twin legacies of economic development and political liberalism brought with them a host of social and cultural benefits—improved public health, the formation of education systems, the articulation and documentation of cultural diversity, the rights of women and minorities, and much else. It is no wonder, then, that colonized peoples by and large supported colonial rule. They migrated closer to more intensive areas of colonialism, paid taxes and reported crimes to colonial authorities, fought for colonial armies, administered colonial policies, and celebrated their status as colonial subjects. Without the willing collaboration of large parts of the population, colonialism would have been impossible. One scholar called this "the non-European foundations of European imperialism."[33] Were this not true, it is hard to imagine how colonies could have survived since the number of expatriate policemen, soldiers, and administrators in most colonies was vanishingly small relative to land areas and populations. The Swiss historian Bouda Etemad estimated that there were 3,300 colonial subjects for every *one* European soldier in the European empires in 1913, a figure roughly twenty times greater than the ratio of citizens to soldiers at home. Even if one includes native soldiers in the calculation, the number of colonized people per soldier was still six times greater in the colonies than in Europe. "The rulers remained lost among the indigenous masses," Etemad noted.[34]

Those averages overstate the military presence because most of the time soldiers were concentrated in whatever part of a colony

German colonial trading cards illustrate the cover of this book's German-language edition. *Manuscriptum Publishers*

faced the gravest security threat. European rule was so benign that some natives did not even know they were under European rule. Colonial officials, meanwhile, could go for months without ever receiving instructions from Europe. "In much of Africa, the colonial imprint was barely noticeable," assayed the prize-winning historian Martin Meredith.[35]

While some historians bend over backwards to insist that native collaboration and support for colonial rule were only clever ploys, this "semantic obfuscation," as two scholars called it, cannot hide the fact that many colonies consciously submitted to European rule for purposes of economic improvement, security from rival tribes, and the overthrow of tyranny within their own groups.[36] Whether explained by "self-interest" or "legitimacy," the fact is that colonialism was a welcome intrusion.

• • •

Are there any reasons to suppose that German colonialism did not conform to this more general pattern of European colonialism? Was there anything distinctive about Germany or its colonial approach that would have rendered the benefits of colonialism and its legitimacy absent? The answer is no. If anything, Germany was a typical European colonizer, whether judged by its administrative style, its economic policies, its social and cultural approaches, or its general legitimacy. As two German scholars concluded, "The imperialists, including the Germans, provided peace, settled rule, an expanded trade area, infrastructure, bureaucracy, a tax system—the essentials of a modern state which would rule over a wider swath of territory than would have obtained if African and Pacific ethnic rivalries had been allowed to persist." Faced with similar circumstances, "Germans acted much like their French and British imperial counterparts."[37]

If there is anything distinctive about German colonialism, other than its short tenure and unusual legislative oversight at home, it is that the German state never tried to incorporate its colonies into the mother country, even as part of some loose federation. Indeed, they were not referred to as *Kolonien* but as *Schutzgebiete*, or "protected areas." A united Germany was just a few decades old, and it was hardly time to think about digesting newer and more culturally distinct peoples. Hoisting the German flag always made for an awkward moment in the colonies because Germany still did not have a national anthem. Sometimes, a German ditty was sung to the tune of "God Save the Queen," which led some locals to believe they had been colonized by the British.

This meant that German colonialism entailed "a certain respect for local institutions,"[38] since it was assumed that German rule would always be at arm's length. Unlike the education systems in British and French colonies, education in German colonies offered instruction in local histories, cultures, and geographies, alongside the normal "technical" subjects that reflected the technical nature of education in Germany itself. This meant, unusually, that local language instruction, whether Samoan, Swahili, or Chinese, took precedence, unlike in other European colonies where the official language of the colonizer was used.

Not surprisingly, local-language media and publications would flourish. The Germans, according to one study based on interviews with the German publishers of Swahili newspapers in East Africa, considered such undertakings to be "cultural institutions" (*Kulturfaktor*) and thus made sure that every word was written by blacks and for blacks, "the property of the black people from the moment the pen was dipped in the inkwell until the written word was published."[39] Indeed, through its formalization and propagation by an official language school in Berlin, Germany transformed Swahili from a coastal language of Muslim elites to the lingua franca for the future country of Tanzania.[40]

Of course, for the modern Woke warriors, the Germans are damned no matter what they did in the realm of language and culture. They are accused of imposing "dominating" and "oppressing" German traditions on Africa, while their efforts to embrace and promote local traditions are denounced as "appropriating" and "infiltrating." Radical scholars work feverishly to "deconstruct" the "colonial myth" that Swahili flourished because of German rule. The secret desire of the Germans, according to one conspiratorial professor, was to impose German on everyone. But they were thwarted by the reality of wide Swahili use and thus willy-nilly ended up promoting it, zombie-like, against their better judgement: "They tried to come to terms with coastal Swahili society, and to use the coast as their power base, a decision which could only further encourage the spread of Swahili, no matter what their intentions might be." The German government's active promotion of Swahili in administration, media, and education, according to this professor, was due to a devious plan "to rule effectively."[41]

The conspiratorial professor argues that instruction in German was withheld because the Germans did not want "to demystify the culture which it represented, and to expose the complex tensions within German society." They also did not want "to encourage its use as an *Einheitssprache* (a unifying language), and to encourage a new elite which could fight colonialism on European terms." In the next sentence, we find that the Germans also *undermined* their rule by refraining from education in German. This caused a lack of "trained petty administrators needed to sustain dominance. It allowed, as in the case of Swahili, another language to become the *Einheitssprache*." Worst of all for these incorrigible racists, it "implied a failure in the attempt to spread one's 'superior' culture."[42]

Woke historians try to have it both ways. Cases where the Germans imposed their language on Africans show that they wanted to oppress the native population by erasing their culture. Instances where they did not also show that the Germans were racists and wanted to oppress the natives, this time by denying Africans access to the language of power. Today, the luckless German colonialists are evil no matter what they did or how much support they enjoyed. The intellectual gymnastics are gold-medal quality.

The sniping about language policy is a good example of scholars' squirming and fidgeting to discredit a colonial good with a series of protestations. They say Swahili was already spreading before the Germans arrived; some Germans opposed its use; when it was officially adopted, not enough was done to educate the poor; most of the actual work was done by Africans not Germans; the "true intention" was to sustain colonial rule and its racist project; and so on. Only after a series of such derogations, can scholars at last, very tentatively, and hoping not to be branded racists and colonial apologists, eke out a single sentence of praise, albeit anonymously: "The German colonial authorities and German scholarship certainly made a valuable contribution."[43]

A final quirk of German colonialism was that it did not have much support at home. While Lenin would later insist that colonialism was driven by a voracious greed for profits and imperial egotism, German colonial enthusiasts had trouble overcoming the indifference of businessmen and politicians. Most trade in and out of German colonies was done by the British and French. The business community in Germany preferred to invest in the United States, Canada, South Africa, and Egypt. As the evenhanded scholars Arthur Knoll and Hermann Hiery wrote: "If the German African empire had been measured against the criterion of economic utility, the Reich should have traded or sold it."[44] Other than some oddball adventurers who enjoyed living in places where women went topless, the most enthusiastic constituency for colonialism was found among the Socialists. Following Marx, they believed that colonialism was a boon for breaking down feudal social systems and paving the road to communism.

So while German colonialism differed in some ways from European colonialism more broadly speaking, these divergences were not essential. If anything, the German colonial project was more humane and less self-interested than that of the other European powers. This only meant that German colonialism provided more benefits to natives than the already beneficial European project, something Woke historians will never be able to admit.

CHAPTER 2

The Spirit of Berlin

In the winter of 1884–85, the chancellor of a novice country called Germany, Otto von Bismarck, convened a conference of fourteen European nations and other major powers to discuss colonialism in Africa. Competing claims in West Africa and the Congo set the agenda, but the conference ended up establishing principles that became the guiding ideals of the European colonial mission as a whole. This "Spirit of Berlin" was particularly relevant to Germany because its colonial era was just beginning. There was no "dark past" that needed to be excused, reformed, or forgotten. Instead, the Germans took pride that they had set a new standard for excellence in colonial administration.

It was fitting that Bismarck was the man presiding. Only the previous decade, as president of the old Germanic kingdom of Prussia, he had "colonized" twenty-six disparate territories to form the new state of Germany. Replacing archaic political systems with a modern state was something he knew well. During the meeting at his residence in Berlin, Bismarck engineered a remarkable shift in the rules of the colonial game. This shift would shape every aspect of the German colonial project that followed.

Since founding Germany in 1871, Bismarck had displayed nothing but disdain for colonialism. This was despite the urgings of modernization theorists like Max Weber who famously called the creation of Germany a "youthful prank" (*Jugendstreich*) that would be worthwhile only if the young nation made something of itself on the world stage. German traders were establishing depots, factories, and coaling stations flying the German flag across Asia, Africa, and the Middle East. But when pressed, the chancellor always demurred. No matter what exotic colonial prospects were offered to him—Mozambique, Ecuador, Tunis, Curaçao, Formosa, Morocco—Bismarck showed little interest. "No colonialism as long as I am chancellor," was his oft-repeated phrase.

The absence of German colonialism up to this point is inexplicable from the standpoint of the contemporary illuminati. At its founding in 1871, the economy of unified Germany was larger than that of France and just a third smaller than that of Britain. No other European countries came close. On the Leninist theory of capitalist development, Germany should have been brimming with imperialist agitation to boost profits and loot raw materials from hapless brown people. People like Max Weber should have carried the day. At one point, the French even offered the Germans all of Indochina in return for Alsace-Lorraine, a lordly trinket that would have sent the Frankfurt Stock Exchange sky-high. Yet most German capital invested abroad was in Europe or the Americas. German investors in colonial areas preferred British and French possessions to what eventually became German colonies. The wildcat traders who occasionally sent telegrams to Berlin to announce they were standing by to proclaim a German colony in some tropical port were comical. The theory that colonialism was impelled by greedy big business or bourgeois restiveness is disproven by the German case.

No less confounding to modern professors is Germany's status as the undisputed center of research and knowledge on non-European areas. In the infamous formulation of the Palestinian professor of literature Edward Said, the West's curiosity about other areas "fatally tended towards the systematic accumulation of human beings and territories." In other words, obscure scholarship on the religions, art, literature, cultures, and histories of places like Syria and China would cause countries like Germany to itch for foreign conquest. The flowering of "Orientalist" scholarship in places like Germany, according to Said, could "elucidate subsequent developments," in particular the rise of an "explicitly colonial-minded imperialism."[1]

There are many logical contradictions in Said's theory. His insistence that all Orientalist knowledge was false and distorted sits uneasily with his simultaneous claim that this knowledge was so excellent that it helped Europeans to dominate foreign cultures. In addition, he insists that all claims of "true" knowledge are narratives, which begs the question of how something can be false.

The main empirical problem for his theory is that it cannot account for Germany. It is like a theory of war that cannot account for peace. Said recognized "the great scientific prestige that accrued to German scholarship by the middle of the nineteenth century." Even by 1830, he wrote, German scholarship "had fully attained its European preeminence."[2] If so, we should observe a cohort of German politicians and diplomats brined in Orientalist learning demanding overseas expansion. The problem, as with the Leninist theory, is that the actors do not play their parts as assigned. German officials, like German capitalists, did not lift a finger for colonialism. Both groups demeaned such acquisitions as a waste of time. When it came, German colonialism was modest, and it never reached the Middle East and North Africa where Germany's Orientalist excellence was unsurpassed. "[Edward] Said very conveniently leaves out the important contributions of German Orientalists, for their inclusion would destroy—and their exclusion does indeed totally destroy—the central thesis," wrote the Pakistani scholar Ibn Warraq. Perhaps, Warraq joked, the German scholars were secretly in the pay of imperialists in Britain and France.[3]

The flinty professor Said variously excused, defended, and apologized for his theory's inability to grapple with the German case. The obfuscations came fast and furious, like a mesh of bumper stickers on a hippie's car: Actually the Brits started Oriental studies not the Germans. The Germans had no unified state or foothold in the Orient to carry out their imperialism. All this talk of finding the "truth" about the relationship between scholarship and empire is a delusion of modern thinking that postmodernists like himself have been sent to correct. Perhaps the theory is wrong, for which he apologizes. He is not sure but promises to return to the German case in his later book *Culture and Imperialism,* which he never does. And so on and so on.

Edward Said was an intellectual dandy who pleasured himself by moving to New York and reading the great books of the Western canon, and then, gripped by self-loathing, he wrote darkly of their nefarious purposes. Of the many deplorable consequences of his enduring influence on understandings of the Western intellectual inheritance, none is so great as its blanket condemnation of Germany's contributions to Orientalist scholarship, now dismissed as "greedy," "racist," and "imperialist."

The German Orientalist achievement is not our concern here. But having dismissed both Leninist and Saidist cavils, we are left with the more obvious explanation of why Bismarck convened a conference of major powers in the winter of 1884–85 to discuss colonialism: benevolence. By that I do not mean that a sudden bout of charity and love for others overcame the Germans, although the country's deep Christian tradition would often appear in the subsequent rollout of colonial rule. Rather, I mean a practical benevolence: Bismarck understood that there was no shirking Germany's involvement in the world given his new country's size and wealth. He knew that overseas areas were being colonized because, by and large, natives wanted them to be colonized; and he knew that Germany, at the very least, would be as good as the other major powers in exporting its governance system, developing native economies, and sharing in global peace operations. Colonialism came to Germany not because of its greedy capitalists or its racist Orientalists but because of its maturing politicians.

The newly created country simply could not ignore the responsibilities that flowed from its growing trade and security interests abroad. Bismarck was already talking to Britain and France about German interests in West Africa. There were complex discussions about Germany's role in Egypt. Bismarck's top advisor urged him to get more involved in these disputes to improve relations with France (which cohosted the conference). As if he needed any reminders, a German Colonial Union had been formed to represent the country's outward orientation in the tropics.

Bismarck also recognized that countries engaged in high-minded activities abroad were less likely to descend into low-minded political wrangling at home. "Colonies depend upon a home country where national sentiment is stronger than party feelings," he noted in 1883. "We would need a national legislature with a higher sense of purpose than nettling the government and making grand speeches."[4] German nation-builders such as Bismarck saw that France had emerged from a squabbling post-revolutionary mess into a broad-minded, united country with vast global knowledge as its colonial empire expanded. The same civilizing influence of colonial stewardship on the home front was obvious in Britain, whose cross-party consensus on the country's need for steady rule was inseparable from its imperial responsibilities. They hoped Germany could chart a similar course, and the German colonial episode would create a brief moment—from

1884 to 1914—when just such conservative national unity prevailed in Germany.

• • •

Bismarck's ironclad indifference towards the colonies cracked in 1883 when a failed tobacco merchant from Bremen named Adolf Lüderitz wired to say that he had run up the German flag on a thin strip of land on the Atlantic coast of southern Africa. Lüderitz had bought the land from natives of the Nama tribe for two hundred loaded rifles and a box of gold. The Nama needed the rifles for their ongoing wars against their historic enemies, the Herero. Bismarck at last gave in. Following his recognition of Lüderitzland (population twenty), Bismarck told the Reichstag that henceforth he would fly the flag whenever established German merchants requested the protection of the state. "We do not want to install colonies artificially," Bismarck sighed. "When they emerge, however, we will try to protect them." His hope was for empire on the cheap: "Clerks from the trading houses, not German generals," would handle the functions of government.[5]

Since Germany was a colonial newcomer, it had the neutrality to convene the 1884–85 conference to set new ground rules for colonial endeavors. Being sensitive to publicity, the Germans invited some Africans from the Niger river to join their delegation, at first calling them porters, then river navigators, then caravan leaders, and finally "princes." Other European powers hastened to bring their own "loyal Africans" to wintry Berlin to demonstrate their own legitimacy.[6]

During the meetings, Bismarck oversaw a major redefinition of colonialism. The Germans spoke most frequently and thus their views had tremendous influence on the final agreement. While the immediate issues were the Congo and West Africa, as well as free trade, the broader question was on what basis colonial rule could be justified. Initial fears that Bismarck planned to make vast claims on unmarked territory proved unfounded. His aim was simply to promote European trade in a way that did not bring the European powers to blows and that delivered uplift for the natives.

The Spirit of Berlin was embodied in two principles. First, colonial powers, whatever else they did, had a responsibility to improve the lives of native populations. European powers, the agreement stated, should be "preoccupied with the means of increasing the moral and material wellbeing of the indigenous populations." When a colony was established, the powers "engage themselves to watch over the conservation of the indigenous populations and the amelioration of their moral and material conditions of existence." That included putting an end to slavery and the slave trade. It also meant supporting religious, scientific, and charitable endeavors to bring the "advantages of civilization."[7] Bismarck praised the "careful solicitude" the European powers showed towards colonial subjects. Native uplift was now an explicit rather than implicit promise of colonialism.[8] A British delegate noted that "humanitarian considerations have occupied a prominent place in the discussions."[9] Words only. But words that would create norms, and norms that would shape behavior.

The second principle insisted that any colonial claim needed to be backed up by "the existence of an authority sufficient to cause acquired rights to be respected." Merely planting the flag or signing a treaty with local chiefs for a box of cigars was no longer enough. Colonialism required governance so that "new occupations . . . may be considered as effective." This was later known as the principle of "effective occupation." With this idea, Bismarck introduced the expectation that colonialism was not mere claim-staking or resource development—even if those things were still better than no colonialism at all. Rather, as with his newly created Germany, political institutions needed to provide the means to deliver the end of good governance.

The "effective occupation" principle applied at first only to coastal areas since the powers did not want to set off conflicts over border demarcations in inland areas.[10] But as mapping of the inland proceeded in subsequent years, it crept willy-nilly into the bush as well. It "became the instrument for sanctioning and formalizing colonial occupation even in the African hinterland," noted a legal historian.[11]

One result of the Spirit of Berlin was a surge in trans-colonial cooperation among the major colonial powers. British, French, and German officials, especially in Africa, acted as if they were part of a common European project. They regularly swapped bits of territory, shared tips on governing, and got gloriously drunk to cement the bonds of colonial friendship.[12] Germany's top colonial official hosted a dinner to honor the retiring British governor of Uganda when they found themselves together aboard a homebound German steamer in 1909: "We made flowery speeches, vowing eternal friendship between our two nations," the governor recalled.[13] In German Samoa, the governor in 1901 appointed a Brit who did not speak German as the top official of the largest island. At the outbreak of war in 1914, the Brit was still expecting to draw his civil service pension from the British colonial office, arguing that European colonialism was a unified endeavor for the betterment of other peoples.[14]

● ● ●

The Berlin conference has been subject to a relentless campaign of debunking by modern intellectuals. One claim they make is that the assembled delegates "carved up" Africa like a bunch of gluttons. This is wrong. For one, the carving was already happening when

Local officials establishing the border between German Cameroon and the French Congo area, 1903. *Bundesarchiv*

Bismarck acted. The conference was a *response to*, not a cause of, expanded colonial claims. Critics seem to think that absent the conference Africa would have been left untouched. Quite the opposite. The scramble for Africa created tensions, suspicions, and fears on all sides. Bismarck wanted to set some ground rules.

Second, if "carving up" is taken to mean staking territorial claims on a map with a view to gobbling up resources, this is flatly untrue. Of course, economic interests took a prominent role in colonial expansion as a way to pay the costs and reward the effort. But the attendant responsibilities were new. Expansion now required an explicit commitment to native uplift alongside economic development, and this commitment required the creation of effective governing structures.

Finally, the notion of "carving" conjures images of high-handed mandarins in Europe ignorant of local conditions absent-mindedly drawing boundaries on a map while playing a game of whist. The myth of "artificial boundaries" drawn by ignorant Europeans is one that dies hard. In fact, as the French scholar Camille Lefebvre has shown, colonial administrators went to great lengths to figure out where boundaries should be drawn. In doing so, they made use of extensive local knowledge.[15] Later demands by critics to redraw borders along ethnic lines, she argued, "had the paradoxical effect of erasing the history of African political structures and the role of the local populations in defining colonial boundaries." This reflected a racist idea "that the essence of Africans is to be found in their ethnicity."[16]

The final border between German Cameroon and neighboring British and French colonies, for instance, was the result of tortuous field surveys carried out with native guides between 1902 and 1913. "The boundary is, as far as possible, a natural one, but, whenever practicable, tribal limits have been taken into consideration," a *Times* of London correspondent reported on the arduous demarcation, noting "no opposition was met with by the natives, who realize the advantage of having a definite chain of landmarks between English and German territory."[17] In German East Africa, the Germans allowed the neighboring British territory to control all of the lake between the two in order to protect native trading patterns. The treaty of 1890 also allowed that "any correction of the demarcation lines that becomes necessary due to local requirements may be untaken by agreement between the two powers."[18] Critics forget that drawing borders on a map would mean little if they could not be enforced, and enforcement in turn depended on local social and economic conditions.

What *is* true is that these political boundaries did not always coincide with ethnic boundaries. Many ethnic groups ended up on different sides of borders because carving up "ethnic homelands" would have been both impractical as well as, in Lefebvre's view, racist. If there is a "high-handed" assumption at play, it is the assumption of later critics that Africans are essentially tribal and need to be organized on tribal lines. Thus borders should be redrawn not based on political, social, and economic logic but on ethnic essentialism. When the apartheid state of South Africa created such ethnic "homelands," they were roundly derided because they created ethnic ghettos cut off from modern lines of economic and political life. Yet the "artificial boundaries" critique of the borders resulting from the Berlin conference is an appeal for just such apartheid-style "homelands."

Broader criticism of the Spirit of Berlin is even more hyperbolic: *no* white man, German or otherwise, the critics avail, had a right to march around the world oppressing helpless brown and black people at gunpoint. One Harvard professor wrote that the British and French should be equally blamed for the rapacious Spirit of Berlin even though the Germans hosted the conference. There should be no *Sonderweg* or "separate path" theory that explained why only Germans were evil. Any suggestion of a "German (colonial) *Sonderweg*" would exculpate Britain and France from their fair share of the blame for the great evil that was European colonialism.[19] Scholars like him censure as racist the idea that Western civilization had anything to offer to non-Western peoples. The so-called humanitarian principles of the conference were so much hypocrisy, a clever cloak for self-interest, they charge.

Not one of these claims withstands scrutiny. Civilization is a *descriptive* concept that emerged in the field of archaeology to measure the progress that cultures achieved towards the universally common ends of intensive agriculture, urbanization, state formation, the division of labor, the use of machinery, civic government, and a written tradition with record keeping. If Europeans truly believed that black Africans were inherently inferior, why would they try to raise them up to European levels of civilization? It would be impossible. The assumption that European progress was accessible to all was based on a belief in the universal human potential of all peoples.

As to the inevitable coercion that this entailed against dominant local elites, critics forget important lessons from the past in their sermonizing. World history is a story of more civilized nations conquering less civilized ones because they are better organized and thus able to create and sustain more lives, production, and material wealth. Nowhere in the world at the time was it assumed that conquest was bad. Certainly, powerful African groups like the Fulani and the Buganda assumed they had a right to conquer nearby peoples. As Jörg Fisch wrote: "Strictly speaking, the colonial acquisition of Africa needed no justification. The Europeans had the necessary strength and, even within Europe, the right of conquest was widely accepted both in theory and state practice."[20]

Claims that no African was involved or that colonial expansion ignored African interests are rather bizarre given that such norms were alien to Africa itself. The Fulani, Buganda, Bantu, or Ngoni had not asked whether they should "consult" the African peoples they subjugated before the Europeans arrived. With the Spirit of Berlin promising high living standards, Europe's conquest of Africa was justified, not just legally but also ethically, and just as much it was unavoidable. The idea that it was "arbitrary" for Western civilization to spread (or that such a spread was based on ill intent) simply ignores the fact that human societies *all* strive to be more civilized.

Civilization isn't racist and violent; denying it is. Anti-civilizational discourses that wish upon non-European peoples a return to the five thousand–year developmental gap that they faced when the European encounter began deny the humanity of non-Europeans. These Woke theories embody the racism they decry. As the Canadian scholar Tom Flanagan asked in rebutting claims that the "First Nations" (Siberian migrants to North America) should have been left in their primitive state in Canada, "Though one might dislike many aspects of civilization, would it be morally defensible to call for a radical decline in population, necessitating early death and reproductive failure for billions of people now living?"[21]

The "civilizing mission" was both proper and reasonable as an aim of European colonialism. Germany more than any other colonial power took that mission seriously, as shown by its extensive training academies for colonial administrators and special institutes to understand native cultures, geographies, languages, and economics. As one American historian wrote:

> Of all the European powers engaged in colonization in tropical territories before 1914, the Germans made the most extensive efforts in the direction of preparing themselves for their colonial responsibilities. Though their emphasis on colonial education had developed only late in the history of the German colonial empire, it was one of the determinants of their stature in 1914 as one of the most progressive and energetic of all the colonial powers.[22]

In 1988, American historian Suzanne Miers claimed to have "uncovered" a dark secret about the Spirit of Berlin: the conference participants did not give a fig about the civilizing mission (an odd critique when set against the charge by others that they did, but that this mission was racist). Her evidence? The powers were also motivated by self-interest, and they did not try their hardest to enact their altruistic ends. Miers writes, for instance, that the British agreed to limit liquor sales in the Niger River region only "if all powers agreed to it, as, if they refused, British traders would be excluded from a lucrative traffic." In the next sentence she states: "The Colonial Office certainly was not contemplating British self-denial for humanitarian reasons."[23] Yet her own sentence shows that they *were* contemplating this *if* it could be achieved. Like other scholars, she seems to think that Quixotic and ineffective romantic gestures are what was needed. Thank goodness the Colonial Office was staffed by men of practical bent.

None of this will convince colonial critics, of course, who hasten to point out that the abolition of slavery came slowly, liquor imports continued despite prohibitions, wars were fought using brutal tactics, and all the blessings of civilization like the rule of law, health systems, roads, and education came only piecemeal. Having set up a high standard, the European powers immediately fell short of it, thus "proving" in the eyes of the critics that they never meant it in the first place. Yet these critics never seek to establish what "best effort" would have looked like: What was fiscally, technically, and organizationally feasible circa, say, 1885, even if we wish away all political obstacles? A more accurate view, propounded by the Stanford economists Lewis Gann and Peter Duignan, is that Western colonial powers like Britain and Germany exceeded "best effort," and the costs that this effort imposed eventually forced Europe to abandon the colonial project altogether.[24]

● ● ●

The first country forced by the Spirit of Berlin to change its colonial practices was Germany itself. Bismarck's wish for colonialism on the cheap now stood in violation of both principles the conference had established. When German colonial founders in the Cameroon and in New Guinea applied for "subventions" (money) to build roads and establish police, Bismarck could not refuse. Progress came rapidly as a result. So too did net outlays on the colonies from German taxpayers. By 1912, the last year when figures were tallied, the expenditures by all German colonies were £6 million while revenues were just £2.4 million.[25] Trade with Germany, meanwhile, was miniscule. Africans and Asians were exploiting the German taxpayer.

The Spirit of Berlin also tripped up one of its leading acolytes, the Belgian King Leopold II. His experiment in private rule in the Congo had been approved at the Berlin conference because the powers believed the place was impossible to formally colonize and that Leopold's rule would be preferable to local rule by warlords like the feared Msiri or by Arab slave traders in the east. Rebranded the Congo Free State in 1885, the private fiefdom was anything but free and anything but a state. An investigating magistrate would describe it as "no colonized state, barely a state at all but a financial enterprise."[26] This opened the way to wide abuses that Leopold was either unwilling or unable to control. In 1895, an Irishman working for the government in German East Africa trekked into the Free State and was summarily executed by lawless local officials on false charges of illegal ivory trading and of supplying arms to Arab slave traders. The murder prompted an international investigation into wider abuses. Later critics have made wild claims about the brutalities of rubber harvesting being the main cause of high mortality rates in the Congo. These claims have *no* evidence. The area did however suffer from depopulation due to disease, migration, and falling birth rates. Leopold undertook reforms but too little, too late.

The crusading Belgian lawyer who revealed the abuses in the Congo Free State, Edmund Morel, proposed that Germany take over. German colonial rule had met the highest standards, Morel wrote. "Nor must we forget . . . the outstanding fact that the first great international conference called to deal with the future of the non-colonizable area of Africa was summoned by Bismarck, and held at Berlin."[27] The area became a formal colony of Belgium in 1908 instead. Leopold's fiefdom, "both legally and morally became subject to the full rigor of the provisions of the [Berlin] Act," wrote a British official with satisfaction.[28]

The Germans justifiably believed that they had brought order and civility to the colonial enterprise. Under the Spirit of Berlin, colonialism was now based on a "dual contract." The first was between European powers including a clause saying that in the event of a European war the colonies would remain at peace. The second was between the colonizer and the colonized. The idea of "solidarity" with native peoples made the Germans feel good about their colonialism. In *The Heart of Darkness*, Conrad has his narrator famously declaim that what redeemed colonialism was "an idea at the back of it; not a sentimental pretense but an idea; and an unselfish belief in the idea—something you can set up, and bow down before, and offer a sacrifice to."[29] That idea, in a nutshell, was the Spirit of Berlin.

Understanding German pride in this new spirit in 1884–85, and in their subsequent record of colonial rule, is key to understanding the sense of betrayal when the colonies were seized in 1919. As a German economist later wrote: "The only colonial power that professed the idea of solidarity with practically all of the consequences of that word is the one that paid the price for its attitude by losing all of its colonies."[30]

And with the disappearance of the colonies, the conservative national unity that prevailed in Germany would give way to the domestic dissension that Bismarck was eager to prevent. The Weimar and Nazi eras that followed would show the consequences of losing the national sentiment that came with the colonies.

CHAPTER 3

Who Shot Off My Thumb?

The history of what is today Namibia looms large in contemporary debates on German colonialism. Indeed, it might be said that the *only* thing most people know about the German colonial past is that "something terrible happened" in what was then German Southwest Africa. Scholars eager to emphasize colonial mistakes and ignore colonial successes are happy to oblige this selective memory. At last count, there were over fifty full-length books in German and English on the tragedy that unfolded among the Herero and Nama peoples between 1904 and 1908. By comparison, there are around ten general histories of the colony itself. Much as Americans think of "Vietnam" as a war not a country, Germans think of "Namibia" as a genocide not a former colony. Any attempt to make a positive case for German colonialism is invariably met with the response: "What about the Herero?" Well, what about them?

German missionaries, traders, and settlers began arriving in the territory north of the British Cape Colony in the nineteenth century. They found a place that was in every respect anarchic and violent. The various groups inhabiting the region occupied shifting centers without demarcated borders.[1] The future Namibia was a dangerous space of

41

cattle raiding, slave raiding, and war *long before* the Germans arrived. In particular, the Herero and Nama, both of which had migrated to the area only a generation before the Germans, had tense and violent encounters over pasture lands and enclosures.[2] The Herero were part of the extensive Bantu expansion into southern Africa that displaced or wiped out most of the indigenous Khoisan groups, of which the Nama were one. The later land commissioner of the colony, Paul Rohrbach, called the Herero a "predatory indigenous tribe."[3]

Fighting for survival, the Nama massacred a fifth of the Herero population in a single day on August 23, 1850, at a place now known as Murder Hill.[4] Another Nama raid of 1890, recorded by the newly arrived Germans, resulted in the burning of the entire southern territory of the Herero in what can only be described as an attempt at genocide.[5] The Herero also displaced and enslaved the indigenous Damara people, who fled into the mountains. The Germans called

Artist's rendering of the prairies of German Southwest Africa, showing native ranchers, a German soldier, and German settlers, 1903. *Bundesarchiv*

them the Berg or "mountain" Damara and created a protected homeland for them in 1906. Missionary reports from before the German
annexation described constant Herero raids on Damara and Saan
villages. "They spared only the young and strong so that they could
use them as slaves," explained one report.[6] The mutual antipathies
and traditions of cattle and slave raiding in this area predated European contact. Honest historians, wrote two Tanzanian scholars,
"should be able to discuss the atrocities committed between African
communities in the precolonial period."[7]

Contact with European traders intensified but did not create these
local rivalries. As the weapons shipment that led to the founding of
Lüderitzland reminds us, local groups armed themselves with the new
weapons traders had to offer. The Herero became what one scholar
called a "gun society."[8] The settlers complained that the new German
colonial government did not stop the incessant cattle raiding of the
Herero and Nama. The Nama leader, Hendrik Witbooi, explained that
he was a vigilante by birth and thus could not be expected to settle
down and raise cattle. Portrayed as a victim, Witbooi was first and
foremost a legendary rogue, leaving corpses and devastation everywhere he went. He had gained ascendancy over the various factions of
the Nama (or Hottentots) because of his skill in battles against the
Herero. He had a missing thumb as a souvenir from one gunfight.[9]
When his pastor tried to persuade him to make peace with the Herero,
he responded that God had ordered him to make war. Anytime the
Germans got within sight of Witbooi's forces, dozens of his slaves and
black prisoners would rush to freedom on the German side, along with
any women who dared.[10]

Legislation introduced by German authorities after 1884 outlawed
the arms trade. But the tensions between the two seminomadic groups
did not relent. In 1886, German soldiers witnessed a grisly battle between
Herero and Nama after the latter tried to occupy a water well claimed by

the former at the settlement of Osona. (Today, oddly, this is the site of a Namibia Water Corporation vocational training center.) As soon as the battle ended, the Germans moved into the field to assist the wounded. The new governor, Heinrich Göring, "did not seem to tire of extracting cannon balls and sewing up wounds," one officer recalled.[11]

One imaginative American professor insists that Witbooi's constant raids on the Herero were a clever form of anti-colonial resistance rather than a continuation of pre-colonial behavior: "At no time did the supposed threat of the German military dissuade him from seizing land, cattle, and trade rights from the Herero," the professor writes with admiration. The raids, he continues, were "a significant problem for the German imperial government," forgetting that they were first and foremost a significant problem for the Herero victims.[12] The initial German contingent set at twenty-six soldiers (six Germans and twenty natives) was powerless to stop the Herero-Nama wars, which led to the addition of another twenty-five by 1892. At the time, the Nama alone had three hundred men under arms.

When German settlers began looking for land to graze, the Herero were all too happy to dispose of their holdings. The Herero became willing partners of German efforts to modernize agriculture and, when minerals were discovered, to build railways.[13] The Herero's enduring love of German-style military uniforms was one odd result of this partnership, and cooperating with the Germans strengthened their position vis-à-vis the Nama. Witbooi, seeing that the good old days were over, laid down his arms and was given a civil-service salary. He pledged to enlist in the German forces anytime he was needed. At first then, German colonialism seemed to be taking the region from violence and poverty towards peace and prosperity. Warring tribes were pacified, and the construction of a modern state had begun.

The Nama too became willing partners of the colonial project. Among the many housekeeping tasks performed by the state was the shrinking of Lüderitzland back to its agreed-upon dimensions because the wily founder had used an archaic definition of "mile" to extent his holdings well into Nama territory. Witbooi was pleased, and he even provided twenty of his troops to the colonial forces to help them apprehend a band of thieves terrorizing the countryside.[14] Such collaborations were later ignored by scholars because, as a 1999 thesis written by a German military officer noted, "the image of Africans and Germans serving together in field companies did not seem to fit into their cliché of German colonial history."[15]

German colonialism, then, was effective in transforming the region from violence and poverty towards modernity. These changes were necessary to pull Namibia into the modern world. The enclosure of grazing lands and the building of railways were inevitable shifts that would have occurred irrespective of which regime—German, British, private European, northern Ovambo—gained ascendance. Even if left to their own devices, the Herero and Nama would not have lived in idyllic bliss tending healthy herds of cattle and hosting multiethnic community barbeques. Economic globalization, health transitions, cattle diseases, security dilemmas, a communications revolution, and many more changes were coming no matter what. The only question was *how* modernity would come. Even under the implausible scenario in which some independent, pan-ethnic, native government magically emerged in the area, it too would have faced the same incentives to marketize land, create cattle markets, and offer railway concessions. But no such indigenous governing capacity existed. The likely counterfactual to German colonization in Namibia was either colonization by another European power or a private colony led by the German Colonial Society for Southwest Africa. Absent European rule, the area would have reverted to civil war.

The German settlers were not aid workers, and thank goodness they were not. They were motivated by bettering themselves, and when this motivation was properly governed, it brought good out-comes to the native communities. The Germans literally brought the dusty, desert land of the future Namibia to life. Water holes were dug, paved roads built, port facilities expanded, and a railway laid from the coast to the capital that reduced travel time from three weeks to three days. Of course, all this brings sneers and caustic asides from the modern scholar who has never had to do without a spicy latte each morning as she sits down with a high-speed Internet connection to denounce "modernity" (always in quotes).

In 1896–97, a *rinderpest* epidemic struck the Herero and Nama region's cattle. The German administration drew a quarantine line dividing Hereroland from the northerly section of Ovamboland and built a 550-kilometer string of monitoring stations. Without German settlers to provide employment and food, a large part of the Herero population would have died of starvation and malnutrition. Certainly, the Nama and other groups would not have set up soup kitchens. South Africa's white-owned diamond companies paid for Robert Koch (then a little-known German scientist) to visit, and he quickly discovered an effective cattle vaccine that won him a Nobel prize in 1905.[16] Veterinar-ians assigned to the German military garrison managed to vaccinate most of the Nama and settler herds because they were geographically concentrated. The Herero herds, by contrast, were greater in number and widely dispersed. Half of their cattle succumbed.

The *rinderpest* epidemic, far more than later events, was the key moment that sounded "the death knell of an independent Herero society as a whole," in the words of the leading expert on the group, Jan-Bart Gewald.[17] The Herero split into factions. The faction led by Samuel Maherero began raiding other Herero for their cattle.[18] Others became more dependent on German administration and on German farms.

The "passing of traditional society" was a universal experience in which personal relationships and assumptions of individual disempowerment were replaced by impersonal institutions and assumptions of individual efficacy.[19] The Herero and Nama underwent this transition at breakneck speed. The market and trading economy represented a wrenching shift, but German colonial rule eased the change. Samuel Maherero, educated like Witbooi at a German missionary school, negotiated more favorable terms for land concessions and higher wage rates for his faction. The same mediating role was played by Witbooi, who spread Christianity to his people and styled himself a Christian messiah.

The Herero and Nama were objectively better off in the initial stages of German settlement, and as a result they viewed the new rulers as legitimate. The German governor from 1898, Theodor Leutwein, worked closely with both men to restrain land grabs by settlers and to protect native communities. Leutwein described his policy as one of

German Southwest Africa governor Theodor Leutwein with Nama leader Hendrik Witbooi (left) and Herero leader Samuel Maherero (right), 1904. *Bundesarchiv*

"integration" of the various native communities into the new colonial state based on an overriding concern with the "common good" of all peoples inhabiting the territory.[20] A remarkable photo of Leutwein, Maherero, and Witbooi together in 1904 captures the cooperative spirit that ruled the day.

Witbooi exchanged honest and frequent letters with Leutwein about the terms by which a peaceful accommodation might be reached. "It's neither a sin nor a moral offense for me to want to remain the independent chief of my land and my people," Witbooi wrote to the governor in one letter. "I am at peace because I am innocent, and I know that you know that I stand before you without guilt." Indeed, Leutwein replied, the historical forces which had brought the two men together to advance their respective causes were not the issue. Witbooi's defiant raiding and roaming was "neither a sin nor a moral offense." It was, however, "a threat to the existence of the colony" and thus "I can leave you in your independence only if you remain peaceful in your place."[21]

The Germans took a "policy of diplomacy" towards the native groups that helped them to withstand the strains of modernity without resorting to arms. But peace and development can also bring conflict if disgruntled actors take advantage of their freedoms to foment rebellion. As the German defense ministry wrote in an admirably even-handed assessment (a more accurate rendering of history than what was achieved by later professional historians),

> The policy of the diplomacy produced results; the basis for peaceful development was laid, and isolated uprisings were relatively easily suppressed with the active participation of other tribes. German settlers—mostly cattle breeders and traders—came into the country in increasing numbers. Military stations were founded, port and railroad facilities were created, and the arms trade was restricted. In short, German

rule seemed to be strengthening itself in such a way that even many former opponents of this peaceful policy became its staunch supporters, and even long-time experts of the country and its people were proven wrong. The colony experienced a visible boom. . . . And yet the effects of the colonizing endeavors penetrated deeply into the life and habits of the natives who felt their independence and freedom threatened with the advancement of culture. They took advantage of German colonization with its peace, order, personal security, and job opportunities. But under the apparent external calm they became disgruntled with the foreign intruders and awaited a favorable opportunity for a violent outbreak.[22]

Whatever their various causes for complaint, neither the Herero nor the Nama had a right to rebel against German colonial authority itself. German settlement provided a more just and equitable solution to the region's many tribal conflicts, developmental challenges, and social pressures than could possibly have emerged from a feasible alternative source of political authority. To rage against German colonialism, as today's professoriate does, is nothing less than to rage against the modern world, or humanity itself. German rule in the area was ethical by any reasonable standard in light of the standards and constraints of governance in early twentieth-century desert Africa, even if we wish the area had been a land of milk and honey. To rebel against it was to invite a *justified* counter-insurgency, with all the dangers and uncertainties that such campaigns implied in desert conditions. Setting this moral compass is critical because without it there is an unspoken assumption that the rebels were on the side of justice and the colonial authorities the side of injustice. Reversing that assumption puts the tragic events that followed in the proper light.

• • •

In 1903, German settlers lobbied Berlin to allow faster land acquisition to solve looming food shortages. Berlin overturned the governor's
limits on land acquisition, and settlers began arriving in greater numbers, rising to fourteen thousand in total. This was a mistake by Berlin,
as it failed to anticipate the consequences of making the Herero and
Nama wholly dependent on German farms. The colonial government
opposed the new policy vigorously, but to no avail. Samuel Maherero
was by this time an alcoholic, so his deputies stepped forward to offer
Herero land for sale, while lining their own pockets. This led to internal
disgruntlement. Seeing his position at risk, Maherero rallied his people
to blame the Germans for their woes.

Late in the year, when the German militia of two thousand troops
was in the south of the colony, the Herero rose up. They attacked
ranches, farms, and mission stations and sabotaged telegraph cables
and railway lines. The major atrocities carried out by the Herero in
January 1904 included wanton destruction not just of 120 German
settlers but also of farms and infrastructure. These were not wars of
defense but wars of annihilation. If there was a genocidal intention
evident anywhere in this colony's history, this was it. Maherero's
battle cry was plain: "Kill all Germans!" A few days later, he amended
the battle cry: "Do not kill women, children or missionaries, no Boers
and Englishmen." The German response was predictably forceful and
uncompromising. German officials could respond *only* by defeating
the rebellion that sought to throw the region back into turmoil and
to exterminate one of the resident groups.

The task for German colonial authorities after the initial rebellion
was to restore order, reform land policy, and address the tensions
among the various groups. But governor Leutwein's hopes for a short
campaign followed by a negotiated peace evaporated under the

scorching sun when it became clear that Maherero's forces wanted a fight to the death. Maherero famously wrote to Witbooi enjoining him to "fight to the death," even if it meant their respective groups would be annihilated by the difficult conditions and loss of access to life-sustaining water and food. After German forces escaped a Herero encirclement through a daring nighttime flight in April 1904, Leutwein wired to Berlin for help: "Accusation of failure hits me hard . . . [I] believe we have saved the troops from catastrophe by a night march. I am asking for replacement by a high officer who enjoys the full confidence of the general staff because it is the only way."[23]

In response, the new German emperor, Wilhelm II, made a second policy mistake. He sent a war-hardened outsider, General Lothar von Trotha, to the colony. A veteran of counterinsurgency in German East Africa, von Trotha had most recently been in China helping the Chinese governor of northern Shandong province suppress the murderous Boxer Rebellion there. He saw in the Herero uprising a threat similar in scale and nature, one that could not be solved by negotiations. The decision to send him into the delicate situation went against the advice of the cabinet, the minister of war, and the director of the colonial department.[24]

Trotha planned to use German troop reinforcements to wage a single decisive battle. Large amounts of barbed wire were prepared for POW camps. But the decisive battle eluded him. Trotha now pledged to defeat the Herero at any cost, worrying that the racist rhetoric of Maherero might give rise to an "Ethiopian movement" that sought to exterminate all non-blacks in the area.[25] Having failed to apprehend, defeat, or gain the surrender of the Herero, Trotha at the very end of the conflict issued an order for all Herero to leave the colony for neighboring British Bechuanaland (now Botswana), where they had been allowed to settle by the local chief since 1896. All men not complying would be shot on site. Women and children who did not surrender would be shot or imprisoned.[26]

The Nama at first joined the German counterinsurgency against the Herero. Witbooi fulfilled his promise to fight for the Germans despite being eighty years old. His group might have remained loyal had not an itinerant African preacher convinced him that the Herero defeat was a sign from God that he could regain his former glory. The Nama rebellion he led was short-lived, as he soon bled to death from a gunshot wound. The Nama surrendered on pain of an order similar to that issued against the Herero.

By the time the rebellions ended in 1906, the officially enumerated Herero population in the colony had fallen by 75 percent from eighty thousand to twenty thousand. The officially enumerated population of the Nama had fallen by half from twenty thousand to ten thousand. In addition to 150 murdered settlers, the Germans counted their losses at 1,400 dead and another 1,000 wounded or missing.

So was Lothar von Trotha responsible for the death of seventy thousand people? Without doubt, hundreds of Herero and Nama people died in battle as well as from starvation and thirst during the campaigns. A large number also died while fleeing the colony or in the inadequate conditions of German detention camps.[27] The Herero fell victim to their own poisoning of water wells as they fled into the desert. How many, however, remains a mystery. Without exception, contemporary scholars trot out the figures above without *any* inquiry into their origins. One must search footnotes to find embarrassed little asides like "No precise fatality numbers can be ascertained."[28] Calling out this basic lack of descriptive evidence that lies at the center of the "genocide" thesis, the military historian Gunter Spraul wrote: "How high the losses of the Herero were and to what causes these losses are due will probably have to remain unclear due to the sources. Shouldn't this be admitted frankly rather than insisting on certain figures and giving the appearance of precision?"[29]

To take a comparison group, the enumerated population of the Berg-Damara, who were under close German protection and were *not* targeted by the Herero, also fell by roughly the same proportion as the Herero and Nama from thirty thousand to twelve thousand between the 1904 and 1911 census estimates. The same officially enumerated decline of over 50 percent was recorded for another group, the Rehoboth Basters, that was *not* involved in the conflict.[30] Why did the enumerated populations of groups not at war decline at nearly the same rate as those at war? Did Lothar von Trotha steal from his tent in the evenings to commit genocide against these groups too?

Most demographers have a better explanation: migration away from the conflict zones; falls in female fertility; increased mortality due to the disruptions of the conflicts, the effects of recurring epidemics, and reduced food supply; and changing census definitions and weak census capacity after the conflicts. To take one example, the German military estimated the total Herero population at between fifty thousand and sixty thousand before the war, rather than the official eighty thousand. The fact that only twenty thousand were counted after the war tells us merely that somewhere between thirty thousand and sixty thousand Herero disappeared from official counts, but not why. The biased reasoning of German progressives eager to attribute a high body count to the German counterinsurgency has created a myth that no one dares to question. Yet if the enumerated declines of the other groups are used as a baseline, then the excess population declines of the Herero and Nama were more like ten thousand and, more to the point, were largely unrelated to the German counterinsurgency.

What happened in the deserts of German Southwest Africa remains the subject of sustained and angry debate among Germans. There is no doubt that Trotha's use of force was sometimes disproportionate to the threat, and that German soldiers were sometimes lawless and barbaric under his command. Trotha was eventually condemned and recalled and his policies rescinded. As the German diplomat and colonial governor Heinrich Schnee would write: "Military methods were adopted in combatting the revolt *which were not sanctioned by the German government and were formally repudiated.*"[31]

Yet minor failings to not constitute evidence of major war crimes. The standard academic account is that Trotha and his troops intentionally pursued the Herero to death, either by gunfire or expulsion into the desert. This amounts to a charge of an intentional act of genocide (even ignoring the dubious data about deaths). Susanne Kuss of the University of Bern found that instead, the orders "emerged entirely independently of any conscious decision for or against a strategy of concerted racial genocide." Trotha, she argues, "did not intend to bring about a situation in which the Herero would be subject to a slow death through adverse natural conditions."[32] German actions were an improvised field tactic in the face of chaos and uncertainty. Not only were they not sanctioned, but they were not intended to wipe out either group. Trotha's intention was to defeat them in battle or exile them (and to subdue the Nama). There is no evidence that German troops actually pushed the Herero into the desert because by the time the great migrations began, the Germans had already abandoned the chase because of supply limits. The expulsion order was Trotha's admission of failure, not some major new offensive. Genocide requires both an intention and a decision to wipe out a group *as a policy aim*, neither of which existed here. Moreover, as noted, it is doubtful that either group actually suffered a precipitous population decline as a result of German actions.

A more scathing critique of the genocide thesis was offered by the German military officer Karl Lorenz, who wrote a master's thesis on the subject in 1999. He agreed that the war evolved through "field tactics" as argued by Kuss. Trotha's goal was "to militarily destroy the fighting part of the Herero" and to eliminate the Herero "as a power factor in South West Africa" who did not recognize the colonial state. "A man who prepares prison camps is not a man intent on exterminating a people."[33] In fact, Lorenz argued, using field diaries from soldiers, the war ended mainly through mutual exhaustion. The German forces barely waged war at all given their own grave deprivations in the harsh conditions. The decline of the enumerated Herero, he argued, was mainly due to migration and miscounting.[34]

Of course, German establishment intellectuals are quick to cry "Holocaust Denial" against anyone who points out the flaws in their genocide thesis, thus foreclosing the argument altogether. But there is no comparison at all. The Holocaust is all too evident in the data—names, places, methods, intentions, policies, multiple estimates, horrific first-hand accounts. None of this exists in the case of the counterinsurgency wars against the Herero and Nama. Rather, all the evidence points in the opposite direction—to a conflict *without* genocidal animus or behavior (with the possible exception of the Herero themselves). It is a dishonest and demeaning act of Holocaust trivialization to invoke the sacred memory of the Shoah to stand up this flimsy Woke crusade.

After the rebellions, the commissioner for land disputes who had been appointed in 1903, Paul Rohrbach, warned against any "false philanthropy" that would treat the Herero and Nama as permanent victim groups.[35] Rohrbach was a scathing critic of Trotha's failure to negotiate with the groups.[36] But he also saw their rebellion as unjustified and reactionary. The progressive governor of German Cameroon, Theodor Seitz, was sent to German Southwest Africa to restore the confidence of both and restart development. He oversaw the process of bringing German officers accused of abuses to justice.[37] He promised "to reinstate in the natives a confidence that they will find protection against the brutal excesses of a few individuals."[38] The overall population of the colony began to recover by 1910.

The conflict with the Herero and Nama was a tragedy for all parties. It was unplanned and inconsistent with German colonial policy, and German Southwest Africa was only a tiny sliver of the whole German colonial experience. If we use the measure of "people-years"—meaning the sum of people living under German colonial rule in each year of its existence—German Southwest Africa was only 1–2 percent of Germany's colonial rule. If the tragedy here reflected German colonial policy in general or was an inevitable result of it, then this small percentage would reflect something rotten at the core of German colonialism. But that is not the case. The Herero and Nama tragedy was neither a systematic nor a predictable result of German colonialism.[39] For that reason, it should not be used as a general measure to assess the German colonial record. That record should no more be held hostage to the Herero-Nama war than an assessment of British colonialism in India should be held hostage to the similarly tragic and criminal actions of a single British army officer who ordered his troops to open fire on protestors in India in 1919, killing four hundred (and who, like Trotha, was similarly condemned, recalled, and punished). On such a "group-guilt" theory, every contemporary country is illegitimate, genocidal, and evil because every country has at one time experienced major policy lapses that have had terrible consequences.

When the Herero leader Samuel Maherero died in 1923, the Herero held a German-style military funeral for him and professed themselves to be Germans through and through. Clearly, they had not received their official acting scripts from radical professors telling them that they were supposed to denounce German colonialism and declare themselves eternal victims of Lothar von Trotha. It was only with the passing of this generation and their replacement by "Woke grandchildren" that both groups turned themselves into cargo cults hoping that trillion-dollar reparation packages would drop out of the sky from the white man.

Scholars who insist on giving this tragedy pride of place seem to know implicitly that it deserves no such position. Chief antagonist Jürgen Zimmerer unintentionally absolved Trotha when he told *Der Spiegel* in 2016 that he was "a war criminal by today's standards" and that "today he would be put on trial."[40] Well, by today's standards, virtually every pre-colonial *and* post-colonial leader in Africa, Asia, and the Middle East was a war criminal who should be put on trial. Zimmerer has equated Trotha's crimes with other contemporary "crimes" including the use of fossil fuels and unequal voting rights in the United Nations. This anachronistic imposition of one radical scholar's contemporary ideological code to *scold* the colonial past speaks volumes about the inability of most historians of German colonialism to do what historians are supposed to do: namely, *understand* the past.

The political scientist Klaus Bachmann argued in a 2018 book that the battles fought by German colonial authorities to maintain order in German Southwest Africa would never fall under the concept of genocide and blamed the "misleading academic agenda-setting" of contemporary academics intent on using the past to pummel the present. He did however charge a violation of humanitarian law in the raids, deportations, and imprisonments that came *after* the formal cessation of hostilities as chains of command broke down and chaos ensued.[41] If so, then the claim that this tragedy reflected something "systemic" about German colonialism is even weaker.

In the 2000s, a series of revisionist books were published by amateur historians, several of them German Namibians, based on new sources.[42] The general claim was that the casualties on the Herero and Nama sides were not intended as genocidal but reflected the harsh theater of war, a finding given academic respectability by the likes of Kuss and Lorenz. Nonetheless, these "hobby historians" who "write in newspapers" get the full up-turned nose treatment by the credentialed experts in the German academy for whom the genocide claim has become a major source of grants and status, no matter what new evidence turned up. The work of Brigitte Lau, for instance, caused gasps from the German academic establishment because, following the truth, she reached conclusions that differed from the anti-colonial narrative.[43] "Those whose interventions are taken up today in quarters one suspects they may be reluctant to associate with," warned one scholar darkly about Lau's work, "still have a duty to at least pause and reflect on the potential, if unintended conse- quences of their contributions—even if, in the case of Brigitte Lau at least, they clearly run counter to the intention of her life work."[44] In other words, politics comes before truth for these academics.

In the *Der Spiegel* interview, Zimmerer declared that any attempt by a European to judge the colonial past, especially if he uses scientific standards, is itself a form of colonialism. Of course, the work of Herr Professor Zimmerer is excused from such calumnies. When voices of reason dissent against the orthodoxies about the Herero-Nama wars, as occurred when I spoke in Berlin in 2019, it is an occasion to further declare that all scientific inquiry should be banned. "That such an important issue as the legacy of the colonial era is now in the gutter of party politics," Zimmerer declared about my talk, "is in part the fault of the federal government and Bundestag to clearly declare colonialism a crime against humanity and to recognize the genocide against the Herero and Nama."[45] History is something to be "declared" and "recognized" not investigated or debated. That is the gutter of academic history today.

CHAPTER 4

The Culturally Competent Krauts

I f we judge German colonialism by the place where most of it occurred, then German East Africa should receive most of our attention. This colony of eight million people which mostly became Tanzania (other bits are now in Rwanda, Burundi, Kenya, and Mozambique) accounted for about 57 percent of the German colonial experience in terms of people-years. It is far more noteworthy than any other part.

Why do we hear so little about German East Africa? For a simple reason: it was a resounding success, bringing prosperity to a region long wracked by internal conflict and the slave trade. It was a rare episode of "overseas development" that actually worked, and it enjoyed a high degree of popular legitimacy as a result. While on safari in the colony in 1909 after leaving office, U.S. president Theodore Roosevelt remarked on the "men of evident power and energy, seeing whom made it easy to understand why Germany in East Africa has thriven apace."[1]

The justifiably heroic figure here was Carl Peters. An adventurer par excellence, he signed twenty-five treaties with local chiefs in the course of just a few weeks in 1884 that put an area the size of India under German control. Peters has been dubbed a German *conquistador* because of the swagger he showed while scooping up territory for the German empire. But most of the time he was wracked by tropical disease, carried in a hammock by black porters while waving his pistol to indicate the direction he wanted to go. The German presence was welcomed by most groups because the region had long suffered from plundering and slave raiding. "[Our chief] welcomed them. All they wanted was to live in his country, so why should he abhor them?" a Luguru elder told a researcher in 1968. The Germans, he explained, offered protection from their historical rival, the Mbunga.[2]

Peters congratulated himself with youthful exuberance and wrote many silly things about the struggle for mastery in global affairs. Of course, later critics have pored over those youthful writings as evidence of the psychopathic drive at the heart of German colonialism.[3] The malarial musings of a young man swinging in a hammock somewhere in tropical Africa in the 1880s have become the basis of a *Götterdämmerung* tale of rot at the heart of the West.

The main resistance to German rule, not surprisingly, came from the Muslim elites of the coast who ran the major slavery and ivory trades in the region. The slave and ivory raider Rumaliza and the slave and rubber tyrant Tippu Tip made common cause against the German interlopers. They recruited black mercenaries from the interior with promises of plunder. Bismarck at first showed no interest in the territories claimed by Peters: "I don't want to hear about more land acquisitions, I prefer to see economic results."[4] Facing attacks on its factories in 1888, the German East Africa Company thus had to find its own mercenaries. It turned to Sudanese and Mozambican soldiers later known as *askari*. Under German command, they easily defeated the coastal rebels. In 1890, Bismarck relented, and a formal German mission took control of the private interests.

Under German dominion, a law-based, civic peace was extended to all parties, even the former rebels. One rebel leader, Bana Heri, surrendered in return for a title as sultan and a civil-service salary.[5] Rumaliza fled to the British island of Zanzibar, but he returned to file suit against his erstwhile ally Tippu Tip in a German court in 1902. "He gives the impression of having reconciled himself to circumstances and was in Dar-es-Salaam only a short time ago, when he introduced himself to me," one German governor wrote about Rumaliza.[6]

The Spirit of Berlin was implemented quickly in German East Africa. "Effective occupation" meant establishing government stations in the interior, but this had to be done with carrots rather than sticks. "I would rather give up the whole East Africa colonial endeavor than agree to imperial military undertakings in the interior," Bismarck warned. "In order to maintain friendly relations . . . we will need to gain the cooperation and support of the natives."[7]

Two military campaigns in the interior in the 1890s have been cited by critics to show the hypocrisy of those words: one on the slopes of Mount Kilimanjaro and one on the Iringa plateau. In both cases, the German aim was not to wipe out warring tribes but to establish a common set of ground rules and a civic peace. On Kilimanjaro, the Germans were first seen by Africans as hapless pawns in the long-running skirmishes among the region's dozen or so competing chiefs.[8] But military superiority soon allowed the Germans to prevail. They established a single paramount ruler for the region dependent on the German state. Trade and human life flourished as a result, making possible the building of a railway to the mountain region.

On the Iringa plateau, the Germans confronted the Wahehe tribe that had been driven there after waging no less than twenty-two wars against rival tribes in the previous decade.[9] From there, the Wahehe had continued assaults on their main rival, the Ngoni. Their leader had the delightful habit of murdering his own advisors and cousins, and the tribe was wracked by constant coups and familial disputes.[10] The Wahehe repulsed the first Afro-German expedition of 1891 (which included Lothar von Trotha). The Germans returned in 1894 and prevailed. The absconded Wahehe chief shot himself rather than be captured, despite an offer of amnesty and exile by the Germans. A bounty hunter tracked down the corpse and presented the local German district officer with the skull as proof of his death. Many Wahehe people began to treat the officer as the reincarnation of their leader because of the skull. The alarmed officer sent it to a museum in Bremen and resumed his duties as a mortal.

After suffering defeat, the Wahehe abruptly ended their war-like ways and became loyal German subjects. The deceased Wahehe leader's son was sent to Germany for education and on his return was put in charge of a district. The group provided substantial recruits to subdue the later Maji Maji Rebellion in the colony, relishing a chance to resume their fight against the Ngoni. "I spoke with a number of elderly [Wahehe] men who proudly told me of their service in the German administration," recounted a historian of the 1950s. "They brought out commissions, decorations, and equipment they had been issued; sang German military songs; and read passages to me from [German] books and papers in their possession."[11]

The events that unfolded on Kilimanjaro and on the Iringa plateau were repeated elsewhere in the colony. In the feudal kingdoms of Rwanda and Burundi, Germany recognized the existing tribal leaders after they agreed to lay down arms. As three scholars argued, Germany's state-building process in East Africa was motivated by the need to establish peace, not by the "economic results" sought by Bismarck.[12] Heinrich Schnee, who became governor of German East Africa in 1912, wrote: "Serious fighting was necessary before the Germans could enforce peace."[13]

The other piece of evidence often cited to show the evil origins of Germany's greatest colony was the so-called "Peters Scandal." After staking out the new colony, Carl Peters accepted a position in 1891 as an inland district commissioner on the slopes of Kilimanjaro. The governor told him that he should "establish peaceful relations with the tribes and chiefs in the hinterland" and "use money and good words . . . more like a diplomatic intermediary than a military dictator."[14] Peters managed the job well and became obsessed with the completion of the Kilimanjaro railway. He refused offers to bolster his scanty detachment of forty troops, consistent with Bismarck's admonition.

In 1892, Peters was accused of murdering his black lover and a black manservant because, the rumor went, he thought they were having an affair. Critics also claimed that he razed their villages for good measure. After a conservative member of the Reichstag allied with missionary groups raised the allegation in 1896, it was taken up with vigor by the Socialist legislator August Bebel. The debate on the charge seized the Reichstag for three days. The main thrust of the criticism was that Peters had failed to act on Christian principles and had instead followed local practices. As an appeals court said: "One can't concede that ideas about justice and decency that are substantially different than in Europe are allowed in Africa."[15] In today's terms, Peters was accused of being too "culturally competent." You would think that academics today would celebrate his rejection of "Eurocentric" notions of justice.

The Reich colonial office replied that it had already conducted two full investigations that had exonerated Peters. Nonetheless, it undertook a *third* one to satisfy the critics. The third inquiry found the same facts: Peters had sent one man to the gallows for theft, and several months later he had executed a woman who was spying for a rebellious chief. The inquiry concluded that the execution of the man was excessive and was motivated because he had won the affections of Peters' black lover. This was not the same woman as the spy, who had indeed been passing information to a hostile chief. Peters had burnt down a few huts in her home village, not the entire village, as a show of force. Under pressure, Bebel admitted that his British informants had been mistaken.

Since the records of the three separate official inquiries were destroyed in an air raid on Berlin in 1945, scholars have felt free to praise the initial, sensational allegations as more truthful. But detailed archival investigation by the American historian Martin Reuss, and later by the German journalist Arne Perras, turned up the truth. "No concrete evidence had been brought forth to substantiate the charge that Peters had had two people hanged because they had committed 'adultery.' Nor had anyone challenged Peters's legal right to impose capital punishment on thieves and spies, especially since Peters, at least, thought his station imperiled," concluded Reuss.[16]

Despite the debunking of the Peters Scandal, the allegations have been repeated by anti-colonial historians ever since. The scandal showed the "wrathful vengeance" and "violent repression" at the heart of the German colonial project, wrote one credulous American professor as recently as 2019.[17] Peters held a "brutal colonial *Weltanschauung*" charged another modern academic.[18]

Peters himself was not far from the mark when he remarked later that the "real scandal" of German colonialism his dustup revealed was the "philistines and old women [who] search with a magnifying glass for all sorts of things" with which to discredit the colonial project. The rebuke for Peters was sufficient to drive him out of the colonial service despite the slap on the wrist. "International attention and criticism made life uncomfortable for the government and increased their desire to close the Peters chapter as soon as possible," wrote Perras.[19]

If there was anything redeeming about the fake scandal, it was the efforts that ensued to improve the rule of law in remote stations. *The Times* called Peters "an anachronism" and suggested that Berlin convene another conference on colonialism to deal with "the abuse of powers" by colonial officials so that "acts of oppression shall not pass unknown or unrebuked."[20] Thus the "scandal," as with the Leist scandal, emerges more as a vindication than an indictment of German colonialism. The Germans had provided a viable pathway to peaceful and civic life in the Kilimanjaro region. That is why so many people sought to live at the government station where it all took place. What scandal occurred was less than it appeared. Even so, wide-ranging investigations and publicity prompted beneficial reforms. As Reuss concluded: "It was instrumental in stimulating the cry for colonial reform which eventually resulted in the creation of an independent Colonial Ministry in 1907. Beyond that, even those opposed to colonies became convinced that the Reichstag must become more deeply involved in colonial development if the rule of law was ever to replace that of men in Germany's far-flung possessions."[21]

● ● ●

Having first established peace in East Africa, the Germans proceeded to establish prosperity. A 1,250-kilometer railway was built linking Lake Tanganyika to Dar es Salaam. To this day, the railway remains the lifeblood of Tanzania's economy and of Zambia's trans-shipment traffic. The German colonial railway was not just economically beneficial. It also led to the documenting of the region's geography, vegetation, minerals, and peoples—much of which was carried out by the German-English railway engineer Clement Gillman as he surveyed the new line. He published voluminously, tying his studies together under the concept of *Zusammenhang* ("coherence" or "connection") that sought to understand each place as an integrated whole.[22] Along with the Leipzig professor Hans Meyer,[23] who was the first to record an ascent of Mount Kilimanjaro, these German-era colonial scientists brought Tanzania as a distinct place into existence.

For the green conscious, it is especially noteworthy that German colonialism discovered the knowledge and crafted the regulations that protected the great forests and fauna of today's Tanzania, Rwanda, and Burundi.[24] In 1896, the governor Herman von Wissman passed laws prohibiting unlicensed elephant hunting and created the first game reserves. The naturalist Carl Georg Schillings proposed "nature protection parks" (*Naturschutzparke*) that the British would eventually realize as the Selous and Serengeti nature reserves. In 1900, Berlin and London convened a trans-imperial Conference on the

A native public-health team and a female settler distributing medicine to children in German East Africa, 1903. *Bundesarchiv*

Preservation of Wild Animals, Birds, and Fish in Africa. The 1959 film by the German naturalist and Frankfurt Zoo director Bernhard Grzimek, *Serengeti darf nicht sterben*, which sought to preserve the Serengeti nature park from settlement and dismemberment after independence, achieved enormous critical and commercial success and became the first German film to win an Academy Award.

Of course, since such good works were carried out in colonial times, scholars are duty-bound to treat them with contempt and suspicion. Rather than admired as attempts to protect nature, conservation policies are derided as attempts to force hapless Africans who lived in the forests into wage labor. Not motivated by a genuine love and concern with East Africa's ecology, this conservation reflects the unresolved psychological problems of the German male. Once loved by critics, Grzimek's film is now denounced for using such offensive cinematographic techniques as filming out of the back of an airplane, as in a Nazi bomb-run flick.[25] He is also charged with using high-altitude shots that reflected "a measuring, calculating imperial gaze over an unclaimed colonial territory."[26] By that standard, every nature filmmaker who uses an airplane or drone is a closet Nazi or imperialist. Any educated person can easily see past these intellectual gymnastics. The truth is that Germany laid the basis for ecological and environmental protection in Tanzania.

Perhaps the most important development was the Africanization of the government through Swahili-language schools that trained native colonial administrators. By 1910, there were 3,494 elementary and 681 middle- and upper-school students in the state schools, compared to only 1,196 in the mission schools. Roughly 6,100 in total passed through the state schools from 1902 to 1914. In neighboring British Kenya and Uganda, by contrast, there were still no state schools. "The Germans have accomplished marvels," a British report on the colony's education concluded in 1924.[27]

The German colonial model as it emerged in East Africa was a hybrid of the hands-off British and the hands-on French approaches. Native rule was encouraged, but only through new integrative government structures rather than existing tribal ones. Military stations in the inland were replaced by government departments, staffed by the children of local elites who had been educated at secular schools teaching in Swahili. The educational policy reflected a pro-native orientation among the German administration. "For its time, this seems in retrospect to have been a unique investment by a colonial administration in the intellectual, and ultimately in the political, capacities of a subject people," wrote the Columbia University historian Marcia Wright, who was miraculously free of the Afro-radicalism of the American academy when writing in the 1960s. Local governors, she wrote, made a conscious decision to develop the colony for and with Africans rather than through settlers. "This policy amounted to a commitment to keep Africans progressing with the country as it became more developed and integrated."[28]

Settlers came. But their land acquisition was constrained in order to allow natives to develop their own agricultural capacity. The value of agricultural revenues of native-owned farms tripled between 1894 and 1913, as German rule made new inputs available and opened access to new markets.[29] Prosperous and stable coffee kingdoms emerged in places that had been slaving kingdoms wracked by internal conflict, such as Buhaya.[30] As Wright noted, "Steam power superseded porterage and cultivated products supplanted those of plunder and raiding."[31]

Anti-slavery policies, which had been a key factor in the decision to formally take over the colony, slowly eroded the power of local slaving interests. But there were some unforeseen difficulties. As early as 1891, the then governor Julius von Soden remarked that one of the main obstacles to abolition was that slaves would rather remain in their current state than become "free laborers" on a plantation, where they would have to work harder.[32] The German diplomat Heinrich Brode noted that slaves were considered part of the family in most instances and given only light work while "domestic servants at home appear much greater slaves than the natives who bear this name."[33] Therefore, German policy adopted a gradualist approach, eradicating slavery with a combination of incentives and economic development.

In 1904, a new colonial policy stated that all children born to slaves from 1906 on were to be regarded as free. Moreover, between 1891 and 1912, 52,000 slaves were freed by legal, social, and financial means.[34] Through these efforts, coupled with the growth of the capitalist economy that made it more profitable to hire labor, the roughly one million slaves in the area at the time of German colonization in 1890 fell to two hundred thousand by 1914 and would disappear entirely by the 1920s.

One of those freed was Martin Ganisya, who rose to become a senior teacher at the Lutheran mission school in Dar es Salaam: "Formerly its condition was one of injustice.... But now there is peace everywhere. There is none who terrorizes, for all are under the Kaiser's rule," he wrote in 1910.[35] As two Tanzanian scholars wrote in 2017: "The old concern of security against slave raiding and the internecine wars was giving way to normalcy and different concerns of life. Now instead of being wary of warring neighbors, the leaders of the local societies had worries such as wild predatory animals, the consolidation of exchange relations, new diseases that were emerging brought by foreigners, and increase of population in village settlements."[36]

In the Berlin legislative debate on the colonial budget of 1914, parliament passed a sweeping plan of progressive reforms that included medical spending, doctor training, property rights, protections from

coercive labor practices, health surveys, minimum wages, and maximum working hours.[37] The American scholar Woodruff Smith called
the resolution "the most complete statement to date by any colonial
power of its self-conceived obligation to subject peoples and of the need
for limitations on the exercise of imperial power."[38] The Spirit of Berlin
was at work. The resolution's "provisions for indigenous people went
further than those accepted by any other colonial power at the time,"
added the Stanford economist Lewis Gann.[39] The British would inherit
a colony in which the term "African bureaucrats" could be used without
irony: there were specialized officials with both the autonomy and
capacity to carry out functions of the modern state.[40]

Faced with such objective evidence of colonial beneficence,
anti-colonial scholars retreat to postmodernism. They argue that
so-called "improvements" were just another form of violence, a kind
of killing by kindness. As Eva Bischoff of the University of Trier
writes in typical high-mandarin style: "Instead of ruling by the
sword, German colonial officials aimed to control, regulate, and
optimize the lives of the indigenous population." Building hospitals
is rekeyed as a devious plot to find subjects for unethical medical
experiments and to supplant traditional quack doctors with
"Western" medicine. She then invokes the patron saint of academic
nonsense, the French theorist and sadomasochist Michel Foucault,
to support her claim that the patently beneficial actions the German
government took for natives were in fact harmful.[41] But if critical
scholars must retreat to Foucault, then the case for German colonialism has been made.

The American scholar Sean Andrew Wempe devotes a whole
chapter of his book on German colonialism to sniffing at ideas like
"rational emancipation, technological prowess, medical miracles,
and proper German industry." Wempe does not deny that Germany
brought emancipation from slavery, technological knowledge,

medical miracles, or modern industry. Far from it, he accepts that the Germans did this. But for a modern intellectual, valuing material and economic development is evidence of a paltry mind. What *really matters* to academics is how the German presence reflected dark, psychological, male flaws or the exasperating human desire to show one's worth: "Not only did this have the effect of asserting German moral superiority over both Arabic and other Europeans civilizations in the area, it also allowed German males to portray themselves as opening doors for Africans to develop and civilize."[42] That Germans *did* open doors for Africans to develop and civilize is not questioned; the real evil was the horrible act of taking pride in the endeavor.

Current scholarly assessment of the location of the German East Africa capital provides another example of academic perfidy. The traditional trading center of the area was the coastal port of Bagamoyo. The Germans decided to establish their capital thirty miles down the coast at Dar es Salaam. The fact that Dar es Salaam was a better harbor, that the Germans needed land for their new administrative capital, and that German merchants wanted only the chance to compete with the traders of Bagamoyo on fair terms apparently all pale in comparison to their nefarious plan to "gradually lure interior trade to a new site." Leaving the traders of Bagamoyo to carry on as usual was, in the words of one imaginative historian, an attempt to "outmaneuver" them.[43] And yet, had the Germans set up their capital at Bagamoyo, it would be maligned as an act to "displace" or "destroy" the local community.

Commandeering and razing the Bagamoyo port would have been the unfair course of action, and it was well within German capacity. If the Germans wanted to crush Bagamoyo they could easily have done so. But they did not. Both places became free ports and "in Bagamoyo there was more freedom to conduct business much the same way as had been done prior to the German takeover," one scholar noted sheepishly.[44] What eventually tilted the balance was the construction of the railway from the interior to Dar es Salaam and of course the administrative presence of the German government. The "socio-economic struggle" that academicians espy is simply humans doing well by doing good. Africans were content to see shabby and overpriced goods "outmaneuvered" by better quality and more competitively priced ones.

● ● ●

At this point, the critic of colonialism rolls her eyes in boredom. Can't we talk about hippo-whip floggings, exclusionary colonial clubs, and photographs of black breasts? All this talk about basic social needs is boring. What about queer liberation and cultural appropriation?

Like much of the academy, scholars of German colonialism today pour their hearts into studies of sexual fantasies and laundry detergent commercials. The trend is captured nicely in the title of a 2010 article by the American scholar Daniel Walther entitled: "Sex, Race and Empire: White Male Sexuality and the 'Other' in Germany's Colonies." In German East Africa, white men outnumbered white women by seven to one. Walther's research breakthrough in his article is to show that German men had sex with local women. That was bad, in his view, because sex "became an instrument for European conquest." How exactly? Because the women liked the Germans more than they liked native men. Professor Walther has another research breakthrough: some German men *did not* have sex with local women. That was bad too. Why? Again, because it was an instrument of European conquest. Efforts to limit sex were "invoked to extend further German control over the colonial environment."[45] To discourage sex, the colonial bureaucracy established public health systems, a population census, regulations, and all those other hateful things of modern government.

Chief colonialism inquisitor Jürgen Zimmerer has also insisted that attempts to limit interracial sex were racist. By denying black women access to the boudoirs of white men, he asserts, German imperialists denied them access to European civilization. "Thus, the principle of biology had pushed aside any civilization-missionary interpretation that Africans would have to be educated as Europeans," laments Zimmerer. Wait! Wasn't the "civilization-missionary" impulse what scholars find morally repugnant? Indeed, in other moods, Zimmerer condemns that impulse.[46] Self-contradiction is never a problem as long as the anti-colonial viewpoint is unchallenged. It's hard to keep up with this intellectual *Cirque du Soleil*.

The scholarly schizophrenia—colonialists are evil when they do *A* and they are evil when they do *not* do *A*—is also found in studies of how German rulers dealt with tribal organizations. In a 2010 essay, Frank Schubert of the University of Zurich argues that German rule entrenched tribalism in Africa. The result, he explains, was that German colonial areas could never develop *national* political movements.[47] So according to Schubert, African ethnicity is a Western invention, a pretty demeaning claim if you are an African. But Schubert also admits that his theory does not apply to German East Africa because a pan-ethnic national movement, the Tanganyika African National Union (TANU), later became the leading force in politics. As we will see below, his theory also does not work for German Togo. To put it politely, if your theory fails in two of four cases, including the most important one, it is probably not correct.

A district officer attends a local assembly meeting in Usambara, German East Africa, n.d. *Author's collection*

Other critical scholars hold an opposite theory: German colonialism was wicked because it did *not* entrench tribalism. It denied ethnic groups their indigenous institutions, agency, and political parties, forcing on them a "Western" conception of national movements and a modern state, and "carved up" Africa with "artificial" boundaries that did not create ethnic ghettos.[48] Aside from this being a false account of how African borders and institutions developed, most native kingdoms never developed the capacity or institutional forms that would allow them to survive the ups and downs of modernity even if they had been protected. The kingdom of the warlord Chief Mirambo had been built on warfare, plunder, and slavery. It collapsed the moment he died in 1884, *before* the Germans arrived in East Africa.[49] If German rule had done "violence" to traditional ruling structures such as Mirambo's empire, it no doubt would have been welcomed by the Arabs, Buganda, and other groups under its thumb. Such native institutions usually collapsed under their own weight once these societies encountered a better alternative.

• • •

Were African people satisfied with German rule in East Africa? Did they consider it legitimate? In addition to testimonies like that of Martin Ganisya, the dozens of major tribes that rallied around German rule prove the loyalty the colonial government was able to inspire in its subjects. The two principal chiefs in the coffee-growing area of Buhaya, Chief Kahigi and Chief Mutahangarwa, for example, were "on the best of terms with the German Administration," concluded the Anglo-German scholar Alice Werner. The latter chief "was living in a neat house, built of bricks made and burnt by his own people, and roofed (alas!) with corrugated iron."[50] Werner was reviewing a photo book published by the local district officer in Buhaya, a young lieutenant Max Weiss, who is revered in the region to this day.[51] Across Africa, concluded the American scholar Woodruff Smith in 1978, there was "considerable evidence" for the German claim that they enjoyed a good reputation among the natives.[52]

Chief Kahigi of the Kianya people is an instructive example of the respect locals had for the Germans. Kahigi's kingdom had sunk into civil war when the Germans arrived. When he provided workers to build the government station (or *boma*), the Germans guaranteed his position among his people. Over time, his own court took on a fully German flavor, with uniforms and a military band. In 1907, a delegation from the Reichstag and the colonial ministry visited his residence, where the two sides pledged eternal loyalty to one another. The region "served as a model for a successful native policy," wrote the University of Hamburg historian Michael Pesek. Of course,

modern-day scholars like Pesek have to cavil and sniff at any suggestion that the people of Kianya *actually* found German rule to be
legitimate. Such beliefs can be written off as false consciousness.
"Germans often tended to take the behavior of the Africans in the
contexts of their performances as an expression of their loyalty and
acceptance of colonial rule," he writes. But wise contemporary
scholars know better. When parading or taking target practice, the
tiny little military detachments led by one or two German officers,
in Pesek's view, "evoked a 'space of death' as a possible future reality
for disobedient Africans."[53]

The "space of death" supposedly conjured up by the evil Germans
was one impressive feat considering how few of them were on the
ground. In 1904, the entire colonial government of German East
Africa—a sprawling territory three times larger than Germany
proper and populated by nearly eight million people—consisted of

Askari troops of German East Africa at play, 1914. *Bundesarchiv*

just 280 whites and 50 native civil servants.[54] There were an additional 300 German or European soldiers. By 1913, the combined government and military staff of Germans totaled just 737.[55] Native elites ran the colony, operating out of thirty government/military *bomani*.[56] In population terms, the numbers are similar to what they would be if New Jersey was run by 320 civil servants (New Jersey had 432,000 state and local employees in 2019). By 1914, the number of German and European soldiers had *decreased* to 200, alongside 2,500 enlisted native soldiers (*askari*).[57]

The same pattern was true in other German colonies in Africa. One scholar estimates that there were 4,400 people for every single German soldier in Africa, more than the 3,600 and 3,700 for French and British possessions respectively, and roughly twenty-five times as many people per soldier as in Germany itself at the time.[58] To illustrate, today's Bolivia has roughly the same population and area as German East Africa and maintains a military of 32,000 soldiers. If a small government and the absence of coercive forces is the hallmark of legitimacy, German colonialism was fantastically legitimate.

Some scholars insist that these numbers conceal pervasive violence that gives the lie to legitimacy claims. Alongside those martial parades evoking a "space of death," they point to corporal punishment (mostly floggings), citing detailed records kept by the German administration. These floggings were used in place of jail sentences for convicted criminals, since jail time removed men from their productive roles in their families. They were carefully recorded, monitored, and evaluated. As a result, we have a wealth of archival data on floggings, which gives anti-colonial critics many happy hours poring over the data. How much more humane German colonialism would have seemed if it had not kept records! Between 1903 and 1913, the average annual number of flogging sentences per one thousand persons in German East Africa remained consistent at about 0.73

(that is, less than one flogging per thousand people per year).[59] If contemporary Germany were to convict just 10 percent of its reported crimes and to punish them by flogging, the similar rate would be seventy-seven floggings per one thousand people per year, roughly one hundred times more floggings than in colonial East Africa.

But anti-colonial scholars never consider such contextual and comparative questions. Do they think that the German administration should not have upheld the rule of law? Do they think that jail sentences would have been more humane? Do they think that the floggings were not legitimate? Do they believe that the detailed statistics were compiled and monitored because the German authorities were trying to cover up the whole system?

Moreover, the floggings elicited strong shows of support from natives. To refute this, scholars twist themselves into logical and empirical knots. In writing about the full cooperation that native leaders gave to German officials in the investigation and prosecution of a case of native murder and cannibalism in 1908, Eva Bischoff of the University of Trier insists that the response "can be seen not as collaboration but as an act of cultural and social resistance." Come again? The native leaders, she ventures, cooperated only in order to outwit their political rivals by gaining German praise. Her evidence? The speculations of a single German missionary who was not present at the trial. Since none of the court records have survived, Bischoff feels free to accept these random speculations as true and to ignore the legal records still extant in Germany that show the opposite.[60]

If German colonial government was not considered legitimate, it would have taken very little to overthrow it. The Muslim Egyptian and Sudanese *askari* soldiers were soon joined by native blacks as the backbone of the colonial military. It became a prestige appointment with its own esprit de corps. The "loyal *askari*" became fanatically loyal not just to the German colonial authorities but to their own comrades and regiments with institutional histories, insignia, and rituals. The term was sometimes extended to include soldiers who did duty as tax collectors, messengers, guards, clerks, and laborers. They "fulfilled German colonial interests, while also creating new opportunities for East African men, women, and children to improve their access to status, wealth, and security," in the words of one specialist on the cohorts.[61] Colonialism in German East Africa worked because so many people found it preferable to the alternatives. When German recruiters came to town, natives rushed to enlist because military service offered an escape from the poverty, oppression, and stagnation of traditional life. The departure of a man from his family to join German forces was a moment of pride and celebration, often captured in a staged photograph.

Anti-colonial scholars studiously ignore such legitimacy and native collaboration, preferring a Eurocentric dogma of German oppression and native resistance. "The history of collaborators and intermediaries has been expelled from scholarship," noted three scholars about the amnesia, because "studies foregrounding such interactions might be interpreted as exculpatory."[62] In other words, if the facts support the case for German colonialism, those facts need to be suppressed. To cover up and distort evidence is to fulfill one's sacred duty as a professor.

● ● ●

There is one final redoubt for the anti-colonial critic of German East Africa: the Maji Maji Rebellion of 1905–07. Like the Herero and Nama campaigns, this rebellion absorbs an inordinate amount of scholarly energy because it is seen as the Achilles' Heel of the colony. If you can discredit German East Africa using this single event, then you do not need to bother with the rest. Yet the argument here is farcical. Not only was the counterinsurgency campaign against the Maji Maji justified (as was that against the Herero and Nama), but it was carried out in a way that was proportionate to the threat (unlike that against the Herero and Nama). Moreover, most natives in German East Africa supported the German side.

As with all violent attacks on governing authorities during colonial times, the Maji Maji Rebellion has been cast as a "liberation" movement. One hyperventilating German progressive wrote a book describing the rebellion as "the first joint uprising of black African peoples against white colonial rule."[63] The loose federation of warlords and Arab slave traders that tried to oust German rulers in this rebellion was not seeking to liberate anyone. Its *explicit* goal was to reclaim ancient privileges like looting and pillaging weaker tribes, taking and trading slaves, female trafficking, and excluding new trading elites from power. As scholar Heike Schmidt summarized: "Attacks against Germans appear to have been chiefly motivated by the goal of removing the frail colonial monopoly of violence and thus re-opening the territory to slave raiding, and also by personal revenge. Most attacks were directed towards raiding and looting, a return to the economic staple activity before colonialism."[64] A detailed empirical study by Alexander De Juan of the German Institute of Global and Area Studies confirms that it was not "oppressive taxation" that caused the rebellion—a favorite trope of critics—but the fact that taxation was creating a modern and durable state that threatened the political power of premodern elites. German colonialism threatened to liberate common people (especially women) from their feudal dependence on such elites.[65] Colonialism was the true "liberation struggle."

Tanzanian scholars Eginald Mihanjo, director of studies at the National Defense College of Tanzania, and Oswald Masebo, chair of the Department of History at the University of Dar es Salaam, noted that the Ngoni warlords who led the rebellion were vicious militarists who plundered and killed lesser tribes until the Germans stepped in to establish order. The Ngoni were imperialists afraid of the liberating force of German rule: "The emergence of a younger generation that included Christian converts, western educated youths, well-travelled traders, and even ex-slaves all becoming part of the social fabric was perceived as a challenge to their traditional authority," wrote Mihanjo and Masebo.[66]

The number of deaths caused by the rebels was horrific. The colonial government estimated that thousands of rebels were sent to their deaths by the warlords and voodoo men who claimed their "water water" oath would deflect German bullets. The casualties on the German side, which was composed mostly of African troops, numbered only in the hundreds. The best that scholars can bring themselves to admit about the large number of African traders, clerks, soldiers, teachers, workers, and farmers who rallied to the German cause is a blasé dismissal of their relevance for being on the wrong side of history.

The colonial government estimated that 75,000 Africans died either in battle or as direct civilian casualties. The death toll was not because of some willful policy of maximum damage by the Germans, but because the geographic, social, and economic characteristics of this "theater of war" (*Kriegsschauplatz*) led to rebel battle tactics that cost lives.[67] Rebels hid in villages, used human shields, and sent hundreds into gunfire with orders never to surrender. Governor Heinrich Schnee compared the irrational fanaticism of the Maji Maji rebels to the "Fuzzy Wuzzy" dervishes armed with only spears and Islamic prayers who were defeated by the British general Sir Herbert Kitchener in the Sudan between 1896 and 1899.[68]

Anti-colonial and Tanzanian-nationalist historians have inflated the civilian death toll by factors of three or four. They do this by adding in the later deaths from famine, disease, and inter-tribal conflicts that erupted after the campaign ended. Whatever this post-rebellion civilian death toll, the blame for it rests with the rebels, not with the German counterinsurgency. The normalcy that had been established by German rule was destroyed by the rebels. This is especially the case because the rebels destroyed the Christian mission stations that had traditionally provided food and safety for women, the elderly, and children who later became the main victims of postwar famine and disease.

After the defeat of the Maji Maji Rebellion, Berlin initiated efforts to rebuild the region through development, as the British had done in South Africa after the Boer War. The "age of improvement"[69] that followed left behind one of the most progressive colonies in Africa. German desires to prevent another Maji Maji uprising and African desires to reap gains from colonial rule combined to create one of Africa's most well-run colonies.

Anti-colonial scholars insist that the Maji Maji rebels were good nationalists who were repressed by bad colonialists. Nobody saw it that way at the time. It was only in the 1960s when a British historian, John Iliffe, was working in Tanzania under orders from the post-colonial dictator Julius Nyerere that the distortionary story of Maji Maji virtue was spun. Nyerere wanted to use the Maji Maji as an origin story for his nationalist movement. Iliffe's graduate students were repeatedly told by local elders that this story was wrong, that the Maji Maji were hated.[70] Nonetheless, Iliffe followed "Jungle Teacher" Nyerere's insistence and called it a "peasant" rebellion that prefigured that "later nationalist movements."[71]

At a conference on the centenary of the rebellion held at the German Historical Museum in Berlin in November 2005, the historian Christoph Sehmsdorf, along with a former German ambassador to Tanzania, scandalized the scholarly attendants by noting that

German colonization of the region was largely beneficial and that the defeat of the Maji Maji was justified and widely supported. True to form, the anti-colonial establishment took to the fainting couch. Stefanie Michels of Heinrich Heine University Düsseldorf declared that she was "ashamed" to attend the conference.[72] One can almost hear the ghost of Carl Peters: the only shame here is the shame of progressive thinkers, the "philistines and old women" who distort the facts to suit their ideological needs.

CHAPTER 5

Rafting the Sanaga in Wicker Baskets

German Cameroon accounted for 30 percent of the "people-years" of German colonialism, the second-largest portion after German East Africa. The scholarly literature on this colony is sparse. Presumably, that's because not much happened other than successful German rule. The main interest that scholars take in this colony is scouring the record for instances of *kraut* brutality—more "colonial scandals"—or for some hapless, fever-ridden, colonial official's diary that they can deconstruct with a postmodern scolding.

German Cameroon was a mountainous and rain-soaked colony of three million people, twice the area of Germany. In the south, German rule operated through the coastal Duala tribes, who became prosperous middlemen as a result of colonization. The Duala consisted of three major factions and were plagued by internecine warfare throughout the nineteenth century. This culminated in 1876 when two of them ganged up on the third and executed its chief. Politics among the Duala never moved in the direction of unity, despite encouragement from European traders to form a single political organization. In 1881, the two remaining chiefs wrote to the

British asking if they would be so kind as to annex the region. "We are tired of governing this country ourselves; every dispute leads to war and often to great loss of lives," they noted.

The British were not interested. So the German consul in Tunis sailed into town and offered his services to the more powerful of the two chiefs, Ndumbe Bell, who had already sent his son for education in Britain. Facing an attack from three of his brothers who were allied with his rival chief, Bell called in the Germans. In 1884, the two chiefs made peace, agreeing to lay down arms in favor of German annexation. As a result, the Duala gained a central political organization for the first time. The murderous and destructive tribal feuds stopped. In the words of Ralph Austen, a University of Chicago historian, the two chiefs agreed "to give up full autonomy in return for more orderly settlement of the endless conflicts at all levels of local political life."[1]

For Austen, the eminent authority on German rule in Cameroon, the Duala appeal for British and then German annexation "does raise questions concerning the confidence of local Africans in their own institutions." There was, he concluded, "a clear statement in all these communications that the local political system was not working." While German rule meant that the Duala would lose exclusive control over trade channels to the interior, they gained far more from the peace and development of German rule. "The Duala monopoly was definitely at an end," Austen wrote. "But the Duala had not resisted the expansion of European enterprise in their hinterland, in part because this expansion had created new opportunities.... for increasing their wealth and cultural influence."[2] Over time, the Duala became wealthy landowners and the backbone of the colonial civil service.

It has often been said that European colonialism was a self-liquidating enterprise because it enriched, empowered, and awakened the societies it governed. For those attuned to the Spirit of

A new governor for German Cameroon arrives at the Duala port, n.d. *Author's collection*

Berlin, this was the whole point. Yet the creative friction between colonial rule and emergent societies could be scorching hot at times. This was the case with the Duala. German rule empowered and mobilized the Duala. The sense of entitlement could easily outrun that of gratitude. Frictions came to a head in 1910 over German plans to build a new port town on Duala lands. In addition to the infrastructure, the Germans wanted to reduce malaria transmission from areas where mosquitos bred. The dispute was over money, not "native sovereignty" or "human rights" as later commentators have extolled. Having been greatly enriched by colonialism, the Duala had become savvy negotiators and balked at the exercise of eminent domain over their now valuable lands.

In March 1914, the Germans imprisoned a Duala chief and his advisor for their failure to accept just compensation and comply with the exercise of eminent domain. The Duala tribal council then hired a German lawyer to represent their property claims in Germany and petitioned the German government. This parlous situation on the coastline would prove a fatal weakness for Germany at the outbreak of war six months later.

• • •

The German presence in Cameroon created similar effects on inland groups such as the Bakoko. At first, some Bakoko members resisted German claims and created a Society of Death to harry German officials. In 1892, a small German force composed of freed slaves defeated them in a short battle. After this, the Bakoko adjusted to the new trading system on the rivers. This adjustment boosted jobs, incomes, and opportunity while increasing markets for their goods by reducing transport costs.

Farther north was an area that had experienced a long and bloody pre-colonial history in which Sudanese and Moroccan empires conquered and assimilated some indigenous tribes and enslaved others. By the time the Germans arrived, there was little left of the indigenous Cameroonian population of the far north. The trade and enslavement of "wives" was particularly rife in this area thanks to the confluence of its Islamic and militaristic traditions. A German doctor undertook a survey of the "wives" of the eight highest-ranking members of five different groups and came up with a tally of 2,307, or 58 wives per man.[3]

Between 1884 and 1902, the Germans and their native allies steadily expanded into this region. The Islamic Fulanis finally bowed to German control and put an end to slavery and trafficking in women. If the Germans had not occupied the area, a Yale historian who conducted fieldwork in the area in the 1920s surmised, the British or French would have. If they had not, then the entire colony would have become a Fulani slave empire, which, given the Fulani record, "might appear to make the native more content with European imperialism."[4]

Having now created a central political organization in what would become Cameroon, the Germans followed the British model. They established native courts and police, native representative councils, a decentralized administration, and training for local elites to serve in central government. By 1913, Christian mission societies in the south operated 631 schools serving forty thousand students. The Germans followed the British example in the north by banning Christian missionaries and leaving Islamic law in place for local matters. As the popular governor Theodor Seitz explained: "We do not want to force our culture on other groups but to help them to properly grasp and cultivate their own cultural values, freed from distortions."[5]

Slavery was outlawed in 1895, and by 1900 it had entirely disappeared, far faster than in any other European colony. Such advances attract little notice from contemporary historians. Colonial official Heinrich Schnee later summarized the achievements:

> Along with robberies and murders among the tribes, so too the acts of violence committed by hereditary rulers against their subjects, not to mention the poisoning murders and other evils of sorcerers and fetish priests, have been brought to a stop with a strong hand. Slavery in its dire forms had been eradicated, and slave robbery and slave trade eradicated. The mild forms of bondage (house slaves) that were still maintained in individual colonies were condemned to extinction by the stipulation that the children of the serfs were free and other regulations aimed at ransom and release, and steps were envisaged that would completely abolish the existing ones. In ever-expanding

areas, the native received his rights from the impartial German judge. Special ordinances were issued to protect the natives against harassment or exploitation by whites and colored people, in particular to protect those who worked as workers on plantations or building railroads and who made ample income. The native, for his part, had to pay the government a moderate poll tax, the collection of which helped educate him to work. A medical staff, equipped with the most modern aids and constantly increasing, brought the natives protection and help against diseases that they previously faced defenseless.[6]

This created an unprecedented period of peace. Native forest-dwellers came into contact with the modern world for the first time. German expeditions of scientists, geographers, botanists, and anthropologists trekked into the mountains without so much as a single guard. They found a ready welcome from local peoples. The main "resistance" was from the difficult climate. "Our film camera went on strike because it had not been packed correctly for the tropical climate," noted one expedition report.[7]

The Germans enacted a robust development program in Cameroon in order to comply with the Spirit of Berlin's insistence on "effective occupation." Starting in 1894, they introduced agriculture, industry, and infrastructure. Two major inland railroads were completed by 1913, which, like German railways completed in other colonies, remain the economic backbone of the modern country today.[8] They created markets for inland farmers of palm oil and kernels, corn, tobacco, livestock, and peanuts. The combined 160 kilometers of inland railway might seem short. But it cost seven times as much per kilometer to build as those in nearby German Togo because of the difficult terrain. Without formal colonial rule, the railroad would

never have been built, as the railroad companies had to borrow
money from the German government for construction.[9]

By 1914, 107,000 hectares of land were allotted to plantations.
Though a relatively small area, the agricultural plots had a massive
influence on the colony. Africans clamored to work on the plantations, which provided a steady income and protection from violence.
African entrepreneurs, meanwhile, joined in plantation development.
Native cocoa-plantation owners of repute became common, such as
Johannes Manga Williams, Samuel Nduya, and Abel Mukete.
German policy was sensitive to the needs of protecting native land
for cultural and subsistence reasons, which is why the plantation
areas remained small compared to the overall cultivable land of the
colony. The colonial government continually rejected proposals from
the main plantation company, the Deutsche WestAfrikanische
Handelsgesellschaft (DWH), for larger estates. "It is also necessary

Students with slates at a mission school in German Cameroon, n.d. *Bundesarchiv*

that the most careful consideration should be given to the allotment of reserves for the Native population and, therefore, the claims of the D. W. H. should not be considered in priority to those of the natives, but the land required by the natives should be theirs for all future time," insisted the last governor, Karl Ebermaier.[10] German efforts in Cameroon would serve as reference points for later African critics of the laissez-faire British and French administrations of the region.[11]

The pace of economic and social change under German rule was head spinning. By 1913, the Duala had shifted from being traders to producers. There were 572 Duala-owned cocoa farms by 1913, and Duala entrepreneurs (including Chief Bell's son) were active in opening land and establishing farms. The sort of black-urban middle class that was long established in British Lagos began to emerge in Duala. One of Chief Bell's ex-slaves, David Mandessi Bell, was the most successful merchant and planter in the region. Chief Bell's grandson ended up as the foreman of a timber company in Germany.

Rubber plantations were established to replace the destructive practices of harvesting wild rubber forests. Plantations were easier to monitor for labor abuses as well. As a Yale historian wrote in the 1920s, "That the Government could not supervise the behavior of traders wandering about the interior is obvious; but, that brutality was punished by the administration is an inference clearly deducible from a glance at court statistics showing the penalties inflicted on whites."[12] Heinrich Schnee added that the sporadic labor abuses in rubber plantations in German Cameroon were far less than those of rubber plantations in the Belgian and French Congo areas. "No one ever heard of 'red rubber' in the German colonies," he noted.[13]

Still, the combined trade of *all* of Germany's colonies never amounted to more than 0.5 percent of Germany's total trade. Lenin's theory that colonialism was driven by the need for trade simply does not apply to Germany's colonies.[14] Its main effect was bettering the lives of Africans, for whom the export trade was an escape from a precarious life in the forest.

• • •

As elsewhere, the legitimacy of colonial rule in German Cameroon can be inferred from the scant military presence. In 1912, government forces amounted to about three thousand German and European soldiers and police, alongside nine thousand native soldiers and police. The combined ratio of police and soldiers to population was one for every one thousand people, consistent with other German colonies when soldiers and police were taken together. For reference, the number of people per soldier and policeman in the modern states of the region is between one hundred and two hundred.[15] Martin Dibobe, the Cameroonian who became a train conductor in Germany and was later misrepresented as "anti-colonial," noted in his famous 1919 petition that German forces in Africa were "assured of the attachment and loyalty of the natives."[16]

Contemporary academics simply cannot sit still when presented with evidence of the strong legitimacy of German rule in Cameroon among native leaders like Johny Baleng, a minor chief about one hundred miles north of Duala in the inland grasslands area. "At first sight, his general attitude seems to have been simply pro-colonial," notes one academic, pointing to the obvious facts that Baleng loyally served the German (and later French) colonial states. Baleng had learned multiple languages from the diverse slaves kept by his father, and thus when the Germans arrived, he was a handy interpreter and problem solver. Nonetheless, when an academic begins his article with the "uneducated" and "simplistic" idea that anyone could possibly have supported German rule for anything other than cynical and calculative reasons, we know we are in for a good old debunking.

In Baleng's case, the debunking is mere speculation: he died a loyal servant of European colonialism, and his family attested to this fact. But the savvy scholar, writing a half century after his death, knows better. His "exaggerated positive way of speaking about" colonial rule "shows the need for Johny Baleng to create and maintain a visible loyal attitude towards the colonial administration and his ability to identify opportune situations and act strategically," the scholar insists.[17] How does he know? Because the editor of the special issue of the journal in which the article appears has arbitrarily framed the lives of people like Baleng in terms of "moral ambiguity" and "opportunism." This is how the nice little racket of anti-colonial scholarship works: someone proposes a theory; someone else fits their evidence to the theory, thus claiming to have correctly interpreted the evidence; and the original theorist then circles back and claims that the theory is "evidence-based."

It is not surprising that academics do not seem interested in debunking "simplistic" descriptions of Africans when they appear to be anti-colonial. There is no deep dive into "moral ambiguity" and "opportunism," nor learned references to complex social-behavior theories and the need to peer beyond the formal record. Far from it. Faced with any mere utterance or act that can be in any way interpreted as anti-colonial, academics rush headlong into overtures about noble "resistance" and celebratory "decolonization," if they can catch their breath amidst all the enthusiasm.

The story of Hans Dominik, the German soldier and inland station head at Jaunde (Yaounde), captures the legitimacy of the German Cameroons. Dominik was loved by his subjects and in turn had a deep love for his adopted land. He wrote two books on government and geography in the region and took a native wife.[18] When Dominik's troops arrived at the inland settlement of Jaunde, they found a typical situation of intertribal warfare. Dominik quickly found allies among tribal chiefs who, as with Chief Bell, saw German rule as preferable to ongoing conflict.

One chief who sided with the Germans sent his fifteen-year-old son, Charles (Karl) Atangana, to study at a German Catholic school in the south. When Atangana returned to Jaunde, he became Dominik's right-hand man, serving as census taker, tax collector, and general problem solver.[19] He often dined at Dominik's house and, in the words of one biographer, was "an unswerving advocate of what he saw of European civilization, customs and religion."[20] At Dominik's urging, Atangana also worked with German linguists to document the local languages that would otherwise have disappeared.

Dominik was at the center of the most infamous "colonial scandal" of German Cameroon in 1906 when it was alleged that native troops under his command had put fifty children of rebel groups into wicker baskets and sent them to their deaths down a series of rapids on the Sanaga river.[21] The allegation filled the German tabloids for months until the Socialist legislator August Bebel (who had made up allegations about Carl Peters in 1896) admitted that his native informant had concocted the story.[22] Nonetheless, the lie was repeated at the Versailles talks and has continued to circulate ever since, taught to naïve German undergraduates by their anti-colonial professors.[23]

Another "colonial scandal" erupted in 1907 when the governor was recalled to Berlin under pressure from the legislature to face three charges of maladministration: profiting from land deals, complaining that a local judge was unfairly harsh on whites, and arranging for a German lady friend to obtain a false passport. After lengthy debates and inquiries, an administrative court rejected the first charge, while ruling that he had made silly errors on the latter two. He was ordered to pay a fine.[24] Seen in the light of pre-colonial and post-colonial Cameroon, this "scandal" is evidence of effective German rule.

Despite their overreach and rumormongering, German legislators like August Bebel played the opposition role that characterizes any liberal democracy. Today, German scholars fall over themselves to claim that such Socialist critics in the legislature were anti-colonial.[25] That is incorrect. In fact, they were mostly committed to colonial rule and were essential to its success. Their "socialist imperialism" differed only from the mainstream conservative imperialism in its prescriptions for how colonialism should be administered—no mandatory labor, more worker education, and so on.[26] "The German nation and its parliament had at all times shown serious concern for the well-being of the native populations," observed the British expert on German colonies William Harbutt Dawson in 1926. "[They] visited with disapproval and condemnation any administrative or other shortcomings which were brought to light in the colonies."[27]

The accountability of the governors to the governed that the people of Cameroon enjoyed under this liberal-democratic tutelage was far greater than any they would have enjoyed otherwise (and any that has existed since). That is why even the harshest critics of colonial abuses in the German legislature were supporters of colonialism. Most believed, to use the crestfallen words of one scholar, that "by exporting the capitalist means of production to Asia and Africa, imperialism was creating for itself new competitors and opponents, awakening the national consciousness of non-European peoples and providing them with the material and intellectual weapons for their own emancipation."[28] Some Socialists legislators were pro-British because they saw in British colonialism a highly liberal model that Germany should follow. The "scandals" that they raised were, in this view, not inherent in colonialism and certainly no reason to abandon the colonial mission.[29] They pushed Berlin to uphold the Spirit of Berlin.

"In the end, our colonial policy boils down to our native policy," declared Germany's top colonial research official on that memorable night in January 1914 when he was in London briefing the nabobs of the British Empire on progress and setbacks in the German colonies:

> It's not really a question of ruling the natives, for in most places they are scarcely ruled at all. Rather, the question is what we will do once the natives have the power to shape their own fate. Our hope is that they become skillful, intelligent, and more numerous. For only then will our colonial empire prove its worth.[30]

As went native interests, so went German interests. There arose in the room at Whitehall a great cheer from the assembled British empire-builders who were engaged in the same project of native uplift. Seven months later, the two sides would be at war.

CHAPTER 6

How Do You Say Class Conflict in Ewe?

German colonialism in Togo—just 8 percent of the German colonial experience—is intriguing because of the desperate attempts by academics to discredit what was seen as a "model colony" (*Musterkolonie*). Mere mention of the term "model colony" is enough to bring forth a righteous froth from most professors and to induce snickering in their graduate students. Facts, however, support the view that German rule here ushered in a miraculous positive transformation.

The colony was founded in 1884 when two main chiefs along a thirty-two-mile strip of coastal land in West Africa (one of whom had Portuguese ancestors) signed a petition asking for German protection from the British. A German envoy promised each "protection to maintain the independence of his West African territories." Berlin envisioned the coastal strip as a trade corridor where European merchants, protected by a limited government, would barter with native groups for mutual benefit. The plan meshed with the long-standing commercial ethos of the coastal groups. Since the neighboring British colony imposed stiff import duties on goods, a free trading colony next door would prosper. "This small area of Togo, in relation to the trade routes to the deepest interior, may be called very promising," wrote the German envoy.[1]

As in other colonies, German colonialism in Togo followed a steep learning curve. The first governor began work with two secretaries, twelve staff, and five rifles.[2] Since Berlin's claims extended well into the interior, the Spirit of Berlin compelled the Germans to make that occupation effective. With only a small contingent (numbering perhaps five hundred) of mostly Hausa soldiers known as the *Polizeitruppe* (Police Force), the Germans pushed inland to compel a civic peace among the twenty-odd rival tribes and warlord families that had beset the region for two hundred years. A ten-day battle against the warlords of *Tové* in 1895 ended after twenty *Tové* fatalities. A fourteen-day skirmish against some clans of the Konkomba people in 1898 was the fiercest battle, leaving one thousand to two thousand Konkomba dead. Most of the Konkomba, a segmentary system without centralized leadership, did not join the battle, and indeed welcomed the German arrival. Since anti-colonial scholars consider *any* colonial authority to be illegitimate, they describe these operations as "atrocities" and the victims as "resistance fighters." But the Germans achieved what no native tribe had been able to: they built a unified, stable, and modern state where human lives could flourish.[3]

If there was anything remarkable, it was how quickly the various groups of the interior accepted German rule. They soon redirected their efforts from clan warfare to productive labor. In the northwest, the Nawuri and Gonja groups, which had overrun and subjugated smaller rivals in the fifteenth and sixteenth centuries, became allies and profited handsomely from German rule. After the Germans entered the region in 1899, both groups took up cotton and mango cultivation, which became major sources of native wealth. By 1913, economic endeavor had so overshadowed tribal conflict as the main vocation of the tribes that the Nawuri chiefs chose a Gonja as their chief liaison with the Germans. The Germans in turn appointed this Gonja as the "head chief" for the region as a whole. The colony became so peaceful that the German military presence shrank to just seven German officers and 150 natives by 1903, rising only slightly in the decade that followed.

• • •

Sparking economic development in German Togo was a *vital* task deemed "essential to maintain life." When the Germans arrived, Togo's "transportation system" involved carrying head loads along bush tracks or paddling canoes through coastal lagoons. Beginning in 1892, a one thousand–kilometer road network was built, and in 1905 the first of three railway lines opened. A wharf and port were constructed at Lomé. This infrastructure created access to markets for agricultural production, a life-and-death concern for the African population. The vision of a thriving entrepôt became a reality: in 1901–02, just over half (58 percent) of the of the 267 vessels that called were German. The remainder were from Britain and France, whose merchants preferred Togo to their own colonial ports.[4]

Togo was a German creation, and its rapid transformation into an integrated economy with institutionalized governance was astonishing. In some ways, we can simply take the dominant Marxist scholarship on the colony and interpret it in a positive rather than negative manner. The successful endeavors by the Germans to establish "capitalist rule of law" and a "capitalist economy," in the telling of a typical book of 2019, led to "the transfer of the most developed capitalist conditions of the metropolis to the colonial-oppressed peoples." In the process, the Marxist tale continues, "the German colonial rulers had railways built, set up schools, intervened fundamentally in the traditional judiciary . . .

and improved health care."[5] At last check, this scholar did not appear to be making plans to move to a noncapitalist country with no health care or schools and a legal system overseen by traditional chiefs. As is so often the case, a more objective account is provided by the German colonial prelates who were actually there. In the words of Alex Haenicke:

> In place of the insecurity that prevented people from even going to the nearest villages, there was now complete calm. Previously, a failed harvest would cause immediate famine because the natives were not accustomed to trade among themselves. The plagues that devoured the negroes had almost completely ceased thanks to the work of our doctors. On my first trips, I met entire villages that were completely extinct due to smallpox. Afterwards there was hardly a man in the entire Togo region who had not been vaccinated. While the natives used to sit idly in front of their huts or under the large Palaver tree of the village for most of the day because they had no buyers for their products, people could now be seen working in their fields from early morning to late at night to give themselves a better life through the work of their hands.[6]

To build infrastructure and clear fields, the German government initially allowed local officials and European farmers to requisition mandatory labor from local chiefs in place of taxation.[7] A law in 1907 outlawed mandatory labor for private works and set regulations for private wages, while regulating public mandatory labor. Under the law, all adult males had to work twelve days a year unpaid for the government, or else pay a tax of six marks. About half of adult men paid the tax, and the other half contributed labor. Some natives in the north of the colony migrated to the British Gold Coast to avoid the service, or because they believed that a mere visit to the British colony entitled them to British citizenship.[8] The chiefs organized mandatory labor on behalf of the government and collected some taxes of which they were allowed to keep 5 percent. Not surprisingly, chiefs often sent a single slave or servant back several times under different names to provide the mandatory labor for members of the chief's family.

In the sedulous industry of German scholars intent on debunking the "model colony" moniker of Togo, this system of mandatory labor has drawn ghoulish attention. Some charge that the colony was little more than a slave state. Prosecutorial scholars draw heavily on the investigations carried out by the scientific polymath and colonial critic Gottlob Adolf Krause, whose travels and research across West Africa were made possible thanks to the political stability, liberal freedoms, and road access of European colonialism. Krause wrote critical articles in the *Kreuz Zeitung* and filed a lengthy petition over mandatory labor in Togo with the Reichstag in 1898. A prickly figure, Krause ended up penniless and friendless living in an attic in Zurich, where his vast research collection was sent to the garbage dump after he died in 1938. He was celebrated by communist propagandists in East German in the 1960s as "anti-colonial."[9] He is better understood as a liberal product of colonialism. An eccentric individualist who spurned his own culture and "went native" in Africa, Krause wandered about dressed as a Haussa chief. His fervent aim, he said, was to bring about "the moral elevation of its inhabitants."[10]

Several pieces of evidence prove that Togo was not in fact a slave state. Britain also relied on mandatory labor in the early stages of development in the Gold Coast because taxation was impractical. Mandatory labor to support the cost of public works was appropriate when taxation was not feasible. Along with German Samoa, Togo was the only German colony that was not reliant on subsidies from Berlin. The government was told to make do with whatever revenues it could raise locally or to find other ways to carry out public works. Berlin was so stingy that one witty district officer would file a report indicating how many bristles of a paint brush had fallen out after each use.

Togo was awash with former slaves and servants who had been freed from the Ashanti kingdom in the neighboring Gold Coast. These freedmen often found themselves without a means of survival, and many put themselves back into service under chiefs in Togo. As the Germans pushed for an end to slavery, the problem of finding a livelihood reappeared. The Germans were asked by chiefs what they were supposed to do with the ex-slaves. The Germans replied that they should be put to use as wage laborers or sent to provide the mandatory labor requirement. The German explorer Ludwig Wolf convinced the chief of Dahomey to use his slaves in new cash-crop endeavors rather than slaughter them in annual ceremonies (just as the Dahomey soldiers and their wives who were at the center of the Heinrich Leist whipping "scandal" in German Cameroon in 1893 had been purchased by another German trader to save them from a similar fate). Public works required public resources. In a colony filled with idle labor due to European success in ending slavery, mandatory work for the state was both justified and effective. A thriving capitalist economy could not be built overnight, and the Germans recognized that economic success, not punitive law, was needed to solve the labor problem in Togo. The mandatory-labor system without doubt was unpopular for many who could not pay, migrate, or send a slave in their place. But the charge that German Togo was a slave state is unfounded.

By the same token, the fact that the colony raised 88 percent of its revenue by taxing imports can hardly be cited as evidence that fiscal policy was "exploitative."[11] After all imports are by definition not the product of local labor, and thus it is hard to conceive how raising their price would be considered "exploitation" of the people of Togo. More likely, anti-colonial critics, because they view colonial rule as *by definition* illegitimate, must insist that any taxes raised were "exploitative." Had the government raised no taxes and thus undertaken no public works, the scholarly critics would cavil about neglect and misgovernance. Ah, to be a model colony!

• • •

One consequence of Togo's small size was that most of the arable land near the coast was already under cultivation when the Germans arrived. There was little space for European plantations, and a law of 1904 banned the purchase of native lands without the personal consent of the governor. The Germans made an exception for the black American Tuskegee Institute, founded to form a model of black integration into the modern economy. Berlin's agricultural attaché in Washington invited the institute to establish an experimental cotton farm and agricultural school in German Togo. Those efforts between 1902 and 1908 led to the foundation of a modern cotton sector and a sixfold expansion of the colony's cotton exports. German officials were attracted to the institute by its philosophy that work brought dignity and cultural uplift, something incomprehensible to the Marxist understanding of labor as a zero-sum tussle over profits.

For Marxists, the Tuskegee efforts were by definition evil since they required wage labor and integration into the global economy. There is a cottage industry of leftist scholars who denounce the institute's experimental farms as "black on black exploitation."[12] The fact that cotton today is Togo's second-biggest export, providing a livelihood for thousands of families, is immaterial to these ideologues of colonial critique.

German colonialism in Togo also brought a vast expansion in access to life-saving health improvements. This included the building of water wells, cemeteries, latrines, and hospitals, as well as campaigns against diseases like smallpox and sleeping sickness (to which we return below). Modest fees were charged at public hospitals for those who could pay, while the poor were treated for free.[13] Of course, sneering scholars insist that improving the public health of the Togolese people was a cynical effort to ensure a healthy labor supply, to make travel easier in the interior, or to reduce political opposition. Call it what you will, the initiative was an appropriate public service that delivered objective benefits and gave legitimacy to German rule. In 1916, a British writer, who was otherwise keen to discredit German colonialism, concluded thus:

> A stable government has been established, the hinterland has been opened up, three railways and many excellent roads have been built, slavery has been abolished and inter-tribal warfare discouraged, and a number of experimental plantations have been formed. The [German] government, by its energetic policy, have developed the resources of the country, established trade and commerce on sound lines, and made considerable progress towards the betterment and prosperity of the people.[14]

The term "model colony" was later defined by the Marxist Ralph Erbar[15] as entailing the following: comparatively few native uprisings, sound infrastructure, social and cultural advance, fiscal self-sufficiency, and progress in health and education. While admitting that German Togo fit the description, Erbar nonetheless derided the naked attempt to "optimize exploitation."[16] This attempt to debunk all successful policies as nefarious projects to boost the labor supply led the American historian Ralph Austen to parody Marxist critics of the German ban on highly profitable imports of brandy. In the Marxist crosshairs, he wrote, the German colonial administrators are "exposed as materialists" whose secret concern was "primarily for labor power rather than the moral well-being of potential African alcoholics." The silliness of such claims, Austen concluded, tended rather to reinforce the idea that German rule in this tiny region had brought untold progress despite setbacks: "Togo's model colony status survives with some reservations."[17]

• • •

German sovereignty in Togo brought an inrush of traders, adventurers, and amateur officials, with its inevitable train of petty abuses. These abuses were the subject of liberal processes of exposure, investigation, prosecution, correction, and monitoring. A key figure in the campaign for good governance was the German trader, farmer, and miner Johann Karl Vietor. Through his Society for Indigenous Protection (*Gesellschaft für Eingeborenschutz*), he lobbied against the liquor trade and the use of flogging and for the protection of native lands. He pushed the colonial government to embrace reforms in areas such as native representation in the colonial government and the protection of native cultures.[18] He embodied the Christian, capitalist, and conservative impulses of German colonialism and their universalizing ethos. He was much loved by his African staff. While on home stay, he served as the colonial-affairs spokesman in the Reichstag for the Christian Social Party.

Scholars gleefully pore over the detailed reports the Germans compiled in investigating the abuses called out by Vietor, seemingly unaware that the system that produced this information justified German rule and gave it local legitimacy.[19] We have no similar evidence on pre-colonial abuses because those societies were too undeveloped to produce it, and even if they could have, they were illiberal and would not have considered such abuses noteworthy. The same, alas, became true of post-colonial Togo.

By around 1905, the apparatus of the liberal and accountable state was emerging quickly in this model colony. The chiefs who continued to exercise authority at the local level were integrated into a common law system. As a Ghanaian scholar explained:

The governor of German Togo, Julius Graf von Zech, hosts his counterpart from neighboring British Gold Coast at the capital Lomé, 1907. *Bundesarchiv*

They had jurisdiction over ordinary civil cases, up to a value
of 200 marks. Appeals against their decision could be made
to the district officials. All criminal cases had to be reported
to the officials. The chiefs were often summoned to the
government stations to have new laws announced or judicial
procedures explained to them. When deciding appeals, the
administrative officers usually summoned reliable local
elders to supply information on local customs of succession,
inheritance and property rights.[20]

The governor from 1903 to 1910, Julius Graf von Zech, was a
Catholic and self-described humanitarian who emphasized Germany's moral responsibility to improve the lives of Africans.[21]
Bismarck encouraged this new humanitarianism as a way to gain
Catholic support at home. "A man of great culture, he was an
authority on African laws and customs," wrote two Stanford historians about Zech. "He was determined to govern through indigenous institutions—as he saw them—and promoted ethnographic
studies in order to acquire a better understanding of African
jurisprudence."[22]

The critical treatment of Zech by later anti-colonial writers reflects
the self-contradictions that usually go unnoticed. Zech's restraint of
plantations by giving Africans as well as the governor a veto on land
sales was designed to prevent the sort of landless peasantry that had
emerged in German Southwest Africa. The consequence, of course,
was that Togo's economy grew more slowly. Had Zech allowed plantations, he would have been accused of exploitation. Since he did not,
he is accused of immiseration.

In Berlin, the high-liberal phase of colonialism was overseen by
the colonial secretary Bernhard Dernburg, a Jewish Prussian indus-
trialist who was only too glad to be accused of having "gone native"

by favoring African interests over German ones. "The government can prosper only if it embarks upon a . . . black-friendly . . . and, as I would say, [black-supporting] policy," he explained to Reichstag critics of his policies to restrain plantation companies.[23] By 1914, German colonialism in Africa was the only serious rival to the British colonial model in terms of legitimacy and efficacy.

German rule in Togo led to the exploration, mapping, and identification of the peoples and places of this hitherto undocumented territory. Governor Zech wrote the first history of the Chokossi people of the north. A missionary did the same for the Ewe. Another missionary, Ernst Bürgi, published no fewer than twenty books about the Ewe language and land.[24] In the words of one scholar, he "did more to standardize the Ewe dialect among Ewe *speakers* in Togo and Ghana than any other individual."[25] There is no reason why Togolese schoolchildren today should not learn the name of Ernst Bürgi, along with the names of other German colonial founders like Heinrich Klose[26] and Valentin Massow.[27] As in other African countries, an honest reckoning with the past suggests that colonial founders, not the pre-colonial chiefs or the post-colonial despots, have the most plausible claim to be the fathers of the Togolese nation *as a nation*.

• • •

As elsewhere, German rule here was remarkably light-handed. Just three hundred Germans ruled one million Africans. The tiny capital at Lomé exerted minimal day-to-day control, while local chiefs carried out most governance. Newly educated Togolese joined the colonial bureaucracy becoming, in the sneering words of one scholar, "men and women who oiled the wheels of the colonial machine."[28]

German Togo is yet another "exception" to the thesis that German colonialism entrenched tribalism. German authorities *rejected* attempts to create ethnically based parties and boundaries, especially for the dominant Ewe group, a policy continued by the British and French. As a French official later noted of attempts to carve out a pure Ewe state, "such a plan would represent a return to the fragmentation which the European colonizers found when they first came to Africa, and which is totally opposed to the general welfare of Africa."[29] German colonial rule worked through ethnic leaderships for pragmatic reasons but intentionally avoided creating ethnically-based jurisdictions because they would be an obstacle to the emergence of a civic, national identity that was crucial to a modern (and self-governing) state. "Artificial" borders reflected a belief in the universal humanity of Africans. They were a direct rejection of the essentializing racism of later anti-colonialists.

In 1981, a project for gathering oral histories in Togo interviewed several people with memories of the German era. Alfred Kwami-Kuma Nyassogbo was born in German Togo in 1895, so his memories of German rule were those of a nineteen-year-old boy: "When they came, our country was nothing but scrubs and forest. First they cultivated, then they sowed good seeds. . . . We are very grateful to the Germans for the tremendous achievement they have performed in various areas in Togo," he told the interlocuters.[30]

Another man, Têtêvi-Godwin Tété-Adjalogo, whose father had welcomed the onset of German rule, explained that the "paradoxical prestige attached to the Germans in Togo" was a result of the increasingly long view of history and a better perspective on the choices faced by people like his father. Seen in perspective, especially with the ravages of despotic post-colonial "independence," he explained, tutelage under German colonial rule was the most just and effective way for Togo to emerge as a democratic and prosperous nation.[31] That is why his father was a founding member of the "Alliance of German Togolanders" (*Bund der Deutschen Togolander*) set up after World War I, which sent petitions to the League of Nations demanding a return to German rule.

Other historians who conducted fieldwork would find curious stock phrases left over from the German period. "And one for the Kaiser!" was bellowed out by Togolese fathers while spanking their sons. "Not in Gruner's time!" was a common sigh of old women referring to better days under a former district officer, Hans Gruner.[32]

One head of the forestry department in German Togo, Oskar Fritz Metzger, noted the "ridiculously small" police force of five hundred in the colony and the "satisfaction with German administration" of the natives. This, he argued, was "the greatest proof to refute the infamous lie of the German inability to colonize." Metzger spent most of his time mapping inland forests and wildlife, so he had a keen appreciation of local responses to German rule. One result, he rued, was an increase in the safety of hunting parties since they no longer ran the risk of being captured and enslaved by rival groups. By 1913 this was leading to a visible decline in wildlife. But any attempt to regulate hunting would "shatter the confidence" of the natives who profited handsomely from the hunting parties, he warned.[33] The solution he proposed was the creation of wildlife and forest protected areas. The idea was taken up by the British and French.

One of those who moved to the new colony because of its economic opportunity and political stability was a mixed-race Brazilian named Francisco Olympio. His son, Octaviano, pushed Governor Zech to undertake political reforms, making use of political opportunities hitherto unknown in the region. In 1913, for instance, when the Reich's secretary for colonies visited Lomé, Octavanio Olympio presented him with a seven-point petition calling for better organization of the judiciary, the

The popular district commissioner Hans Gruner on a scientific expedition in German Togo, 1894. *Author's collection*

abolition of flogging, better prison organization, the admission of natives to the governor's cabinet, the writing of a general code of statutes, a reduction of taxes, and freedom of trade. Olympio's demands were evidence that German colonialism was working, developing a new generation of native leaders who exercised their German political rights and invested themselves in the construction of a strong and liberal state. German colonialism planted the seeds of a literate and economically independent class like the Olympio family. These seeds would grow into the successors to the colonial state and, if given time, that transition would be a success.

● ● ●

When the German press was frothing in indignation about a talk I gave in Berlin in 2019, one newspaper, *Frankfurter Allgemeine*

Zeitung, cited a "well-respected" book by Rebekka Habermas of Georg August University of Göttingen that "speaks of an omnipresence of colonial violence and describes well-documented sources of everyday racism, brutal maltreatment and sexual assault by the German colonialists."[34] It is a good rule that anytime someone cites "evidence" intended to make you shut up, you should go back to the source. Almost always, the evidence is less than what is claimed.

Habermas is the daughter of the German socialist philosopher Jürgen Habermas, and her ideological apple did not fall very far from the tree. "Violent colonial history," she wrote in 2018, is "an essential part of the European heritage."[35] The "well-respected book" that the German press cited to foreclose debate on colonialism is called *Scandal in Togo: A Chapter of German Colonial Rule.*[36] It is about an allegation of misconduct made in 1906 about a young German district officer named Georg ("Geo") Schmidt. The book documents the story of Schmidt's alleged rape of a Togolese girl. She had been force-married to a Togolese man at a young age, who then apparently rented her out to Schmidt on weekends. The allegation (against Schmidt for rape, but not against the Togolese man for polygamy and pimping) was lodged by a local Catholic missionary. It was taken up by the Berlin press, investigated by the Reichstag, and led to the filing of formal criminal charges. Schmidt was tried and acquitted but then removed from his position by the governor.

Habermas called her book "micro-history," which, by definition, does not tell us *anything* in general about German colonialism. This is especially the case when the micro-example has been chosen because it is a "scandal." If anything, we should assume that a scandal is a scandal because it is *not* typical. But let us assume that we *can* learn something general about German colonial history from this incident. What do we learn? That German colonial rule by the early twentieth century had reached impressive standards of governance.

Even in the hands of a dedicated anti-colonial ideologue, the Schmidt story provides a ringing endorsement of German colonial rule. The people of Togo, who under their pre-colonial rulers had been systematically raped, murdered, plundered, and enslaved, experienced under German rule a brief moment in which a *single alleged* rape by a single official became the subject of a wide-ranging national inquiry, public debate, court trial, and ultimately professional sanction. If only the people of Togo could have enjoyed anything like German rule before or after!

The *Frankfurter Allgemeine Zeitung* article was doubly ironic because the illustration the newspaper chose to visualize omnipresent *kraut* brutality in the colonies was a photograph of none other than the German explorer and district officer Hans Gruner ("Not in Gruner's Time!"). If the *Frankfurter Allgemeine Zeitung* photo desk had done a little research, it might have come across the 2013 article in the newspaper *Modern Ghana* noting that Gruner "is still famous in Togo for his remarkable knowledge of Ewe customs" and that the value of the map he drew (still being used, especially for settling land disputes) "cannot be overemphasized."[37] Gruner had converted a military station into a scientific-research center and was widely travelled in the northern areas of the colony, where he carried little more than binoculars and a notebook.[38] The work done by Gruner and his team, *Modern Ghana* commented, quoting one memorial, "will always remain a glorious chapter in the history of German spirit and German colonial cartography."[39]

The photo desk also might have come across another Ghana newspaper article that details how Gruner personally mediated a dispute in 1894 between the indigenous peoples of the town of Krachikrom on Lake Volta and a group of Hausa who had fled persecution from the powerful Ashantis a decade earlier to set up the nearby town of Kete. "No resolution was forthcoming until the intervention of a German,

Dr. Hans Gruner, but for whom there would have been a war in 1894," the newspaper noted.[40] The hyphenated Ghana town of Kete-Krachi stands today as a testament to Gruner's valued service.

White liberals at Georg August University and the *Frankfurter Allgemeine Zeitung* forcing their "progressive" views onto the "barbaric" judgements of native Africans who actually experienced German rule? Not in Gruner's time!

● ● ●

The historical profession has fallen into all the familiar traps in writing the history of German Togo. The field was more or less defined by the state-directed East German historian Peter Sebald, whose first work used Leninist tropes about Western colonialism and the need for the mild rule of the Stalinists.[41] After Sebald regained his intellectual freedom with the collapse of communism, he revisited his earlier conclusions to provide a more balanced account.[42] He argued that German colonial rule in Togo could have done better by being more like British colonial rule. His main conclusion, in the words of one reviewer, was that "colonial history was not necessarily a misfortune for the colonized societies."[43]

Of all the attempts by historians to pummel the "myth" of the model colony of German Togo, some are so plainly dishonest that one need only quote them to discredit them. The American scholar Dennis Laumann, for instance, insists that German rule in Togo was a disaster. His evidence? A quote from a nationalist Togolese historian in 1969 that "the people of Togo were completely disenchanted with the nature of the administration and found it unbearable."[44] This is a *claim* made by a person who was not present and who in the context of "academic freedom" in Togo circa 1969 would have lost his head for saying anything else. Laumann then adds his own declaration that Germans "denied Togolanders their basic freedoms."[45] One wonders exactly what he means by "basic freedoms" in the context of early twentieth-century West Africa. Since fundamental rights such as not being enslaved and having enough food to eat were so vastly expanded under German rule, Laumann must mean things like the right to family leave and gender-neutral bathrooms.

Laumann then sets out to confirm his point by turning away from what he sees as the self-serving colonial narratives of German officials to the enduring "oral traditions" of the people of Togo. For a Marxist who has faith in "the people," popular testimony is guaranteed to support leftist assertions. But alas, the Togolese people do not speak their lines. "The oral history of the German occupation, to my initial surprise, indirectly supports the model colony thesis, emphasizing what oral historians describe as the 'honesty,' 'order,' and 'discipline' of the German era."[46] So what do advanced scholars do when the facts contradict their ideology? They "cancel the people" in Bertold Brecht's famous phrase. In Laumann's words: "Oral history is shaped by the economic and political realities of its present, and thus, as it transforms over time, is a reflection of the specific era in which it is produced."[47] Translation: the people of Togo cannot be relied upon when they give the wrong answers. Again: Not in Gruner's time!

It has become something of a running joke that Western scholars pen evermore anti-German diatribes while the Togolese express evermore fond recollections of German rule. In 1984, on the centenary of the German arrival, the Togo government went out of its way to hold celebrations of the "enduring partnership" between the two peoples. A French scholar huffed about the "anachronistic Germanophilia" that persists in Togo, adding, "This irenic vision of German colonization, of Germany, and of Germans in general is not limited to the cities but can be found even in the small villages."[48] Even worse, this self-identity as inheritors of the German tradition was making life better for Togo! "The current power of Germany, its supposed 'virtues' as regards the rigor of the Germanic organization and discipline, inevitably are having an impact on the Togolese reputation in Africa, on the self-esteem of the inhabitants of Togo, and on their standard of living," wrote another dismayed French scholar.[49] The quandary for such progressives is that they set themselves up as the conscience of "the oppressed," yet they find to their chagrin that all those stupid brown and black people refuse to act as stage props and enact an oppression drama. The scholars then must "decolonize the decolonized," explaining to themselves that those brainwashed brown and black people are yet another sorry example of colonial oppression. Not in Gruner's time!

CHAPTER 7

The Suspicious Dr. Koch

T hroughout its African colonies, Germany was unequalled in its ability to scale up life-saving health interventions against smallpox, sleeping sickness, and other nasty tropical diseases. It also excelled at providing for general public health. Cynics dismiss these accomplishments as a way to "optimize exploitation" or find unsuspecting brown and black people for unethical experiments. The truth is that the German health miracle in the colonies was a sincere and just accomplishment that by itself renders the German colonial era a success.

It is easy to forget that until World War I, German was the language of global science. The German scientific ethos was adventurous and thorough. The famous Schlagintweit brothers from Munich engaged in the singular feat of mapping and describing the diverse cultures of North Africa, Tibet, Central Asia, and the Himalayas, all while creating an indigenous network of scholars in their wake. Their comrades, native and European alike, followed them, even unto death.[1] German doctors took advantage of growing colonial possessions to make major contributions to the science of Africa and Asia. We have already seen two examples: the nature parks created by Carl

Georg Schillings in East Africa (later denounced as the product of the Nazi-bombardier gaze) and the work of Nobel laureate Robert Koch to save the cattle of the Herero from *rinderpest* (presumably just a stalling tactic until Lothar von Trotha arrived). The entire German colonial enterprise was suffused with scientific purpose. In German Togo, the Hamburg research doctor Ernst Rodenwaldt launched the field of "medical geography" as a result of his observations on the relationship between malaria outbreaks and salinity levels in coastal lagoons.

Without doubt, Germany's greatest humanitarian contribution to Africa during its colonial period was the discovery of a cure for sleeping sickness. In terms of lives saved, Germany's colonial achievement could stand on this ground alone. Sleeping sickness originated in nomadic cattle-herding populations in Africa whose movements had spread the disease for hundreds of years before the colonial era.[2] The increase in intensive farming under colonialism accelerated its spread, an inevitable result of policies to increase food supply and modernize agriculture. The disease was ravenous. The British calculated that an outbreak in 1901–07 killed between two hundred thousand and three hundred thousand people in British Uganda, and two million people succumbed in all of East Africa in 1903 alone. "The sleeping sickness problem overshadows everything else in my work here," wrote the governor of Uganda at the time. "The disease rages unchecked and hundreds are dying every month."[3]

Many of the sick fled to Catholic mission hospitals to avoid being thrown into the jungle by their kin where they would be devoured by leopards. In the private Congo estates of the Belgian King Leopold II, five hundred thousand died in 1901 alone. This prompted the king to convene a special commission and to lead international collaborative efforts to slow the spread. Scholars who point out that sleeping sickness was a far-graver threat to the population of the Congo than Leopold's rubber operations are dismissed as "apologists," even though the king's efforts saved hundreds of thousands of Congolese lives.[4]

Robert Koch was a simple country doctor in Germany in 1876 when, in his spare time, he discovered the life cycle of anthrax. In 1882, he identified the tuberculosis bacteria. Next he went to Egypt and India and deduced how cholera spread. After that came the *rinderpest* research and a Nobel prize, and from there he went straight to East Africa to work on sleeping sickness. His first contribution in East Africa came in the field of maritime engineering. Preparing to cross Lake Victoria to a research station, Koch was puzzled by the archaic means used by the natives to maintain their boats:

> Two men have to constantly bail water that penetrates through the joints, because the people do not know how to seal the seams. This is very striking because they have the material right in front of them: they could use the rubber sap of the lianas or the fragrant resin of the incense tree, the canarium edtile, which the natives call Mwaffu. Without this, the boats must be checked thoroughly before each use to ensure that everything is OK, because the journey is already dangerous with the usually high waves. If the boat sinks or a serious accident occurs, you are doomed because the lake is teeming with crocodiles.[5]

The absence of innovation, Koch noted, reflected the universal spirit of *all* premodern societies that acted upon tradition alone. The natives certainly did not complain when Koch taught them the simple means of saving their lives and expanding their fishing success by sealing the boats with readily available local materials. With the boats sealed, Koch turned to his main task.

Between 1901 and 1913, fifteen medical-research missions came to Africa to study sleeping sickness. Under the International Sleeping Sickness Commission convened by colonial powers, German scientists under Koch identified the tsetse fly as the carrier of the disease. Next came methods to identify and isolate patients and to eliminate the tsetse fly's habitat. Germany and Britain agreed in 1908 to prevent infected Africans from crossing borders, and in 1911 they signed a cooperative agreement to combat sleeping sickness in West Africa. The Germans got results: in German East Africa between 1908 and 1911, 62 percent of the four thousand cases treated whose outcomes were known were healed using palliative drugs, a worthy achievement against a disease whose mortality rate was 80–90 percent.[6] Koch headed the international expedition to British Uganda and German East Africa in 1906–07. His account of his research showed the local population's desperation for a cure. Natives streamed into the German camps, many with their sick relatives held in "slave forks" because of their erratic behavior.

The British, French, and Belgians praised German efforts and acceded to German requests for access to their colonies for research and treatment, leading them to plan for a pan-colonial, integrated, tropical-medicine health service. In the major centers of research and treatment, German authorities enjoyed the cooperation of tribal leaders, who understood the threat to their people. Chief Mutahangarwa, the coffee-growing *mukama* of the Ziba kingdom whom we met earlier, hosted a German treatment camp on Lake Victoria. The chief's "very helpful people," as Koch called them, built the camps and laboratories and carried out the population surveys and isolations of cases. At one point, twenty-five young men of this Ziba kingdom acted as trained medical auxiliaries visiting villages to identify cases. They were paid a monthly wage plus incentives for finding cases, more money than most made in a year.

Robert Koch on the shores of Lake Victoria, 1906. *Robert Koch-Institut*

These auxiliaries had learned to read and write at a nearby German mission school, reflecting the "growing interest in modernization" of the chief.[7] The German camp attracted hundreds of victims every day, and the chief basked in the adulation of his people for being a modern leader.[8] The royal family happily exchanged "clan shrines and their ancestral spirits" for modern medicine as the primary mode of healing disease, a fact much bewailed by academics as "cultural disruption."

Eventually, the disappointing results of the early treatments at the camp and the organizational challenges of managing the auxiliaries led to an abandonment of this model. It was a mutual parting of ways as both sides sought to respond to the chaos and uncertainty of a humanitarian catastrophe. But scholars must read dark overtones into the change, suggesting that German relations with the chief had frayed and that colonial medicine was discredited in the kingdom.[9]

If so, it would be hard to explain why the chief continued to work with the new organization that continued Koch's work and then engaged in a robust defense of German colonialism in 1914.

Koch made the breakthrough shortly before he died in 1910. He invented the term "chemotherapy" to describe the use of synthetically manufactured chemicals that would attach to the sleeping sickness pathogen and kill it.[10] Despite being stripped of its colonies at Versailles, German scientific work continued, even though its scientists were often excluded from postwar research in Africa. A new Institute for Tropical Medicine was opened in Hamburg just as the war erupted. In 1916, the successors to Koch's team developed the first vaccine, Bayer 205, which the company patriotically dubbed "Germanin." Berlin offered to share the findings in return for its colonies but was rebuffed. Instead, the French pharmacologist Ernest Fourneau at the Pasteur Institute reverse-engineered the drug on the basis of patents that Bayer had taken out and named it Fourneau 309. The French used it to combat an outbreak of sleeping sickness in the 1920s in French Cameroon and French Equatorial Africa. The French doctor Eugène Jamot between 1925 and 1935 treated "hundreds of thousands" of cases in Cameroon and Upper Volta alone. Germanin continued to be used and was added to the Wolrd Health Organization's list of essential tropical medicines in 1979. The work of Koch "is accounted even by Germany's enemies as work for civilization in the highest sense," wrote the American scholar Mary Townsend.[11]

● ● ●

The achievements of European colonialism in the area of public health command heroic efforts from anti-colonial critics. Their starting point is to assume than absent colonialism, infectious diseases would never have spread to the Third World. This is a bizarre claim since many diseases (like sleeping sickness) were indigenous while others (like smallpox) had already arrived by other means. As the Turkish Nobel laureate Orhan Pamuk noted, these critics leave the impression that "if it weren't for the West, the East would be a wonderful place."[12] He had in mind the critic Edward Said's analysis of venereal disease in Egypt, which Said seemed to assume was a unique European bane upon hapless Arabs. As Pamuk was aware, Egypt's indigenous rulers applauded efforts by Britain to stamp out venereal diseases, which were mainly spread within Arab society. After the establishment of self-government in 1922, they "demanded that their own administration institute the same policing measures for the sake of its own (future) citizens."[13]

Modern colonial critics tend to see things like public health as nefarious systems to control populations, work them to the bone, and implant in them evil notions of modernity. The "hermeneutics of suspicion"—interpreting every action and fact involving the West in the worst possible light (while simultaneously pursuing a "hermeneutics of charity" towards everything emanating from the Rest)—hang heavily over assessments of public health in the colonial era. Germany's efforts to control the spread of sexually transmitted diseases in its colonies, in the estimation of one scholar, were part of efforts at "broadening colonial rule" (which is bad), as well as being "agents of modernity" (also bad).[14] Never mind that the spread of infectious diseases was a serious public-health hazard in all parts of the world (colonized or not), that the measures taken by German authorities greatly reduced them, and that the methods they used were little different from those used in Germany itself (or in the colonies after they became independent).

Not surprisingly, since the German cure for sleeping sickness looms as a great summit of colonial achievement, it attracts frantic efforts from academics to debunk it. The German cure was merely an underhanded way to "establish European dominance" and resulted in "discriminatory practices" such as isolating the infected, in the obtuse thinking of one advanced professor.[15] The historian Sarah Ehlers charges that European efforts to combat sleeping sickness began only when the first cases showed up in Europe in 1900 and were therefore an expression of European racism.[16] This is disproven by early Portuguese efforts that dated to 1870, and more broadly by the fact that tropical medicine was a major sector of research long before the European scramble for Africa, both in the Americas and in Southeast Asia.

Others have questioned whether Germanin itself was such a miracle since another drug appeared in 1940 with similar efficacy. But that was long after the German medicine achieved its major gains. As two Bayer scientists, who are probably more reliable than the supposedly disinterested scholars grinding their ideological axes, wrote in 2020: "The availability of [Germanin] played a significant role in controlling the 1920s epidemic and subsequent outbreaks and in significantly decreasing the number of reported cases until the 1940s."[17]

For another suspicious scholar, the Germans joined in efforts to find a cure because "sleeping sickness threatened potential pools of African labor, necessary for extracting resources and generating wealth."[18] This attitude infuses virtually everything written on the subject (and the tone would no doubt be the same if the Germans had remained indifferent). It misses a basic fact: keeping labor and government effective is the best way to save human lives and achieve justice. Other dons assert that drug firms in Germany and France produced the cure for sleeping sickness only because they saw African colonies as "markets for their products."[19] One wonders precisely on what other basis they would have been able to underwrite the costs of researching, manufacturing, and distributing the drugs.

Still others argue that sleeping sickness would not have spread so rapidly without colonialism, and thus colonial authorities were merely cleaning up a mess of their own making. "This unprecedented outbreak was both a symptom and a result of the social, ecological, and demographic crisis *caused by colonial conquest* in this region," assays one French scholar.[20] But the encounter with the modern world was coming one way or another, and, like the infectious diseases that Europeans brought with them, this encounter cannot be attributed to colonial rule, which was merely the way governments struggled to bring some order and governance to this encounter. It is like blaming the Atlantic Ocean for the property damage caused by hurricanes.

In 2020, chief anti-colonial dogmatist Jürgen Zimmerer called for the Robert Koch Institute to be renamed. According to Zimmerer, Koch's research on Lake Victoria violated contemporary standards of medicine. (Perhaps he was worried about the lack of informed-consent forms.) The claim is both ahistorical—after all, medicine in Germany itself also violated those standards—and insulting, a typical example of a postmodern professor in Germany replacing the considered judgments of black leaders like Chief Mutahangarwa with his own. Would black communities have preferred no Robert Koch? The Koch biographer Christoph Gradmann[21] replied that the institute had "exactly the right name" both because Koch was highly ethical by the standards of his time and because his research resulted in major improvements in public health.[22]

Sleeping sickness continued to haunt West Africa well into the 1950s. The French discovered a new drug called pentamidine that was highly effective in treating the early stages of the disease. They thought it might also work for prevention and thus experimented in its use as a vaccine. Alas, dozens of people died among hundreds vaccinated, mainly because of infected water used to mix the powder. This "misfire" in colonial research has since been elevated to the status of holy myth, a symbol showing the evils of *all* colonial medicine. The French scholar Guillaume Lachenal, while admitting that it is "unfair" to tar the whole history of colonial medicine with the brush of this mishap, nonetheless cannot resist doing just that. "The tragedy thereby appears not so much as an anomaly but instead as a product of the pragmatic and rational norms that governed the practice of colonial medicine."[23] Pragmatic and rational norms! It goes without saying that this French intellectual quickly grasps for the theories of Michel Foucault to justify his horror at "pragmatic and rational norms." Such modern-day critics who enjoy the comforts of "Western" medicine and public-health systems that resulted from "pragmatic and rational norms" are happy to consign brown people to witch doctors and disease in order to maintain their anti-colonial *bona fides*. Foucault, after all, fled to one of the hospitals he had sneered at after he contracted AIDS in the sadomasochist gay bathhouses of San Francisco. Like him, these scholars think nothing of a morning's work in which they write a detailed indictment of Western medicine before nipping out before lunch to pick up their prescription medicine for a skin rash.

What seems to enrage the contemporary academy is the scientific chasm that separated the West from the Rest at the time of colonial expansion. Germany, like other countries, ushered in the modern era of public health in colonial areas, and this contribution is so unambiguous that the only refuge for the critic is to denounce modernity itself. Perhaps we should give the final word to two scholars from Ghana writing about the German cure for sleeping sickness: "On the basis of its achievement in medicine alone, we are of the opinion that the German presence in Africa seemed more than justified ... when Africans strike the balance, they cannot say the German presence did not do them any good."[24]

CHAPTER 8

The Dancing and Feasting Continued
by Torchlight for Two Nights

Germany's Pacific colonies (German Samoa and German New Guinea) were small, scattered, and short-lived. They barely rate a mention in most histories of the Pacific islands. The region's fate had been integrated with the West since the Portuguese sailor Ferdinand Magellan and his crew made landfall in Guam in 1521 after sailing westward around the tip of South America, thus proving that the world is round. While romanticized as a remote paradise, the Pacific was more connected to the global economy than Africa, and, as a result, colonial rule here was mild and uneventful. The region was destined to be brought into the modern world by Japanese and European contact, noted Herman Hiery of the University of Bayreuth, a rare German academic who stayed out of the dungeon for the torturing of colonialism. "There is no place for living people in an ethnological museum," he wrote, chiding the anti-colonial scholars who imagine gentle islanders living in splendid isolation. The only pertinent questions about colonization are "when, who, why and especially how."[1]

As early as 1880, Bismarck, despite his obstinacy on overseas colonies, was impressed by the coffee, spices, and rubber that the

Dutch were importing from Java. He dropped hints to retainers that a "German Java" would be a very fine thing. The result was two colonies spread over thousands of miles where communications were spotty and the German presence barely noticeable. By 1914, there were just 1,500 Germans (and another 700 Europeans) living in the vast Pacific archipelago claimed by Berlin—rare sightings in a native population of about 600,000. Most of these were missionaries, traders, and farmers. Just 180 government officials ran the entire show, the equivalent of one official for every five hundred square miles of land area. The Germans in the Pacific acted more like museum curators and cultural-exchange officers than colonial administrators. The "resistance" they faced was mainly from typhoons and solitude.

German rule came easily and naturally, with none of the arduous state building required in Africa. Colonial officials in Africa looked with envy upon their colleagues in the "peaceful South Pacific." Most political conflict was with European traders and plantation owners who groused to Berlin of the "anti-German" bias of the administration. "The satisfaction of the indigenous people with German rule must be of greater concern" than the profits of German companies, the acting governor of German New Guinea insisted in one note to his staff.[2]

Not surprisingly, there is a diligent industry of critics in Germany devoted to "unmasking" the truth behind the "mythology of the peaceful Pacific." Every poisoned arrow shot at a German clerk by a naughty juvenile clad in grass skirt is contorted into a Wagnerian opera of "anti-colonial resistance." Every exhibition of Samoan canoes is presented as proof of the deep racism and cultural violence at the heart of the German colonial project. In fact, the peaceful Pacific of German times is no myth. It's the truth.

• • •

The main colony was German New Guinea, a scattered collection of islands headquartered on the northeast corner of New Guinea. It was an inheritance of the German-owned New Guinea Company formed in 1884, which maintained trading stations in the area until 1899. Costs outran revenues by a factor of eight, so a government takeover was needed. Another firm, the Jaluit Company, handed over its island stations in 1906. The operations of both houses—like those of other private colonial endeavors—were marred by abusive behavior, cruelty towards workers, heedless land grabs, and a lack of accountability.

One of the first acts of the colonial government was to reverse the default assumption that land not under native cultivation belonged to the Germans. Private settlers and plantations were debarred from buying land except from the colonial government. If an owner of private land was not cultivating at least 75 percent of his holdings, he was barred from acquiring more. "Land speculation of the sort that took place before 1899 was thus virtually impossible," Hiery wrote.[3] This was the "effective occupation" principle of the Spirit of Berlin coming to the Pacific. As with formal colonial rule by Britain in India and by Belgium in the Congo, the German assumption of private concerns in the Pacific brought an age of rapid improvement. Public colonialism was far better than private colonialism, and the private colonizers were mostly relieved to be rid of the unexpected burdens of empire.[4]

Thus, in most of New Guinea, as well as in Samoa, the Germans rejected land reforms that commercialized land. The intent was to ease the transition to modernity—with the evidence from German Southwest Africa often cited—by maintaining communal land even if it meant less income. "If the German colonial administration was primarily interested in economic exploitation and raising efficiency," asks Hiery, "why did it never attempt to sweep away the feudal system" of landholding in the islands?[5] The answer is that most German officials in the Pacific saw themselves as protecting indigenous peoples from the trading companies and plantation developers.

Berlin was not inclined to reverse that course. It never reprimanded an official for poor economic results but frequently upbraided those whose actions might cause tensions with the natives. "We would be satisfied if, under conditions of continuing peace, the maintenance of which is the main task of imperial officials, the indigenous people were gradually to learn that it is in their own interest to multiply and exploit their country's natural resources," Berlin wrote to the deputy governor of New Guinea in 1902.[6]

With little effort, the German authorities also ended tribal blood feuds and imposed their universal civic law and administration on the island peoples. The template for this had been forged in 1888 when the Germans annexed the remote island of Nauru, which had been engaged in a devastating civil war for a decade. It had been prompted by a dispute at a ceremonial feast where, in a quarrel over some coconut oil, the wrong man was shot with an old horse pistol.[7] The war threatened to extinguish the native people, estimated at 1,300 when the Germans arrived, and so the German annexation was a lifesaver. About eight hundred weapons were confiscated after the twelve chiefs of the island were put under house arrest in a copra shed. The weapons secured (along with all stores of alcohol), the chiefs were released. The traditional head chief was then reinstalled, and the islanders turned from tribal vendettas to copra and later phosphate mining.

These acts of asserting authority, in Hiery's words, "conformed completely to indigenous behavior" insofar as the Germans became the strongest tribe demanding fealty from others. The justification, however, was a liberal one: to end tribal warfare, blood feuds, cannibalism, and other local practices in favor of universal rights and opportunities. Whatever the cavils of later critics, Hiery notes, "there is much evidence of local support for German policy," and there was no "conservative-traditional opposition movement . . . in favor of blood feuding and the like."[8]

On the island of Chuuk, the Germans put an end to an internecine war, arresting and imprisoning three disgruntled chiefs for murder. "The turnaround on Chuuk, long renowned for its violence, was near miraculous, as if the Chuukese had been waiting for years for a show of leadership, indigenous or foreign, strong enough to compel their submission," wrote an American Jesuit priest who arrived in the islands in 1963 and recorded the oral histories of those who remembered German rule. The Chuuk people handed over their weapons with "a sense of relief that the constant fighting was over at last."[9]

Likewise, an American historian whose research on the island of Ponape was conducted in 1973, when memories of German colonialism were still firsthand, found that the German elimination of incessant warfare was welcomed. "The Ponapeans especially liked that aspect of the new reforms, for there was a recognized authority which commanded absolute obedience to the law. That, coupled with the emancipating land reform gave Ponapeans a degree of personal security they had not known before. The older people who spoke to me were extremely impressed by the firm German adherence to the law."[10]

After solving basic security issues, officials in German New Guinea did what prudent governors of any isolated island chain would do: they built ports and shipping infrastructure; opened post offices and linked them to the international postal system; constructed telephone systems; laid down cargo railways;

identified products such as pearls, copra, guano, and phosphate that could be successfully exported; and created a uniform governance system. The local police force became the first multi-tribal governing institution in each island cluster, and the Germans intentionally thought of this as "the spearhead of a national institution."[11] A botanical garden was established on Rabaul to study plants for introduction as cash crops. In 1912, its extension service handed out ten thousand plants and two hundred kilograms of seeds to local communities.[12]

As in Africa, the Germans were more efficient and successful than their British counterparts. There were 500 kilometers of roads in German New Guinea by 1914, compared to just 30 kilometers in neighboring British Papua. Even today there is a notable contrast between the extensive road network in the northeast of the island of New Guinea and the single coastal line to Port Moresby in the southeast. Of the 500 total kilometers, 140 kilometers were accounted for by the road on New Ireland, which was eight meters wide and is still known as the Boluminski Highway after the German district officer who worked the modern wonder.

• • •

The provision of modern infrastructure was accompanied by the provision of modern rights. German officials made a point of sending police to stamp out practices of cannibalism, human sacrifice, head-hunting, and inter-communal blood feuding. These policies paralleled those of the British in the Pacific but were more successful because of better cooperation with German missionaries.[13] "Surely no one can object to the 'little wars' waged against native tribes in New Guinea, which had the amiable habit of falling upon a neighboring tribe, making a number of prisoners, and carrying them off to be fattened for a cannibal feast?" asked the redoubtable colonialist Heinrich Schnee.[14]

One of the most detailed descriptions of cannibalism in the South Pacific came from the legendary Austrian anthropologist Richard Thurnwald, who was able to gain the confidence of the chiefs on one island chain in New Guinea. They happily explained the practice in great detail, referring to a recent feast of a victim from the island of Buka. Widows were particularly prized because they could be gang raped while being fattened up. They were then usually traded to creditors or rivals, who would drag them onto a mat, slice them open while alive and roast the contents on a pig spit. The man who struck the fatal blow won the right to display the victim's skull in his home. The meat was divvied up, beginning with the right loin for the chief.[15]

Thurwald was also able to document head-hunting festivities:

> Such celebrations as the completing of a hall for a chief or the ceremony of confederation between two chiefs were associated with organized head hunts. One of the chiefs would sell a [serf] to his friend, for a hundred fathoms of shell money. The victim was killed without warning when the confederate chief appeared with his bondsmen. The head was severed from the body, allowed to disintegrate, and then placed on a sacred spot, on the left pole-plate beneath the rafters of the gable roof of the new hall, or sometimes on the big wooden drums in the rear of the hall. Each chief's hall had at least one skull, generally four or five.[16]

These practices were what sociologists call "malign norms": habits that most people would prefer to kick but cannot because of the costs of doing so alone. Like the prohibition of dueling in nineteenth-century

America, the German proscriptions against head-hunting, blood feuds, and cannibalism were obeyed because all parties could now simultaneously change their behavior without being seen as cowards or risking becoming victims. "The Germans quite clearly filled a vacuum here," wrote Hiery, "responding to a need that indigenous structures and people had not been able to fulfill."[17] In this respect, the Germans quite intentionally "imposed" their liberal culture on colonial subjects, although as Hiery notes "this deliberate interference in internal…affairs was not condemned by [natives] themselves, but [was] seen as something positive." That is because "pacification put an end to the uncertainty which had so far bedeviled people's lives." One additional gain was that "the nomadic way of life, which was a forced result of permanent feuding, stopped."[18]

Modern scholars, of course, insist that these amiable habits were cruelly repressed by the culturally arrogant Germans. Cannibalism may have been widespread in parts of the Pacific, they admit, but the real violence was *to document it* because that was a form of "othering" and "exoticizing" the natives.[19] Legal prohibitions were a mere pretext to extend imperial control. People like Thurnwald, who spent months studying the practice were, on this interpretation, stalking horses for imperialists poring over maps in Europe.[20] Taking the logic one step further, the *real cannibals* were the anthropologists. They intellectually fed on the cultures they studied. Any contemporary scholar who adopts the "colonial" viewpoint that "cannibalism is an uncivilized and sinful act and should therefore be abolished heavy-handedly," in the view of a Dutch professor, needs to be set right because "this is obviously not a healthy point of departure for scholarly research."[21] The unhealthy plight of the poor widow roasting on the pig spit is, at this point, a distant afterthought, obscured by layer upon layer of theory and mumbo-jumbo. The anthropologist today spends hours of devoted time in his study wracked with guilt about his colonizing gaze and wondering how he could ever step foot outside from a "healthy point of departure."

Besides eliminating these barbaric norms, another human-rights policy pursued by the Germans was to encourage monogamous marriage, a key institution to protect women from being traded, raped, or served as a feast's main entrée. Almost miraculously, the shift towards monogamous relationships that occurs long before social complexity in most societies had not occurred in many of the islands of the Pacific. "If two are attracted to each other, they live and love together until they become tired of each other, or until she follows another," one report noted of the people of the Marshall Islands. "All the efforts of the missions and the administration to affect a change have had little success."[22]

The Germans also funded expeditions to document basic facts about the geography, flora, fauna, cultures, languages, and history of

Captain and crew of the German steamship *Langeoog* active in the South Pacific, 1908. *Bundesarchiv*

the places they ruled. The greatest of these was a three-year, $4 million (in today's value) "South Seas" expedition that sailed in a converted steamer through forty-five different island groups between 1908 and 1910. The expedition resulted in seventeen books and a total of sixty-five volumes, the last of which was published in 1954. The invaluable three-volume work written by the senior anthropologist Paul Hambruch laid the foundations of anthropological and historical studies of the region.[23] "For many islands," wrote an Australian scholar, "reliable historical records start with" the proceedings of the expedition.[24]

For critics, everything Hambruch and his colleagues discovered and catalogued was not a fact but a "colonial narrative." Even though the expedition was carried out explicitly to reject notions of racial superiority, the critics charge that Hambruch's writings were "racially tinged"—which of course can never be disproven. The American anthropologist Glenn Petersen claims that Hambruch's unvarnished discussion of pre-colonial tribal warfare in the islands was a protofascist Freudian slip. "What he saw echoed some of the basic tenets of *Lebensraum* theory," Petersen posits. The professor admits wearily that tribal warfare *was* constant, citing the islands of Ponape (Pohnpei) where he did his own research. But the purpose of civil war, he asserts, was not to dominate others but to bring balance to factional strife. This is because "at its core, indigenous Pohnpeian political theory is organized around notions of checks and balances and of resistance to the centralization of power and authority (despite appearances to the contrary)."[25] Since "Pohnpeian political theory" seems to exist only in the mind of Professor Petersen, it is always interpreted as peaceful and humane ("despite appearances to the contrary").

Hambruch undertook his studies at a time when unflinching objectivity was seen as the key to universal equality. Petersen, by contrast, grew up in the postmodern era when the soft bigotry of cultural relativism became dominant. Instead of condemning tribal warfare, Petersen soft-pedals it as part of "Pohnpeian political theory" and, in another book, "a dynamic aspect of Micronesian governments." Indeed, Petersen described the latter book as an "homage" to the people of Ponape aimed at "celebrating" their traditional practices, presumably including civil war, head-hunting, and gang rape.[26]

• • •

As in Africa, the colonial mission's progression from territorial control to basic infrastructure and institutions led finally to the question of governance. Every island group was different, and German rule interacted with local traditions in strange ways. In the Truk Islands, the chiefs of small islands had always sent tribute to the great chief in canoes laden with gifts and paddled by most of the able-bodied men of their island. A capsize would threaten the island population as a whole. At the stroke of a pen, the Germans outlawed long canoe trips in Truk, which had the paradoxical effect of turning the chiefs of minor islands into nettlesome rulers styling themselves as grand chiefs.[27] On the island of Yap, in the most westward island group of German New Guinea, German rule brought an unknown peace. The island's single German police chief and eleven native policemen spent most of their time building roads. An eight-chief council carried out government policies, reporting to the single German district officer. Arno Senfft, the officer from 1901 to 1909, is remembered for implementing governance reforms that sought to modernize the role of chiefs. That makes him red meat for academic critics who make dark comments about the "pathology" and "subversion" of reforms that brought Yap out of the Stone Age. The continuity of Yapese life as shown in the persistence of loincloths, grass skirts, and bare breasts was, in the advanced philosophy of one critic, evidence of "resistance."[28]

Yet Senfft was warmly loved on Yap, not least because of his insatiable curiosity about local people and the priceless knowledge he left behind.[29] He left such a lasting impression of economic prosperity, social reforms, and peace that decades later he was still known as the "Great Father of Yap." Senfft oversaw the opening of a system of roads, a stone pier, and a one-kilometer waterway built through the center of the main island to give better access to people living on the two northern islands. At the celebration of the opening of the canal, a Jesuit recorded from oral memories, "garlands and pennants festooned both sides of the canal, while a flotilla of more than a hundred canoes and twenty boats wound its way through the channel to the strains of a Filipino band and huzzahs for the workers. The dancing and feasting continued by torchlight for two nights."[30]

The most liberal phase of German rule in New Guinea occurred under Governor Albert Hahl between 1902 and 1914. In his early career as district officer on Ponape, Hahl forged a governing system with a council of local leaders answering to a local district officer. This was a more hands-on approach than the British model of "indirect rule" because it maintained a government presence at the local level. Hahl put the thirteen most influential Ponape leaders onto the government payroll. He conducted his work on the island without military escort and left the government compound open to all visitors. His own residence was built outside the remains of the old Spanish fort—no walls, no guards. This was no small thing since as recently as 1888, the Spanish governor and two hundred Spanish troops had been slaughtered by an uprising of two of the five main tribes of Ponape.

When the Spanish relinquished the island to the Germans in 1899, the departing governor told Hahl that he would be dead within a week. "Totally ignoring the advice of the Spanish governor,

Hahl opened the gates of the fortress and began razing the fort. He immediately met with the chiefs of Ponape and, in a number of joint consultations, worked out the principles which were to govern the administration."[31] Ponape never looked back, even after Hahl was recalled to the colony's headquarters in 1901. Land reforms on Ponape in 1910 gave freehold deeds to 1,100 families as part of efforts to free natives from their dependence on traditional chiefs, a rare exception to the insistence on communal land in the German colony. The chiefs were also limited for the first time in their ability to demand labor, as well as in mandatory foods and gifts for communal feasts, whose number was reduced from twenty-two per year to just one.

Hahl saw German colonialism as evidence of Germany's European and liberal heritage, and the native population rallied to the cause.[32] While many Germans, like many natives, retained a prejudiced view of the other as second-rate, Hahl viewed the colonial endeavor as a solvent to such universal prejudices:

> In every colony, anyone who has spent the time to learn the culture, study the language, and compassionately join the customs of the natives and has thereby won their trust, will say the same thing: that they are far from being foolish, primitive, ridiculous savages over which the European is mighty and sublime. They have their idiosyncrasies, like us, like all people have them. But let us be careful not to apply our own standards of civilization to other peoples which we do not understand![33]

Hahl was praised for the "noticeable increase in the influence of the German government over the natives" by the contemporaneous Pacific-islands scholar Richard Deeken. This was evident, Deeken observed, from the ease with which they "consent to pay taxes without protest."[34] In this way, German colonialism sought to transform the role of chiefs from premodern arbitrary despots to modern, rule-following administrators. They retained control over customary disputes and were able to levy taxes.

German attempts to balance respect for local norms with the imperatives of liberal rights were exemplified in one of the "colonial scandals" of the era. A chief's wife in the Marshall Islands had seduced one of her manservants in 1902. After the royal bonking was discovered, the servant was flogged on the orders of the district officer, Eugen Brandeis, following the request of the cuckolded chief. A wider Reichstag inquiry of 1905 found that Brandeis had covered up his use of flogging as a means of rule since the practice was banned in Germany's Pacific colonies.[35] For critics, the Brandeis "scandal" showed that German colonialism was run by a bunch of untethered sadists working out their racism by tapping into the ancient feuds of local chiefs. But attempts to impose the outrage template on this episode fail. The problem for Brandeis, as Hiery showed, was that the chief wanted his wife's *amour* to be maimed for life, if not executed, neither of which was legal. On the other hand, there needed to be an exemplary punishment, not just to save face for the chief but to show that justice was the preserve of the formal authority, not something for private score-settling. Brandeis, in Hiery's view, walked a careful and appropriate line between universal human rights and local traditions, like other German colonial officials. He sums up the approach in this way: "I have carefully studied your laws and listened to your elders, and I thus decide." Slowly, a civic empire of law would replace the personalistic empires of chiefs. If it was "racist" of Brandeis to allow local customs to shape his administration of law, then this was the sort of racism that today's "cultural competence" movement applauds. By contrast, the "non-racist" approach in British Fiji, where each and every capital crime led to a death sentence, Hiery notes, makes "the British 'model colony' look like a police state."[36]

In other words, the Germans were doing exactly what they had set out to do, transforming governance from an "embedded" reliance on face-to-face relationships to a "disembedded" reliance on impartial rules and institutions. One scholar grudgingly admits that, under governor Hahl, "projects considered not feasible only a few years before—had been constructed" and islanders "of later generations looked on the German period as being the most innovative of their history."[37]

The humanist spirit infused Hahl's memoirs.[38] He managed the difficult balancing act of protecting natives against excessive plantation expansion and maintaining chiefly authority while opening up the economy to prosperity and creating a more democratic society. He saw "the New Guineans as individuals," noted one reviewer, and understood "their predicament in the face of advancing colonial rule."[39]

Not surprisingly, Hahl is a target for colonial critics, compelled to reinterpret his humanitarian policies as devious schemes. One Marxist scholar, Margarete Brüll of the University of Freiburg, argues that Hahl's limits on plantation work (which one would expect a Marxist to applaud) were not intended to maintain village life and families so that fathers could return to their villages and help raise their children, as Hahl claimed. Instead, asserts Professor Brüll, he was trying to prevent the emergence of a "working class identity" that would threaten capitalism: "The capitalist mode of production needed indigenous, unpaid subsistence production in order to be competitive and could not afford to create a native proletariat."

Brüll adds the bizarre comment that Hahl's successful policies were intended "to make the locals content and the economy prosperous." All this contentment and prosperity, she explains, would dull resistance to "capitalist ideology."[40] Germans interested in their colonial history, she concludes, should read only Marxist literature that treats the natives as "active and thinking subjects." Marxism may have many analytic merits, but treating working people as active and thinking subjects is not one of them.

The record shows clearly that these exploited proletarians were becoming very prosperous very quickly under German rule. In 1907, the New Guinea government imposed a colony-wide head tax on adult males that could be waived only if a man took paid work on a native or European plantation for at least ten months of the year. It was assumed that, as in German Togo, this would ensure an ample supply of labor. Instead, the natives opened their bulging money chests and paid the tax in cash. Tax revenues tripled in the four ensuing years. "This development can be attributed with a pretty high degree of certainty to the state's encouragement for local copra production and the compulsory planting of palm trees," Hiery notes. Brand new rowing and sailing boats purchased with cash soon lined the shores of every native village. Alas, the Germans were too careful to upset the peaceful Pacific simply to boost labor supply. When European planters demanded an increase in the tax or the imposition of mandatory labor to prompt more labor, the governor refused.[41]

● ● ●

The two main islands constituting German Samoa came under German control under an 1899 treaty ending a failed decade-long experiment treating the region as a loose protectorate of the United States, Britain, and Germany. Intertribal Samoan wars throughout the nineteenth century predated European contact and centered on the rival lineages and factions that contested each other's right to rule. The Scottish writer Robert Louis Stevenson lived his last five years here (from 1889 to 1894) and became a partisan in the internecine struggle. These Samoan civil wars had ruined their communities, and a single political authority was needed. Germany rule provided that single authority, and the Samoan community prospered. Alcohol and gambling were prohibited, and the last governor put a time limit on the intervillage *malaga* partying and cricket matches that went on for days.

Governance on Samoa was comically light-handed. The senior native chief had his own staff, his own budget, and his own palace. The first incumbent insisted on cosigning all government regulations with the governor, mimicking the constitutional arrangements in Germany itself, where both emperor and chancellor needed to sign bills into law. When he died in 1913, the governor appointed coequal chiefs in his place. In this way, the traditional oligarchic rule of competing families was unified and modernized and, as a native council came into being, laid the foundations for democracy. As Hiery noted, "The German administration in Samoa contributed substantially to smoothing out historically-based internal Samoan antagonisms. . . . A Samoan 'national consciousness' came into being only during the German period."[42]

The traders and officials in German Samoa mostly took native wives, and so a culturally distinctive German-Samoan community emerged. The German customs inspector had full-body tattoos and wore a grass skirt when meeting arriving ships, perhaps an unexplored cause of the colony's sorry trade performance.[43] When a young race purist from Germany arrived in 1911 and published an article in the local *Samoanische Zeitung* decrying racial mixing, he was chased down the street by a mob of angry Samoan women wielding sticks and whips who feared losing their valued connections to the German men.[44] Local officials expelled him for disturbing the peace.[45] The governor's reluctant ban on interracial marriage in 1912 was motivated not by race factors but by social and economic ones. Women who married Europeans lost their native land rights and their children tended to abandon village agriculture and become wastrels.[46]

The Germans insisted on the use of the Samoan language in schools and missions and seem to have left behind only one German-derived word, *favaase* (from the German word *Verfassung* meaning "constitution"). Samoans actively complied with the birth and death registries established by the Germans to help track population health. These records showed a growing population despite fears of population decline. Along with the peaceful resolution of feuds among chiefs, wrote scholar Richard Deeken, who owned a Samoa plantation, this reflected a "deeply-penetrating transformation" in which legitimate government replaced blood feuds within Samoan society.[47] The great chief of Samoa was godfather to Deeken's daughter and looked after his family when Deeken died on the Western Front in the early days of World War I.

The Samoan economy was centered on coconut-derived copra that was processed into oil for soap and candles. Samoans worked on European plantations when they needed extra cash, but largely they harvested their own trees and maintained their premodern forms of life, including week-long feasts whenever visitors arrived. To protect this way of life, laws passed in 1899 and 1907 banned sales of Samoan land outside a small plantation area around the capital Apia and promised 1.3 hectares of land to every Samoan. In the last five years of German rule, Samoans provided three-fifths of the exports of cocoa and copra through their household and jointly owned farms, outproducing the Europeans.[48] The income brought bicycles, sewing machines, motorboats, and elaborate village churches. "Prosperity is the first thing that old Samoans remembered when they were asked about their experiences during the German period," Hiery reported from interviews done in 1989.[49]

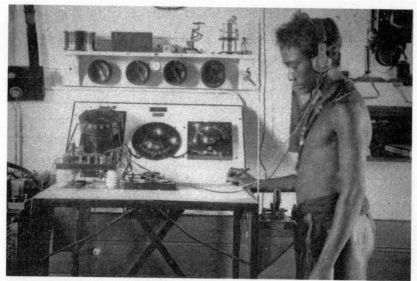

Native operator at the German telegraph station on Yap island, 1911. *Bundesarchiv*

Scholars intent on driving a wedge between German and Samoan interests insist that the Samoans' sporadic acceptance of work on European plantations reflected "resistance" to the copra economy. For good measure, when Samoans ran their own copra plantations, this too was "resistance" (for showing up the Europeans). When they did a little of both, this was *Übermensch* resistance.[50] A better interpretation is that the Samoans saw the opportunities and protections of German rule as preferable to any feasible alternative and acted accordingly.

The Germans saw that, denied a traditional warfare "economy," Pacific societies needed to transition to the economy of labor in order to survive. "Labor was even justified as being *beneficial* for local people," one horrified scholar writes.[51] The Germans were right. Despite abuses of labor recruitment, which were gradually brought under control, the problems of labor paled in comparison to the problems of warfare, such as fattening up captured widows for the barbeque and enslaving neighbors. Deprived of those delights, societies needed a new purpose. "Whether by means of the present system or in other ways, the native must be induced to work," noted a report by the Australian administration that took over after 1918. "For the experience of neighboring islands seems to make it clear that unless the native is given both physical exercise and interest in life, to replace the occupations and excitements of his former savage life, he will surely die out."[52] Germany's market economy quite literally offered the only pathway to survival. "Beneficial" does not convey the half of it.

• • •

The academic censure of plantations in the German Pacific—as with that of public works in German Togo—has snowballed into the accusation that the clever Germans hid a slave state in plain view. The claim turns on evidence of mortality rates for the native workers recruited within the islands, along with those of imported workers from China and Southeast Asia. The first spear was thrown by the Australian historian Stewart Firth who claimed mortality rates of 20–30 percent (that is, that one in five or one in three of all the workers expired on the job).[53] He drew mainly on reports compiled by Governor Hahl as part of official efforts to regulate labor recruitment. Yet a close examination of the records by fellow Australian historian Peter Sack showed that the actual figures were much lower, probably no worse than in British and Dutch colonies. Moreover, Europeans on the plantations died at about the same rate. By 1914, the rates had fallen to 1 percent or less, as good as in Germany itself. Sack also found that Firth's claims of low food rations, heedless land grabs, and unaccountable public administration were without foundation. The few instances of forcible labor recruitment, Sack noted, were rare compared to the thirty-seven thousand voluntarily recruited in German New Guinea in the last five years of the colony alone.

Attention to context and accuracy also undermines the claims made by Firth and others about the flogging of workers. As in criminal justice, floggings were first used by the companies to compel workers to fulfill their contracts but then reduced under formal German rule. In 1912, in the district of Rabaul, the center of contract workers, 128 floggings were administered with an average of seven strokes of the cane (the legal maximum being fifteen). In all cases, a doctor was present, and the details carefully recorded. At the time, the total contract workforce in the Rabaul area was eighteen thousand. In other words, far less than 1 percent of the workforce drew a flogging in that year (the last for which records exist). The governor called the use of floggings "brutal and immoral," and a raging debate gripped the final years of the colony over the ethics, law, and legitimacy of the practice. If this is "the ugliest side" of German rule in the Pacific, as Hiery insists, then German rule was remarkably humane.[54]

Clearly, most workers intended to fulfill their contracts because plantation work was attractive. That is why it was so easy to recruit more, Sack noted. Firth's "cavalier treatment of the evidence" along with his "fiery, impressionistic large canvas treatment" suggested the "time is unfortunately still not ripe" for writing a dispassionate history of German colonialism in the Pacific.[55] That was in 1985.

Sack, whose reputation as a spoiler of anti-colonial orthodoxies soon preceded him, later took on another example of "fiery, impressionistic history." At issue was the allegation by Australian historian Judith Bennett that the rapid population decline of the German-controlled Shortland Islands was caused by preventable diseases introduced by European traders and whalers.[56] Sack, digging into the evidence, found the main reason was frequent abortions and widespread polygamy among high-status men.[57]

Population declines in the Pacific islands in the nineteenth century, those under German rule and not, resulted from a confluence of factors: epidemic diseases like dysentery, measles, smallpox, typhus, and malaria; frequent typhoons; plantation work; sexually transmitted diseases caused by unstable marriage norms; infanticide; and contraception. But these factors only reveal a more fundamental cause at work: the vulnerability of the island populations to the above maladies because of their geography and feuding. When German doctors tried to investigate the causes of these public-health threats, encourage preventive measures, and apply vaccinations, they faced strong native resistance. Locals refused autopsies on the deceased, while infected people who discharged themselves from government hospitals were put into hiding by their relatives: "It was almost impossible for the government doctor to control the epidemic," wrote Hiery of one outbreak on Yap in 1912 of either typhus or dysentery.[58]

A similar distortion of history to fit the anti-colonial "moral framework" is evident in the gnashing of teeth that German cultural elites engage in while trying to explain the embarrassing spectacle of a native outrigger boat from the island of Luf in New Guinea on display at the Ethnology Museum (now Humboldt Forum) in Berlin. The population of Luf declined throughout the nineteenth century due to natural disasters and new diseases, as typically occurs when isolated groups come into contact with outsiders. In 1882, after some natives attacked the German trade station on the island, the Germans fought back, and in the ensuing battle three natives were killed. After that, the island was a peaceful redoubt of the German colony. The incomplete boat, a magnificent fifty-two-foot double-masted outrigger, was purchased by a German merchant in 1902 when the locals decided they had no use for it. The Germans returned a few years later to commission missing parts, and the boatbuilders were happy to oblige. Without the purchase, the boat would have rotted unfinished in a shed, perhaps, or been used as firewood. Certainly, documentation of this island's culture would have been lost.

Nonetheless, the boat has become a symbol of German oppression and looting. In 2021, a German journalist published a book on how the boat symbolized German evil.[59] In his embellished telling, the boat was not purchased but "seized" using the "violent appropriation" of a market transaction. Since colonialism was evil, any transaction that took place under colonialism must also be evil: "The boat was appropriated under the assumptions of colonial omnipotence."[60] The boatbuilders who worked on completion were "survivors" of a mini-Holocaust on the island in 1882 (elevated to fifty fatalities without explanation). Western civilization was "syphilisization."[61] The Luf islanders had an "advanced civilization" and a "well-functioning subsistence economy" when barbaric Germans were still living in caves. After the book was released, the museum apologized for its lack of sensitivity in relying so heavily on historical facts. The methods used to establish the boat's provenance, it confessed, were "Eurocentric." In future, the museum would engage "stakeholders" in Papua New Guinea to be re-educated about the "false narrative" of a fair trade for the boat.[62] And so on.

● ● ●

Along with Sack, as mentioned, the most extensive research on the German Pacific colonies was done by Hermann Hiery.[63] Over a long career, Hiery proved himself unwilling to succumb to anti-colonial ideology. He made a general case for German administration while pointing to failures and challenges.[64] One reviewer described his first book as "a substantiated apologia for German cultural and scientific achievements in the Pacific."[65]

Like Sack, Hiery relished cracking the chestnuts of anti-colonial mythology. In a 1993 article, he rejected the myth of twin rebellions that were said to have erupted in Madang on mainland New Guinea in 1904 and 1912.[66] The former was a hoax by German settlers who hoped to attract a more substantial government presence. The latter was a conspiracy among a few disgruntled youths that never got off the ground. No one was ever injured, nor was any property ever damaged in either "uprising." Indeed, with one minor exception, to which we return below, there was no instance of a revolt against German colonialism per se in the German Pacific, despite sporadic protests or complaints against specific policies. In a few instances where islanders held German traders or officials hostage demanding higher wages for carrying copra to ships or mining phosphate, the aim was not "to abolish the overall conditions governing their colonial existence. The German 'superstructure' as such was accepted."[67] The aim rather was to maximize the benefits of the colonial system.

The relatively hands-off form of local government and a consistent application of laws against intertribal warfare and feuding had established the legitimacy of German rule. German rule brought untold prosperity and opportunities. One road project was completed only after the women of the area responded to a strike by their menfolk by taking up the tools themselves with the governor's protection, shaming their men into resuming the project. When natives in the German Pacific raised demands, they were seeking more and better colonialism, not an end to it.

For his misdeeds, the naughty Professor Hiery has been given a good spanking by German academics ever since. Their attempts to insist that the Madang rebellion was "real," even though it was not, would be comical if they were not so alarming. One nanny of the anti-colonial nursery, Klaus Neumann, declared that the writing of history should be guided by a "moral framework" rather than by stubborn facts.[68] A proper "moral framework" would begin with the premise that German colonialism was evil. Following from that premise, all facts and events, real and otherwise, are to be written up as episodes of "anti-colonial resistance." With these accounts in hand, historians could circle back and cite these episodes as "evidence" that German colonialism was evil.

● ● ●

As in other German colonies, the very small police and military presence in the Pacific relative to area and population is *ipso facto* evidence of the legitimacy of German rule. There was widespread compliance with colonial laws despite minimal monitoring or enforcement: high levels of enlistment in colonial governments, support for expansion of colonial governance systems, payment of taxes despite easy evasion, and support for measures against crime. As a governor of Samoa noted, "If the governor engages in follies, if he appears indecisive, or if he handles the Samoans improperly, that is too strenuously, too weakly, or too unjustly, the Samoans will react quickly."[69] Many radical scholars pin their hopes on finding angry denunciations of the Germans from oral histories and memories. But as in Africa, the people do not read the anti-colonial scripts they have been assigned by the professors. Instead, noted one deflated don, "they often respond with a rosy or misty light."[70]

As in Africa, tribal chiefs in the Pacific found German rule preferable to the constant warfare and instability of pre-colonial days. The chief Zake, who ruled one of the ethnic groups on the main island of New Guinea, formed a deep friendship with German authorities. The German station chief brought the chief's people education and medical care and the chief social prestige.[71] The mission chief was known locally as "Chief Zake's best friend" and the missioners in turn called the chief "diplomat" and "chief of Papua."[72]

Then there is the legendary Henry Nanpei, a missionary-educated businessman on Ponape. He was the man-about-town of the island with a finger in every pot. No mere yes-man, Nanpei, according to the ethnographer Hambruch, wanted to "establish a parliament that progressively intended to represent the interests of Pohnpei's natives and would in time free them of the government of the foreigners."[73] He found many allies for this reformist agenda among the German administration that, like other European colonial powers, saw its remit as limited in time. He was awarded the Prussian Order of the Crown in 1905. Still, critics must strain and stretch to force Nanpei into the "resistance" mold. "Though, outwardly, he remained faithful to the German regime until 1914," insisted one scholar with exotic psychological insights, "it was probably because he was satisfied that it provided him with the best possible support for his position and influence."[74] What is forgotten is that Nanpei's loyalty to the German administration is precisely what made him a leader of his community. As another scholar who interviewed those of the German era noted, Nanpei "would not have been successful without the support of other Ponapeans."[75] When asked later which colonizer—Spanish, German, or Japanese—he thought best, Nanpei opted for the Germans.[76]

There was, in the totality of German rule in the Pacific, *one* minor jacquerie of note that was a rebellion against German rule itself. Since the "rebel force" consisted of a minor chief named Samuel and perhaps thirty of his friends, the so-called Sokehs Rebellion of 1910 has more than an air of light comedy. It seems that Samuel did not like the pay he was receiving for a road construction project on Sokehs, a one-kilometer-wide island on the north coast of Ponape. Some were forced into labor since they could not pay a poll tax. The local German officer, who previously served in Africa, used corporal punishments (floggings in this case) to prompt the men to deliver the labor, which unbeknownst to him was not a form of punishment used in the islands. The bigger issue was that land reform throughout Ponape had stripped feudal lords, even minor ones like Samuel, of their status in order to benefit "the peasants." In any other situation, historians would assail the Sokehs uprising as a "reactionary" defense of feudalism.

After murdering a half dozen of his fellow Ponapeans along with some Germans, Samuel and his friends fled into the hills. The German officer held parlay with the other chiefs and agreed to put on hold attempts at land reform and constitutional change. The chiefs then took up arms against the rebels, contributing six hundred warriors within days.

It took more than two months for news of the rebellion to reach Berlin and then another month for instructions to be given, so this was hardly a fast-moving event. While waiting for instructions, the German officer died and his number two, the well-loved doctor of the island, became the face of German colonialism. A German counterinsurgency force arrived armed with swimming trunks and beach towels. The soldiers took holiday photos as they engaged the rebels, making sure to include their "exotic" native comrades in the frame. The rebels were routed and mostly executed or imprisoned. The remainder of the Sokehs population of four hundred or so was removed to the island of Yap to prevent a repeat performance. One fighter who remained in the jungle until 1913 was adopted by the new governor as his ward, an act of compassion that generated much goodwill.

If the Sokehs Rebellion did not exist, anti-colonial historians would need to invent it. It has been imbued with wide-ranging significance. The Ruhr Museum photo archivist Thomas Morlang, however, cannot help but notice the puny and comical nature of the rebellion. He has the honesty to admit in a photobook on the subject that it is simply false to take the unrest as evidence of broad anti-colonial sentiment.[77]

In the end, the myth of the peaceful Pacific under German rule is no myth. In 1999, the people of Ponape restored their German Bell Tower and recommissioned it at a ceremony attended by the island's king. The bell tower "was a major architectural accomplishment" for the time and place and "remains an important landmark for Ponape," the local restoration committee declared.[78] Compared to the ideologically charged thinking in the academy, the people of the Pacific have made their peace with their colonial past.

CHAPTER 9

Ganbei! *How the Chinese Colonized Qingdao*

The most underappreciated German colonial achievement, and the most tragic example of the perils of decolonization, was Qingdao, a port city in northern China. As part of its Pacific expansion, Berlin signed a ninety-nine-year lease with the decaying Qing dynasty in 1898 to establish a colony at the tip of the peninsula jutting into the Yellow Sea. The perfect setting was no accident: a German explorer had published a book that year with details on the port, and Bismarck was quick to see its potential.[1]

The colony in China was only one-fifth the size of Britain's newly expanded colony at Hong Kong but was intended to serve the same purpose: to open a gateway to trade in the Middle Kingdom. When the Germans arrived, there were only 1,500 people living around the port area of Qingdao, mostly from fishing households, and perhaps another 12,000 in the whole colonial zone known as Jiaozhou.[2] As at Hong Kong, the colonizing was done by the Chinese, who hastened to settle in the new European enclave before the paint was dry on the boundary posts. By 1914, there were 190,000 people living in Jiaozhou (99 percent of them Chinese), including 57,000 in the port of Qingdao (96 percent Chinese). The alien rule of the Germans was considered preferable to the alien rule of the Qing, an intrusion from Manchuria that could not pave roads.

The founding of the German outpost came amidst a wave of internal rebellions against the Qing. The most noteworthy was the Society of Righteous Harmony, known as the Boxer Movement, that targeted Europeans with the tacit consent of race chauvinists in the Qing court. The German ambassador was slain by a Qing soldier, which the dynasty blamed on the Boxers. In fact, the court was losing touch with Chinese society. In the province that contained Qingdao, the governor called for German assistance to subdue the righteous harmonizers. The assistance was rendered by a detachment commanded by the ubiquitous Lothar von Trotha. As during the Sokehs Rebellion in German New Guinea, the German riflemen took holiday photos with their exotic native comrades as they stormed enemy positions. With the defeat of the Boxers, the colony at Qingdao thrived.

Qingdao was run by the German navy, which meant that the territory was furnished with ample resources and highly efficient governors. The port town provided both a refuge and a model for a China undergoing political decay. Its legal and educational systems were far superior to anything in China, and its basic infrastructure and economic opportunities sparked a broader economic expansion in the north. Running water and a sewage system were the first investments, followed by civic amenities such as a hospital and a courthouse. In contrast to the banditry of the inland, Qingdao was safe. The 935 European and Japanese cargo ships that visited the port in 1913 were far outnumbered by the 6,000 Chinese junks and 12,000 sampans.[3] The German colony "fostered agricultural development in rural areas and promoted balanced growth in all sectors of the economy," according to the Hong Kong scholar Fion Wai Ling So.[4]

The German governor from 1901 to 1911, Oscar von Truppel, established an elected committee of Chinese merchants to advise him on business policy, an unknown innovation in the rest of China. A Chinese Affairs Committee made up of Chinese officials handled most civil disputes. Truppel spent lavishly on a new housing quarter for Chinese apprentice workers. His stated plan was to slowly democratize governance in Qingdao by placing representatives (*Vertrauensmänner*) of the Chinese Affairs Committee on his executive cabinet. New provisions issued in 1910 for popular "participation and supervision" over the colonial government showed a liberal enclave taking shape in a most unlikely place. This was "institutional change through colonization," as the German scholar Annette Biener called it, a key benefit of European colonialism worldwide.[5]

As in the Pacific, German officials fell in love with the people and the culture. The native-affairs commissioner declared that Germany's mission at Qingdao was nothing less than the modernization of China.[6] The top German judge, who had been sent to Qingdao from an assignment at the police academy in Tokyo, wrote several papers on comparative law dealing with the complex cultural and legal issues of creating a modern legal system for China.[7] Aspiring modernizers from around China visited Qingdao frequently. As the geographer Heinrich Schmitthenner wrote: "The lively intellectual life and the social traffic, in which the differences in class are less emphasized than in our African colonies, are particularly refreshing."[8] Qingdao was a miracle of good planning, urban sanitation, and prosperity. Chinese culture thrived here—operas, traditional fairs, temple architecture, et cetera—because of the stability of German rule.

Qingdao was the ultimate "model colony" with its good governance and law-abiding citizens. As with German Togo, therefore, German scholars have felt obliged to make heroic efforts to find *any* shred of evidence of misgovernance or "resistance." Failing that, as with their research on Togo, they have retreated to the fairyland of Michel Foucault, claiming that the safety, public health, environmental protection, and economic prosperity were merely a "discourse" intended to "govern."[9] Qingdao is cited as an example of "cultural imperialism" by Germany with its oppressive ideas about such trivialities as clean water and safe streets.

Another tack for anti-colonial scholars has been to argue that Qingdao's success had nothing to do with the Germans. The American sociologist George Steinmetz insists with a straight face that the increased participation of the Chinese community in the colonial governing system was evidence of "decolonization." In his words, the natives "laid claim to the state . . . and in doing so they gained incremental control over the state and actually began to 'decolonize' it." If the Germans had not been ousted by the Japanese during World War I, he asserts, Qingdao "might have eventually lost is colonial character altogether."[10]

Steinmetz, like so many anti-colonial ideologues, treats the ordered rule of the Germans as something that just "happened" magically or that would have existed absent German rule. Yet the system that the Chinese participated in was a wholly German creation. The cosmopolitan, modern, rule-based government with a thriving capitalist economy was the very essence of Qingdao's "colonial" character. For Qingdao to have "lost its colonial character," to use Steinmetz's words, would have meant a reversion to bamboo-stilted fishing huts and rule by family clans amidst banditry and poverty. The Chinese in Qingdao were not "decolonizing" German colonialism, they were self-colonizing the Chinese people. They were embracing German institutions. There was no talk of throwing out the Germans, only of joining them.

There is overwhelming evidence that the German colony enjoyed complete legitimacy in the eyes of both its Chinese inhabitants and

Opening of bakery by German sailors and Chinese assistant in Qingdao, 1899. *Bundesarchiv*

neighbors. Provincial governors from across China visited early and often, praising German rule and taking lessons to apply back home. The governor of the surrounding province wrote to the Qing emperor in 1902 expressing admiration for the German colony and meekly suggesting that the sovereign might descend from the throne to inspect it.[11] After the Qing was overthrown in 1912, a dozen Qing officials fled to the colony, seeking refuge in houses they had bought on the sly while dismissing the colony as an insult to the Chinese people.[12]

The commoners, meanwhile, happily migrated en masse to the city. Many more would have come but for limits set on residency rights. Those who were unable to move did everything to avail themselves of the weal of Qingdao. Chinese from outside the colony voluntarily brought their disputes to be decided by a German judge whose rulings in theory had no legal force.[13] Chinese parents clamored to send their children to the Sino-German College

(*Hochschule*), opened in 1909, the first institution of higher education in a German colony.

Alas, a German middle-school textbook used today takes the migration not as evidence of the legitimacy and appeal of German rule but of the dark forces guiding the whole project: racial mixing was allowed in the colony only because of "the economic benefits"; the thousands of jobs given to formerly poor Chinese "led to class differences within the Chinese population"; rising "anti-German sentiment" in Qingdao was the cause of the virtuous and progressive Boxer Rebellion. And so on.[14]

Not surprisingly, sporadic strikes and boycotts organized by the Chinese Business Association in Qingdao in 1908–10 have been seized upon by some scholars as evidence of "anti-colonial resistance" and "rising nationalism." The truth, as one Hong Kong scholar shows, is more prosaic: they were mafia tactics used by the nearby provincial governor to negotiate better terms on railway development and trade with the Germans.[15]

After a new Republic of China emerged from the rot of the Qing in 1912, the first president and "father of modern China," Sun Yat-sen, visited Qingdao at the invitation of the local Chinese chamber of commerce. Toasts of *ganbei!* (*empty your glass!*) were made over bottles of German "Tsingtao Beer."[16] Sun lavished praise on the German colonial venture. Qingdao under German rule, he said, was a "splendid city" that should be a model for all of China: "In three thousand years, China did not achieve in [Qingdao] what Germany has done in fifteen years," he said, echoing comments he would later make about Hong Kong under British rule.[17] "If every local government in China would send ten people to visit Qingdao and learn about its administrative management, town, streets, wharves, harbors, university, forestation, public works, and government, China would benefit greatly."[18] He scolded Chinese students in Qingdao who had boycotted classes to protest the German insistence that Sun be treated as only a "private citizen" because he had recently stepped down as president, telling them to return to class to "help to modernize China." He left clutching copies of books published by the commissioner for local affairs, Wilhelm Schrameier, on land policy, port operations, and public administration.[19]

A decade later, Sun invited Schrameier to the southern province of Guangdong to formulate a land-reform policy. Schrameier shared his experiences of land reform with Sun's son, who was mayor, before dying in a car accident in the city.[20] Sun Jr. was convinced that the German land policies, which put land into the hands of peasant farmers, were the key to economic success.[21] That insight would travel with the Sun family and the remnants of the republican government to Taiwan after the communist revolution of 1949. Implemented on the island, it has been widely cited as one reason for Taiwan's economic miracle.

The "scandal" of the Qingdao colony, if it can be called that, was that the devoted German officials trying to build a second Hong Kong were ridiculed in the Reichstag for an excess of outlays over revenues. What had begun as a show of force to compel the Qing to investigate the murder of two German missionaries—and then turned into a plan for a naval base—quickly became nothing short of a beacon for the modernization of China. The Chinese people embraced that project with far too much enthusiasm, dragging the German taxpayer into a global-development mission they had not bargained for. Even so, by 1914, the consensus in Germany was that it could not in good faith abandon this expensive *pied-à-terre* in the Middle Kingdom. As elsewhere, German colonialism was too invested in the peoples and places of its authority. All that was about to change.

CHAPTER 10

The "Shabby Annexations" of Versailles

And so we reach the fateful events of August 1914. At the very moment when German colonialism reaches its most fruitful season, it is hewn at the trunk by the axes of European rivalry.

Lenin surmised that Germany's lack of colonies had caused the war because its capitalists needed new places to invest and grab resources. But German investors and traders had done just fine working in British and French colonies, so the explanation has more than a whiff of *ex post* ideological rationalization. Indeed, in the same work Lenin admitted the success of German overseas business despite "inconsiderable" colonial holdings, attributing German success to its "younger, stronger, and better organized" business sector. Never allowing facts to muddy the waters, he insisted on the historical inevitability of colonial wars for capitalist profits. Anyone asserting that free trade would avert such wars had fallen prey to "petty-bourgeois reformism."[1]

Most accounts of German colonial rule thus end in 1914. The military historians step in with analysis of "the landing at Tanga" or "the siege of Kabara." But the history of German colonialism does *not* end here. Rather, it falls to the ground and carries on as rotting fruit with terrible results. Over the next century, this will bring horrific legacies of illiberalism to German society: Soviet-run anti-colonialism, Nazi ethno-nationalism, German communism, academic radicalism, and, in our day, neo-racist Wokeism. The liberal era of Germany that coincided with its colonial rule is ended. The heart of Europe is torn out. For Germany to have any chance of regaining its greatness as a civilizational power today, and for Europe to recover from its self-imposed nosedive, requires us to bring the story of German colonialism forward to the present.

It was not supposed to end this way. Under the Spirit of Berlin, the European powers agreed that if they came to blows in Europe, they would remain at peace in the colonies. Despite a lot of retrospective claims that, for instance, German and French disputes over Morocco in the early 1900s put them on a collision course, these colonial issues created *stronger* liberal bonds among colonial rulers. "We compete, yes, but we are not in opposition to one another," wrote a French nobleman in the main German colonial journal in 1905.[2] The participants saw the Spirit of Berlin as suffusing their colonial disputes with a new cooperation that would serve as a model for the resolution of similar disputes in Europe.[3] As late as January 1914, the director of Germany's main colonial training school was in London giving a talk to an audience of appreciative British nabobs. "Germany is throwing herself into the unfamiliar task of colonial policy with characteristic thoroughness and energy," commented the venerable architect of Britain's southern Africa policy, Lord Milner, "and it would be a great mistake to think we have nothing to learn from their experiences."[4]

But war follows its own logic. Within days of the outbreak of war in Europe, troop movements and war planning began in the colonies that made conflict inevitable. The robust Allied response to German aggression in Europe caused Berlin to adopt a globalized approach to the war from whence the term "world war" (*der Welt Krieg*) derived. Berlin believed that German colonies could be used to tie down Allied armies and resources that would otherwise be deployed to Europe. A British and French quagmire in Africa would help a German victory in Europe.

The British and French, meanwhile, realized that Germany might use its colonies to supply troops and resources in Europe. As a result, they abandoned the defensive colonial strategy in favor of dismantling the German empire. The constituency that prevailed in Britain demanded annexation of all German colonies irrespective of their immediate tactical value. While those in British colonial circles were fond of their German counterparts, war strategists worried that German colonial success posed a danger to British maritime supremacy. Seizing German colonies in East Africa would create a direct link from Egypt to Rhodesia, just as seizing Ottoman colonies in the Middle East would create a direct link from Egypt to India.[5]

Appropriately enough, Britain's first act of war came in Africa on August 7, when a native sergeant of the Gold Coast on patrol near the border with German Togo fired on his counterparts. A few days later, two British cruisers in the Indian Ocean diverted to Dar es Salaam and took out the German wireless-transmission station with a heavy bombardment. The war in the colonies was begun.

The fighting abilities of German colonies largely reflected their prewar conditions. German Southwest Africa was still reeling from the Herero-Nama conflicts and was in little position to defend itself. Without native support, the German settler-based army fell easily to forces from British South Africa in 1915. German Togo was just as unprepared, with a threadbare defense corps of eight hundred natives and a dozen German officers. Sensing the hopeless situation, the local chiefs of Togo rebelled, and the German garrison in Lomé was overrun. When the war erupted, the Germans were putting the finishing touches on a massive twelve-tower radio transmitter in the inland, a marvel of modern telecommunications.[6] They demolished the transmitter with tears in their eyes and waved the white flag. The colony was split into French and British sectors. The natives went back to trading.

Things at first did not look any better in German Cameroon. The dispute with the coastal Duala over the new port project left the colony vulnerable to insurrection. As hostilities began in Europe, the Germans hastily convened a show trial for the imprisoned chief and his advisor and hanged them both. An uncle of the chief fled to Lagos and placed himself at the service of the British. The British put him back ashore to gather information and stir rebellion among the Duala. When a joint British-French expedition arrived in September 1914, the Duala mutinied.

The same was not true inland, where the Hausa and Jaunde tribes proved loyal to Germany. In their first attempt to seize the new inland capital at Jaunde (today's capital of Yaoundé), the British and French lost 900 soldiers. The colony was not defeated until late 1915. What ensued was one of the more bizarre events of the war in Africa. Over 6,000 native soldiers and 12,000 other natives along with 117 Cameroonian chiefs and their entourages chose to leave the colony with the 95 surviving German officers. The delegation marched into neutral Spanish Guinea (today's Equatorial Guinea). Another 20,000–30,000 Africans sought to join them but were immediately expelled by the Spanish.[7] While cooling their heels on the island of Fernando Po, the 117 chiefs petitioned the King of Spain to intervene to reestablish German rule in Cameroon. If the royal petition had assailed colonialism and demanded liberation from the unbearable oppression of the white man, there would be bookshelves of anti-colonial invective dedicated to the document by now. But it said the opposite, which is

why it has been ignored: "We have left behind in Cameroon our families and households along with the love for and trust in our government. We hope soon to return with the German government. This love
and loyalty is unchanged. We have only one wish: to join the German
government to return to Cameroon."[8] The epic trek of the natives to
Spanish Guinea and the dogged loyalty to Germany over the next three
years is one of many untold stories of German colonialism.

The most tenacious fight by Africans for German colonialism
came in East Africa. This came as a surprise, as the colony was still
recovering from the destruction of the Maji Maji insurgency. As
Heinrich Schnee, the last governor noted: "No one knew to what
extent we had succeeded in gaining the trust and loyalty of the
natives." Even lukewarm support, he calculated, would not have been
enough: "A major uprising or even the passive resistance of the native
population would have crippled the whole campaign. We were just
6,000 whites (including women and children) among eight million
blacks and we depended on the cooperation of our natives as soldiers,
porters, and suppliers."[9]

But as the American scholar Woodruff Smith noted, the defeat
of the hated Maji Maji had brought a groundswell of support for
German rule, unbeknownst even to the Germans.[10] The result was a
sticky quagmire of war across East Africa that pitted an agile
15,000-man *askari*-based German army against 130,000 British,
Indian, Belgian, South African, and Portuguese soldiers. So revered
were the *askari* that when the Germans were forced to scuttle a navy
cruiser on a river in 1915, the German sailors were put back into service as "European *askari*" sporting native garb.[11] The native *askari*
figured prominently in C. S. Forester's 1935 novel *The African Queen*,
centered on the sinking of another German cruiser in the campaign,
and the loyal *askari* enjoyed considerable screen time in a later film
adaptation starring Humphrey Bogart and Katharine Hepburn.

Heinrich Schnee's memoir recalls the tireless efforts of African soldiers, porters, and tradesmen during the East Africa campaign.

> Hides were brought in, leather tanned, shoes made, cloth fabrics made by hand spinning and hand weaving, as well as wax candles, soap, petrol, petroleum substitutes, gold and brass coins, and quinine, which is important for combating malaria in the deep areas. The procurement of all these things and many others had to be improvised and that would not have been possible without the willingness of the colored people to work. During the war we reaped the fruits of our long-standing humane native policy and achieved things that our opponents could not match.[12]

Most of the time there were no German commanders on hand. Large African platoons and thousands of civilians labored away with little or no pay, as payment was made in a new currency printed on the spot—in effect an IOU.[13] "Only the sentiments of genuine fidelity and devotion, could have produced these results," Schnee wrote.[14] The French were so impressed by the loyalty and effectiveness of the native troops that they translated German military documents for use in their colonies.[15] "Is it not obvious," asked Schnee, "that the invasion of the enemy in all colonies should have been the signal for a general uprising had the natives wished to free themselves from German rule? If blacks had been held down in brutal tyranny, wouldn't they have used the opportune moment to shake off the yoke?"[16]

Instead, they did the opposite, yoking themselves ever more tightly to the German cause with a spirit that put the Prussian military tradition to shame. Not until November 23, 1918, when word finally came through that Germany had surrendered in Europe, did the loyal *askari* lay down their arms. Just 155 German officers, 1,200 native *askari,* and 1,600 porters were all that remained of a force that had menaced the British for four years.

In the Pacific, Germany was in no position to resist. The island colonies fell quickly as soon as Australian or New Zealand warships dropped anchor, although the German colonists had a naughty habit of running the German flag up again as soon as their new rulers had departed, as happened on Nauru. In the north, Japan rolled like a tropical storm over the northwestern areas of New Guinea, seizing islands it would later use in its march on Asia.

The greatest tragedy came at Qingdao. When the war erupted, the new president of China was none other than Yuan Shikai, the former governor of the nearby province who had worked with the Germans to suppress the Boxers and promote railway development. Yuan declared neutrality because Japan had entered the war on the side of the Allies. When it became clear that the Germans could not defend the port, Yuan offered it to the British, much as Octaviano Olympio had feverishly sought British control of German Togo. Had the British accepted, this Hong Kong of the north would have become a second miraculous gift to China's development. Alas, the British ceded the tactical initiative to Japan. London hoped to emerge as an honest broker between the United States and Japan in their Pacific ambitions, and it believed that Japan would behave nicely towards British colonies in Asia in return.[17] This small decision would produce a catastrophic shift in world history.

The Japanese sent an ultimatum demanding the surrender of Qingdao. The German governor had only one airplane and a small detachment, eventually augmented with five thousand reinforcements. The Japanese blockaded the port with the help of British naval ships before bombarding the town. While the British studiously observed China's neutrality, the Japanese had no such qualms. Their

A British advertisement of 1914 celebrates colonies seized from Germany. *Wellcome Collection*

illegal assault began on Chinese territory eighty miles to the north, and so the Japanese view of China as ripe for conquest was born. Eventually, the Japanese deployed sixty thousand troops as the Germans dug in. After scuttling ships, blowing up the docks, and destroying port facilities, the "heroes of Qingdao," as they were later called in Germany, surrendered in November.[18] Their dogged defense of the colony had cost two hundred lives on the German side and perhaps five hundred on the Japanese side.

The entire German naval band at Qingdao was shipped off to a U.S. Army camp in Georgia where its talents were put to use in a prison symphony. It offered concerts to locals under the baton of the interned Austrian conductor of the Cincinnati Symphony Orchestra, Ernst Kunwald. In Qingdao, the results were less melodious. A few months after the battle, the Japanese issued a series of secret demands for special rights across northern China. When Yuan Shikai acceded and it became public, his popularity plummeted. The Chinese Communist Party was birthed in 1921 by nationalists outraged at Yuan's capitulation to Japanese demands.

Qingdao might have remained a thriving and humane northern version of Hong Kong if the British had taken the lead in battle. Instead, it would spark the rise of an ugly totalitarian movement and dash hopes for a democratic alternative to the catastrophic policies of the Chinese Communist Party. Needless to say, world history would have turned out much better if colonialism had survived at Qingdao.

• • •

With the armistice in 1918, German colonialism shifted from the realm of practice to that of politics and memory. Debates about the everyday issues of colonial rule were replaced by debates over theory, history, ideology, and national identity. One big change was the attitude of foreign powers towards German colonialism. Bitter recriminations on both sides replaced collaborative and friendly relations. Propagandists in Britain, Belgium, and France dug up every scurrilous rumor they could find about the German colonial record—including August Bebel's infamous lies about children in wicker baskets being sent over waterfalls and Carl Peters's alleged "confession" to his crimes of passion—in order to justify the seizure of German colonies.[19] The Allies styled themselves knights-errant rescuing helpless natives from the wiles of the *krauts*, despite clear native preferences for German rule.

When the Ottoman Empire collapsed, it could not of course resume control of its colonies. The same was not true of Germany. Thus, the Allies needed another reason to seize German holdings. "The Allies fell back on the false assertion that the German colonial record proved that she was unfit to govern dependent peoples," wrote the Cambridge economic historian David Fieldhouse. As an economic historian, Fieldhouse did not think it much of a loss since colonies had been a net drain on Germany.[20] But the manner and fact of losing its "status" as a colonial power would exert a profoundly negative influence on German domestic politics.

Almost from the moment the German colonies fell, the Allied press was filled with horror stories supposedly gathered from "liberated" natives. The native press in the British Gold Coast, for instance, began printing accounts of German Togo that were almost as purple as its regular commentary on affairs in the British colony itself. "No advantage would accrue from any attempt to comment upon them," sniffed a British scholar.[21]

British propaganda recalled the worst excesses of England's "We are the best colonizers" tradition, going back to the Cromwellian opera *The Cruelty of the Spaniards in Peru*.[22] The French historian René Puaux asserted that returning the colonies to Germany would be "a crime against humanity."[23] Any and every charge levelled against German colonialism was assumed to be historically accurate, an approach that prefigured what would later become mainstream German scholarship on colonialism. Sir Hugh Clifford, then governor of the Gold Coast, published "a plea for the native races" to bolster the British justification for taking over Germany colonies. Germany, he wrote, "has besmirched the escutcheon of Europe in Africa" and as a result "white men" and "Germans" were considered by the natives to be two different races.[24]

The British went to great trouble to cover up strong native support for a resumption of German colonial rule. A British cabinet memo sent to the relevant occupying colonial governments in January 1918 warned that "it has not been possible to secure general acceptance" of the view that occupying forces should seize the colonies. Thus the cabinet would "be glad if it could be furnished with a statement suitable for publication, if necessary, containing evidence of anxiety of natives ... to live under British rule."[25] A functionary in East Africa, Charles Dundas, was instructed by London to write up an "atrocity report" on German rule, which eventually came out in 1923.[26] The cottage industry of "unmasking" the horrors of German colonialism soon extended to the Pacific, where an Australian journalist published a trilogy of books premised on the idea that "the Germany of the African atrocities and horrors is the Germany of the Pacific."[27]

In Togo, the British suspended all taxation, mandatory labor, and court trials during the war, which not surprisingly led to an outburst of support for British rule. In Cameroon, the repatriated chiefs first asked whether the British would promise never to give the lands back to Germany. With those assurances offered, they burst forth with gushing demands for British rule. Thus the report on "native wishes" found ardent support for British rule and lurid stories of German misrule. Any formal referendums, the British East Africa commissioner told parliament, would be "injudicious," since most natives would assume the question was some sort of trick to root out *kraut* sympathizers. Better to stick to the less contentious justification, he suggested, that "European control, which ensured the safety of life and property, was preferable to the state of anarchy which must otherwise prevail."[28]

A blue-book report on German colonies written by the Foreign Office in 1918 was a violation of the sober and empirical blue-book tradition that had informed British colonial rule for a century.[29] The report was kept secret by the British until just before the Versailles talks, ensuring the Germans had little time to prepare their rebuttal.

The British expert on Germany, William Harbutt Dawson, who participated in the British delegation at Versailles, called it a concoction of "lurid stories based merely on native testimony." The same Foreign Office, he noted, had issued positive reports on German colonialism before the war.[30] The Treaty of Versailles blamed Berlin for "dereliction in the sphere of colonial civilization."[31]

The most depraved picture was painted by a separate blue book on the Herero-Nama conflict in German Southwest Africa.[32] The Germans had left behind extensive documentation of the conflict that the British plumbed for salacious details. The main British author, an Irishman and Herero advocate, compiled selective and purposeful facts. The Congo campaigner Edmund Morel, no pushover for colonial rule, wrote of the British report: "Without minimizing in the slightest degree the action of the Germans in Southwest Africa, we should do well to have at the back of our minds the sort of indictment which would have been drawn up by a successful enemy in occupation of Rhodesia and Bechuanaland, desirous of demonstrating our iniquities to the world in order to make out a case for retaining those territories for himself."[33]

Berlin in 1919 rushed into print its own blue book on atrocities and misrule in British colonies as part of an attempt to have the colonies returned.[34] Schnee warned that by abandoning objectivity and fairness to gang up on Germany, Britain and France were dooming their own colonial enterprises. "If Europe remains sick under the calumnies and threats of the Treaty of Versailles, Africa will remain sick and undeveloped for the same reason."[35] Schnee's warning that the foul attacks on German colonialism would doom the European project proved all too prescient over the next century.

The victors were deaf as posts and carried out what Dawson called the "shabby annexations" of Versailles.[36] An American proposal to add some international supervision prevailed. These "mandates" from the new League of Nations would provide "the tutelage of . . . advanced nations" as part of the "sacred trust of civilization."[37] It was a direct restatement of the civilizational arguments of the Spirit of Berlin. In practice, the British and French managed the territories as part of their colonial holdings.

Germany had thus been stripped of its colonies on the basis of evidence and principles that its own colonial era had generated. The colonies of Berlin and their fourteen million inhabitants were seized under the pretext of standards first established by the Spirit of Berlin. Hence the bitter emanations from a German middle class that felt abruptly expelled from liberal civilization. "The only colonial power that professed the idea of solidarity with practically all of the consequences of that word," wrote the German economist and colonial advocate Arthur Dix in 1926, "is the one that paid the price for its attitude by losing all of its colonies."[38] Dix had previously written positive articles about globalization and European integration, coining the phrase "the global village" (*das Dörfchen Erde*) four decades before its popularization by the Canadian philosopher Marshall McLuhan. His next book in 1928 had different tone: *Schluss mit "Europa"* meaning *The End of "Europe,"* or perhaps in more colloquial language, *We're Done with Europe.*

CHAPTER 11

Why the Loss of Colonies
Doomed German Liberalism

The seizure of German colonies at Versailles was one of the great diplomatic blunders of the twentieth century. Many wise owls on the British side recognized the German colonial achievement and worried about the implications of casting this noble people out of the comity of nations. "German unrest will never be overcome without some solution of this question," cautioned the British colonial deity Lord Lugard, who served on the League of Nations mandates commission. Failing that, he warned, "the deprivation of all her colonies must lead to a new war with Germany."[1] British Versailles delegate William Harbutt Dawson counseled that the annexations were "the sure prelude of future armed strife" and "will inevitably lead to another war."[2]

If Germany had not been shorn of its colonies at Versailles, German politics would have been delivered from a major source of resentment in the Weimar era that followed. The unifying and liberal colonial project would have continued to draw together center-left and center-right parties. A broad-minded cosmopolitanism would have remained at the center of German politics. Support for fringe movements like communism and fascism—two heads of the same totalitarian monster—would have been weaker.

The American war correspondent William Shirer would later refer to "the shadow of Versailles" to describe the noxious effects of the treaty on German political life.[3] Like other authors, Shirer focused on reparations and disarmament, failing to mention the stripping of colonies. But the loss of overseas possessions was a key factor in the rise of the Nazi party. The "shadow of Versailles" would throw into darkness the German colonial mission that was one of the bulwarks *against* a bitter fanaticism. German colonialism reflected and reinforced the liberal spirit of this new nation. Its termination would usher in an illiberal disaster.

The collapse of German liberalism after World War I is one of the most researched topics in European history. Yet few historians have ever drawn a causal link between the forced cessation of German colonialism and the rise of illiberal politics. To be sure, the antagonisms arising from World War I, the economic effects of the Great Depression, German anti-Semitism, and military designs on Central Europe would have remained latent sources of a terrifying turn in domestic politics. The new communist menace in Russia would still have roiled the geopolitical scene. In part, then, this oversight reflects the compelling significance of other factors.

But historians have their blind spots, and few are more eclipsing than their anti-colonial bias.

In part, this is a failure of logic. Historians tend to examine factors that are present in order to explain some outcome, not paying attention to factors that are absent but which could plausibly have been present. Social scientists are more adept at including "absent factors" in their explanations, but few studies consider the absence of colonialism as a possible explanation for the rise of the Third Reich.

The bigger failure is ideological. Scholars wish ardently to believe that colonialism and fascism were two heads of the same monster. They desperately insist that the fifteen years from the ceasefire in East

Heraus mit den Kolonien!
Ohne Kolonien keine Rohstoffe!
Ohne Kolonien kein Rechtsfriede!
Der Reichsverband der Kolonialdeutschen

The German Colonial Society warns of "no peace" without
a return of German colonies, 1919. *Bundesarchiv*

Africa to the rise of Hitler were merely an interlude between one form
of German nastiness and another. They cannot imagine how the
abrupt Allied termination of German colonialism was anything but
a good thing. If anything, the Allies should have more thoroughly
purged the colonialist idea from the German public square in order
to avert the rise of the Nazis. If only the Allies had perhaps jailed all
the members of the old colonial lobby like Heinrich Schnee or perhaps put all the returning colonial settlers into thought-reform
camps. Then those colonial ideas with their high-altitude bombardier
gazes and "othering" of the natives with new capital cities and limits

on German-language instruction would have been stamped out once and for all. World War II could have been averted with a little more anti-colonial zeal shown at Versailles. This at least is implied by the academy's silence on the question.

There is a troubling little datum in this logic: it was *decolonized* Germany, not *colonial* Britain or France, that turned illiberal and marched on Europe. The Allies fought in support of liberal civilization with the extraordinary voluntary efforts of their colonized peoples. By anti-colonial logic, fascism should have gripped Britain or France, not Germany. Accounting for this role reversal requires some intellectual gymnastics by the professoriate. On one theory, Germany's loss of opportunities to kill and repress non-white people in the colonies—a pastime that the sadists of Britain and France continued to enjoy—led to a search for second-best prey in Europe.[4] The theory falls apart on many counts, not least because of the popular revulsion in Britain and France (as had been true in Germany as well) every time an obscure news dispatch or missionary complaint suggested an untoward act had been committed in the colonies. Unlike Germany, the fascists in Britain and France remained a fringe outfit because the mainstream was too liberal and too international—in a word, too "colonial"—to entertain such nonsense.

The fact is, colonialism was a critical bulwark *against* the rise of fascism. A continuation of colonialism by Germany would have strongly, perhaps decisively, averted the rise of the Nazi party. Over seventy-five years of scholarship has ignored this critical explanation for one of the great calamities of Western history, largely because over that same period, the Western academy has been gripped by an anti-colonial moral panic. Thus to the grand diplomatic blunder of seizing German colonies at Versailles must be added the grand intellectual blunder of ignoring this event's role in Germany's political conflagration.

It was not just pro-colonial figures like Lord Lugard who predicted the odious consequences of abolishing German colonialism. The anti-colonial fanatics of right and left expected it with gleeful anticipation. What better way to end the sickness of liberal civilization at home than by ending the liberal mission abroad? The former naval captain, prolific journalist, and later Nazi legislator Count Ernst Reventlow made the case as early as 1907 that German colonialism was an obstacle to a manly war of expansion in Europe. If Britain and her allies were to seize German colonies, he wrote hopefully in that year, it "would create in Germany a bitter feeling of rancor which might be turned to good account." The anti-Semitic and illiberal Count Reventlow saw how the angry energies of the far left and far right in Germany would be energized, "certainly *not* for the purpose of celebrating, after a fashion to which we have been accustomed all too long, universal peace, international civilization, and human progress as the highest blessings and as the sole objects of 'national' ambition."[5] To our contemporary ears, Count Reventlow's strictures against "human progress" and "civilization" sound a lot like the postmodern professors who dominate academic life in the West. This is a parallel to which we will return below. For now, we will focus our attention on *how* the German loss of colonies led to the disaster of fascism for Europe, a disaster that would ultimately shutter the entire European colonial project.

• • •

The severing of colonies led to a "phantom limb" syndrome in Germany. The colonial lobby acted as if nothing had changed or as if the nightmare of colonial amputation would soon end. The redoubtable Heinrich Schnee, recovering from the battles of East Africa, published a three-volume "lexicon of German colonies" in

1920.[6] A Colonial Department was created in the new federal Foreign Office in 1924, reflecting more cross-party consensus on colonialism than had existed even in colonial days. Two law professors who had been detailed by the Reichstag in 1907 to conduct a study of indigenous laws in the colonies brought their work to fruition in 1929 with a two-volume reference on "customs and customary rights in the former German colonies."[7] An odd provision of the Treaty of Versailles had required Germany to repatriate to East Africa the skull of the Wahehe rebel leader that had been sent to Germany in 1898 because of the occult sway it held over the natives. The Germans refused. These scientific and anthropological artifacts were all that remained to support the colonial vision. The skull remained in a museum in Bremen.

The economist Arthur Dix's 1928 book *The End of "Europe"* predicted that the loss of Germany's colonies would doom the pan-European project. The American historian David Thomas Murphy finds the impassioned advocacy of Dix "ironic" because, on the one hand, he was clearly a liberal and a political moderate, but on the other hand he was "unable ultimately to break from the obsolescent colonialist concepts of world order."[8] In fact, there is *nothing* ironic about his position. Dix's liberalism perfectly complemented his advocacy for colonialism. To be pro-colonial in the Weimar era was to understand the foundations of liberal freedoms at home and abroad, a link later historians fail to comprehend. The ones who broke with "obsolescent colonialist concepts" were the race hustlers and Leninists who wanted to tear liberal freedoms to shreds. Murphy is clearly disappointed that Dix, "for all his insight," still believed in "the old colonial mission" as a mutually enriching encounter between Germany and its former colonies.[9] But as we have seen, the encounter between Germany and its former colonies *was* mutually enriching. Murphy, like most academics, "for all their insight," cannot grasp this most basic historical truth, falling back on sneering intellectual dismissals of "the White Man's Burden" and "the civilizing mission" as the sorts of stock phrases of disapprobation that one utters in the faculty lounge to bring knowing nods of assent from the assembled Ph.D.s.

A dwindling colonial lobby fought to uphold the Western tradition of humane universalism that the colonial project exemplified. Decrying the injustice of Versailles, these Weimar-era politicians and colonial organizations portrayed the new French and British stewards of German colonies as falling short of high German standards. Probably the most bungled takeover of a German colony was New Zealand's of German Samoa. With just 38,000 people, New Zealand's Samoa mandate was hardly important, but it provided a clear contrast with the gentle and efficient administration of the Germans. The first achievement of New Zealand was to wipe out 20 percent of

German colonial veterans protest in Munich against the loss of colonies in 1929. The sign reads "Never Forget Our Colonies!" *Mary Evans / Sueddeutsche Zeitung Photo*

the population by allowing a ship carrying troops with the Spanish influenza to debark without quarantine in November 1918. Thereafter, relations with the main chief and the new guardians deteriorated, leading to a "Black Saturday" tragedy in 1929 when twelve were killed and fifty injured by police trying to disperse a Samoan protest in the capital city of Apia. A rosy view of the German era became "almost an obsession" among the Samoans, according to one native at the time.[10] Schnee, among others, was quick to declare a Kiwi "tyranny" (*Gewaltherrschaft*) in the former colony.[11] Expelled from the paradise of colonial rule, German statesmen became embittered and biased.

Overall trade in German colonies had grown by 17 percent a year from 1903 to 1913, but growth fell to just 2 percent year in the same territories from 1914 to 1929. This was in part because German planter families returned to Germany, leaving agricultural sectors in crisis. Along with them went missionary teachers, health workers, engineers, and accountants. German society united to support the return of their colonial settlers—*Kolonialdeutschen*—after they were expelled or made unwelcome by the mandate powers. Long before France had its *Pieds-Noirs* or Portugal its *Retornados*, Germany dealt with the trauma of decolonization on domestic politics. That trauma would have far worse consequences for Germany than for any other major colonial power.

Heinrich Schnee coined the phrase "the myth of colonial guilt" (*Die koloniale Schuldlüge*) to refute the charges made at Versailles and to buck up pride in colonial achievements.[12] German colonies had been beneficial and legitimate, he argued, and the League of Nations system was a failure. The mandate powers should be "honorable" and return the colonies to Germany (with the exception of Qingdao, now restored to China). A "colonial friends" (*Kolonialfreund*) movement of the 1920s was part of this ghostly apparition in German politics. A popular series of commemorative publications about German colonies in Africa, the "Afrikabücher," included war stories and fictionalized accounts of the colonial era.

Germany made half-hearted efforts to get its colonies returned at the Locarno negotiations of 1925, without success. The delegates agreed that Germany could in theory take over as a mandatory power. But the British considered the mandates to be a legal fiction and integrated Togo, Cameroon, and East Africa into their colonial system.[13] Rebuffed, German politicians became critics of colonialism rather than aspiring governors.

• • •

Shorn of its cosmopolitan colonial project, Germany succumbed to a vengeful anti-European mood. The embittered public turned first to Bolshevism and then to Nazism as balm for its wounds. Both of these plagues attacked the old colonial lobby and its liberal ideals with deadly menace.

The communists were the first to recognize the potential of anti-colonialism to gain adherents in Germany, breaking with the pro-colonial views of their master, Marx. From 1927 to 1933, Berlin was the operative center of the Soviet Union's main anti-colonial organization, the League Against Imperialism and Colonial Oppression. Moscow chose Berlin because Germany had been stripped of its colonies and was seen as ripe for revolution against everything that colonialism had embodied.[14] The international communist organization (or Comintern) in Moscow hired the German communist Willi Münzenberg to head the League. From Berlin, Münzenberg ran a sprawling and chaotic movement with one purpose according to the League's official history: to "establish a channel for communism to the colonial and semi-colonial countries" by serving as "a distributor for Bolshevik propaganda." Seeding communism in the colonies would serve the ultimate purpose, according to the official history: "To create a 'Solar System' to realize the building of world communism."[15] Those external pressures would help the communists to gain power in Germany itself, where they polled just behind the Nazis as the German center collapsed.

Moscow treated Africans, Arabs, and Asians as "a strategically important element in communist activity," as Lenin wrote in 1921.[16] If the entire Third World swooned to the overtures of Moscow and overthrew colonial governments in favor of one-party regimes run by Moscow, then Europe would be helpless in the face of world communism. The Berlin-based League thus set out to recruit what the historian Mary Grabar would later call "black mascots for the red revolution."[17] Black, brown, yellow—all were useful. The League offered material support to an armed insurgency against Dutch rule in Indonesia that erupted in 1927. As the official history explained: "The uprising provided the communists with the opportunity to infiltrate and assume control over the Indonesian nationalist organization."[18]

The official opening of the League in 1927 coincided with the tenth anniversary of the Russian revolution. The purpose was "to portray the international communist movement as the real supporter of the [anti-]colonial struggle" and thus to serve the bigger goal of a "support campaign for Soviet Russian foreign policy" in Europe.[19] The invitation list included Mohandas Gandhi, who preached the superiority of Oriental values against the decrepit West. "To add spice to the ethnic mix, black American delegates would be recruited . . . to come to Europe and denounce racial oppression in the United States," noted the American historian Sean McMeekin. "Münzenberg planned to add noncommunist 'fellow travelers' with no particular connection to imperial regimes or opposition movements, who wanted to demonstrate their right-thinking opposition to colonialism, racism, and all the rest."[20]

The formation of the League turned Berlin into a haven for Moscow-controlled, anti-colonial activists from across Europe. Eminent anti-colonialists like Manabendra Nath Roy and Jawaharlal Nehru from India, Mohammed Nafi Çelebi of Syria, and Mohammad Hatta of Indonesia flocked to the headquarters on Friedrichstrasse. German colonialism had been liberal and democratic. German anti-colonialism was at birth illiberal and totalitarian.

Like all totalitarian movements, German anti-colonialism soon fractured into ideological schism and personal vendettas. The second League conference in Frankfurt in 1929 ended in chaos as the Stalinist faction purged the moderates. According to the official history: "The chaos had been carefully planned at Comintern headquarters in Moscow solely to steer the League into a more radical direction that suited the ambitions of the agenda-makers in Moscow."[21] Nehru, whose anti-colonialism bordered on the psychotic, was happy to join the board of the purified movement, now more than ever in the control of Moscow. The Bengali radical Virendranath Chattopadhyaya won Nehru's support for the establishment of an India-affairs section of the League in 1929. He would be executed in a Stalinist purge in Moscow in 1937.

Nehru's willing and considerable work on behalf of international communism and proto-fascist Indian nationalists operating out of Berlin has been lovingly praised by academics as evidence of his progressive views. His "collective mobilization against imperialist powers and capitalist classes," in the words of a cooing American historian, makes him an icon of the left.[22] But the radical movements of which Nehru was a part were anything but progressive. The anti-colonial nationalism and socialism that Nehru and his ilk

encouraged would find its logical end in the National Socialist cata-
clysm of German politics and world history.

● ● ●

As a consolation prize for losing its colonies, Germany was given
a seat on the Mandates Commission during its seven years in the
League of Nations from 1926 to 1933. It was an attempt to bring Germany
back into the comity of Europe and into pan-European debates on
modernity, civilization, and humanitarianism. While contemporary
academics sneer at those concepts, they were the only thing standing
between Germany and Nazi rule. Participation in the Mandates Commission had the potential to keep German nationalism on its liberal
path, undergirded by an alliance of conservative and moderate-left
parties: "The German colonial lobby and individual colonial bureaucrats . . . looked to the League as the defender of imperialism and the
sustainer of the European civilizing mission to which Colonial Germans had dedicated their careers and ideologies," wrote the American historian Sean Wempe.

Britain and France feared the move would allow Berlin to
counter the calumnies of Versailles with "even more vitriolic
condemnations . . . by giving the dead empire an official setting
in which to point an accusing finger from the grave." To avert that,
no former German colonial governors were allowed to hold the
German seat. London and Paris were particularly anxious to keep
the outspoken Heinrich Schnee at bay.[23] The two successive
German representatives were experienced officials who had
worked both in the German colonial office and in the African
colonies. They earned a sterling reputation and became a source
of pride for the old colonial lobby in Germany. But hopes that this
would result in a return to colonial rule for Germany were dashed.

"It was seven lean years in every respect," Schnee grumbled in a 1935 book. "Discrimination against Germany was upheld in colonial affairs."[24]

Schnee's only cameo came when he was put onto the League commission investigating Japan's takeover of northeast China in 1931, the fulfillment of Britain's tactical mistake at Qingdao in 1914. Schnee saw the parallels between the march on Asia by Japanese fascists holding high the banner of anti-colonialism and a similar movement taking shape in Germany. One can almost hear his trumpeting pleas over the dull bureaucratic bass lines of the League's inquiry: "Please, for the love of God, let us back into the colonial world, or there will be far worse things coming out of Germany!" The efforts by Schnee and others to rejoin the liberal project of Europe took on a desperate tone as an ugly fascist specter gained stature at home.[25] The "ecumenical internationalism" of German colonialism, as one scholar called it, was now clinging to the hopes of just one man on an obscure committee.[26] Schnee's "willingness to appropriate the political languages of internationalism and liberal imperialism," wrote Wempe, was a Hail Mary from the colonial lobby to save German politics from a dark turn.[27] German colonialism had been embedded in a liberal European civilizing mission. Spurned by Europe, Germany would turn illiberal and anti-Western alongside Russia.

Too little, too late. Hitler was made German chancellor in January 1933 and took Germany out of the League in October. Schnee's cameo was, in the words of Wempe, "the beginning of the end for the heretofore ongoing influence of Schnee and Colonial Germans like him in Germany's colonial policies and international relations." The Spirit of Berlin was defunct. On the long voyage home, Schnee reminisced with French colleagues about the better times of the colonial days.[28]

• • •

In the street brawl that became German politics, the only question was whether the communists or the fascists would prevail. The schisms and purges on the left, which had brought the League Against Imperialism into disarray, provided the opportunity for Nazi preeminence. The Nazis realized that they could capture embittered constituencies by being more anti-Western than the communists. Nazi propagandist Joseph Goebbels was jealous of Willi Münzenberg's gift for anti-colonial propaganda.[29] With the chancellorship in hand, the Nazis styled themselves the true champions of anti-colonial agitation. The Gestapo chased the LAI out of Germany and ran up the flag of anti-colonialism itself.

The anti-colonial movement saw in Adolph Hitler a powerful new sponsor: "The Nazis' rise to power led to a reorientation of anticolonialists' alignments from the left to the right of the political spectrum," wrote the historian Daniel Brückenhaus. The Nazis drew parallels between their "national revolution" of 1933, which they argued had freed Germany from the oppressive regime of Versailles, and the national aspirations of colonized peoples everywhere. Like Nazism, this anti-colonialism was illiberal, reckless, and an imminent threat to the lives of those who might be put under its rule. Nazi politicians positioned themselves as vigorous, young emblems fighting against decrepit European imperialism.

Brückenhaus insists that Nazi support for anti-colonialists in Berlin "was based on strategic considerations, rather than any kind of ideological conviction."[30] But this is contradicted by the flat evidence of Nazi anti-colonialism (more on this below). It was the *shared* ideological conviction of anti-colonialism that allowed the Gestapo to attract the support of the anti-colonial lobby in Germany. The reason the anti-colonialists cozied up to the Nazis is not that they faced "difficult ideological choices," as Brückenhaus claimed. Rather, they *shared* a fundamental illiberal ideology.[31]

The chance to save German liberalism now came down to desperate measures in the form of unsubtle pleas from conservative critics of the Nazis. "The destructive process of war, revolution, and internal disruption have found a starting point in Russia. Now is the moment to stop this destructive process before it reaches Germany," begged Hitler's non-Nazi economics minister Alfred Hugenberg at an economic conference in London in June 1933. Hugenberg then surprised delegates by pulling out a proposal for the return of German colonies in Africa that had not been vetted by Berlin. "We do not want to lose the courage and spirit of our forefathers to the base instincts that are growing among the German people," he explained. "If we go under, other countries of the West will go down with us."[32] This open appeal to allow Germany back into the collaborative world of European colonialism to clean up the toxic political mess at home was a barely concealed attack on Hitler himself. The Führer was furious. Hitler forced Hugenberg to withdraw his proposal, and the Nazis then publicly denounced his talk of a return to overseas colonialism.[33]

In any case, the appeal fell upon deaf ears in Britain, which was in denial about the rise of the Nazis. Any discussion of a return of German colonies, *The Times* opined, needed to be made in writing through the appropriate committees of the League of Nations. The nerve of the Germans to ignore proper procedures! Moreover, all this talk of politics and national spirit was not suitable for a conference on economics: "What on Earth has all this to do with tariffs and quotas and the marketing of goods?"[34] What indeed! If only the British had realized how much it *did* bear on the life and death of Europe. Hugenberg was ordered home and then sacked. He retreated to his family seat on the Weser River and watched a disaster unfold.

Another last-ditch plea from the old conservatives came in 1934 when the general who headed the Colonial Soldiers League—a sort of American Legion of former colonial soldiers—wearily handed over control of the East Africa Protectorate Police (then operating as a stand-alone force) to the new Nazi detachment known as the Göring Police Force. Göring of course was the son of the former governor of Southwest Africa, the one who "did not tire of extracting cannon balls and sewing up wounds" of Herero and Nama men injured in their incessant civil wars. The other powers in Europe "would do well to re-open this outlet for the German people," the retiring colonial commandant begged as he handed over the brigade to the Nazis.[35] Germany's colonial energies—aimed outward at the civilizing mission—were now being perverted and redirected at Europe. The evidence was plain to see. British colonial colleagues of Schnee telephoned to express alarm. "A certain weakening" had occurred in British circles sympathetic to German colonial claims, Schnee wrote in 1935 with barely concealed anxiety.[36] Schnee fully understood the Nazi menace.

The Nazis, noted the American economist Lewis Gann, represented everything that German colonialism was *not*: illiberal, anti-capitalist, and suspicious of racial mixing.[37] William Harbutt Dawson, the British journalist, scholar, and civil servant who was part of the British delegation at Versailles, saw that National Socialism had de-Westernized and "decolonized" Germany, taking it *out of* European civilization much as the anti-colonialist fanatics it supported abroad wanted to be taken out of European civilization and given a free hand to enslave and plunder their fellow peoples.[38] Hitler represented Germany's *rejection* of European civilization and the Spirit of Berlin. We might say that Hitler was a post-colonial despot *avant la lettre*. The road to denazification in Germany, Dawson would argue, lay in restoring Germany to its central place in European life, including colonial life.

The Nazi rise must in part, then, be attributed to the sudden termination of German colonialism. Since anti-colonial scholars can't allow for this, they have to bend facts like clowns making balloon twisters. The Cornell University historian Isabel Hull, for instance, insists that a militarized approach to *all* political questions dominated German colonialism, and the Nazis merely continued the habit. To make this claim, she rewrites the *entire* German colonial period as *nothing more* than total warfare *all the time*, or as she puts it "the colonial situation itself was identical to war."[39] That claim is so false, as we have seen, as to be ludicrous.

Colonial-era officials saw the truth more clearly. One of Schnee's final efforts to restore the lost, pro-colonial center of German politics was *The Book of German Colonies*, an amalgam of encyclopedia, reminiscence, and policy arguments first published in 1933 and then updated three times, finally in 1938.[40] In the book, the former Cameroon and Southwest Africa governor Theodor Seitz asserted that colonialism was the *only* thing that could have prevented the rise of fascism because of "the importance of colonies for the political education of a people." Colonial rule had brought a civilizing influence to the domestic scene, Seitz wrote. It taught the need for compromise and the peaceful resolution of differences. While Britain's politics had remained stable since 1918, Seitz observed, "the Germans tore each other to pieces in all possible and impossible contradictions and parties." The reason was that the two-way "educational interaction that we see between Britain and her colonies" had been cut off in Germany. After losing its abroad holdings, Germany behaved like a squabbling little family.[41] The Shadow of Versailles and the expulsion from colonial civilization would be catastrophic for Germany and Europe.

Similar arguments had been made throughout the 1920s by advocates of a continued world-geography education for German students. Without a global perspective to encourage a broad-minded political perspective at home, one of these colonial advocates wrote, the graduates would throw "the dark shadow of their disharmony on the entire conduct of the state."[42] Moderate socialists and conservatives alike encouraged a renewed global education for Germany's youth as a source of social integration.

Indeed, much as today, the professors railing against colonialism in Weimar Germany were proto-Nazis who attacked "Anglo-Saxon" liberalism and empire, and agitated for cooperation with the Stalinists in the Soviet Union. By contrast, the professors advocating a return to the global and colonial perspective saw more clearly than later critics that the attack on colonialism was nothing less than an appeal for a totalitarian takeover.

Scholars still find it puzzling. "A striking aspect of German colonial propaganda during the Weimar era is the disparity between the actual significance the overseas empire held for German society, which was very small, and the enormous amount of language, paper and ink, and futile energy expended on its recovery," insisted the American historian David Thomas Murphy.[43] Yet the "actual significance" of Germany's colonies was far from small. Economically, to be sure, the effect was minimal, although the loss of colonies did deprive Germany of what would have been a healthy outlet for the continued development of its maritime, aviation, and telecommunications sectors, a major sore point for economists. But politically and socially, the colonies had provided a durable anchor for the emergence of this new nation as the heart of a liberal and integrated Europe. Trying to weigh again on this anchor was far from of "nugatory" significance, as he calls it.[44]

The tragedy of post-Versailles Germany was not that it tried to restore colonial rule, but that it did not try hard enough. By the early 1930s, the German public had abandoned liberal internationalism for the political fringes, leaving the colonial lobby isolated. Too many

Germans were embittered with liberal civilization, turning to illiberal nationalism on the right and illiberal communism on the left. The far right led by Hitler insisted that colonialism was a waste of time, and the far left guided by Moscow insisted that it was oppressive. The cultural relativism of far left and far right replaced liberal universalism. The center could not hold.

German colonialism had been born of the patriotic moderates of the center left and right in Germany. To be a colonialist, often Catholic or Jewish, was to be a centrist standing fast against the siren calls of the radical left and right. This anchor for German politics was now unfixed. The confiscation of German colonies and the attacks on its colonial record beginning in 1919 worked in tandem with other factors to bring to power the staunchly anti-colonial Nazis. The Nazis, as we shall see, prefigured the contemporary race hustlers of the radical left with their insistence on racial essentialism and their disparaging of liberal civilization. Disillusioned Germans, much as contemporary Woke activists, saw themselves in Third World guise, fighting against the liberal values of the West.

Bismarck, recall, had observed in 1883 that colonialism would help create a bipartisan and mature politics at home because of the onerous responsibilities to those abroad. The result of being stripped of colonies and humiliated as a pariah of Europe, as ex-colonial governor Theodor Seitz saw with horror, was to reignite bitter divisions and petty politics at home, stoking support for radicals of left and right.

Academics, who are supposed to be smart people, are puzzled by what Nathanael Kuck of the University of Leipzig calls the "rather unexpected convergence" of anti-colonialism and fascism.[45] But there is nothing unexpected about it. The Nazi doctrine was perfectly aligned with the doctrines of anti-colonialism. The happy alliance between the two makes perfect sense. The anti-colonialists of the

Weimar period understood the confluence of their illiberal visions with both communism and fascism. Hitler and Stalin were for them equally useful in their fight against the West. Thus when the Nazis and Soviets struck up a friendship in 1939, anti-colonialists considered the new alliance a most natural thing. The totalitarian vision for tearing down liberal civilization had brought together these otherwise strange bedfellows.

The argument that a continuation of German colonialism would have averted the rise of the Nazis was made by the legendary German historian Gerhard Ritter in his 1948 book *Europe and the German Question*.[46] His work documented the decline of liberalism that set in with the end of colonial affairs. It pointed to the failed centrist resistance to the Nazis. (He was jailed in 1944.) Revolts against liberal modernity, he insisted, were a result of illiberal movements that began with the violence of the French Revolution and found full expression in the attack on the Spirit of Berlin. It was *anti-colonialism*, not colonialism, that was the wellspring of fascism. But such "reactionary" ideas were no longer *au courant* in the academy of the 1960s (where revolution was an idol of worship) and died with the likes of Ritter. Scholars labored instead to stand up the ludicrous claim that colonialism was somehow implicated in the Nazi revolution.

German colonialism, as the Stanford professor Russell Berman argued, had been among the most liberal of European models.[47] Once deprived of this liberal practice rooted in the Western tradition, Germany was left with only a parochial version of nationalism to cling to. The "myth of anti-colonialism" in progressive circles, as Berman called it, was that ending colonialism would advance liberalism in Germany. It did the opposite. It fatally undermined the civilizational arguments made at the Berlin conference on which liberalism depended. The attack on German colonialism at Versailles was nothing less than an attack on German civilization. The proof would emerge tragically over the next twenty years.

CHAPTER 12

Nazi Anti-Colonialism and the War on Europe

For the ideologues of the National Socialist German Workers' Party, the repudiation of colonialism was part of a much-longed-for return to German purity. Adolph Hitler opposed the seafaring "colonies and trade" lobby in favor of land-based expansion in Europe. At most, he saw colonial claims as useful bargaining chips. Unlike Bismarck, whose reluctance towards colonialism was practical, Hitler saw colonialism as the preserve of odious Jewish capitalists and Christian missionaries. Africans, Hitler wrote in *Mein Kampf,* were not fit to be ruled by Germans, for they were no better than "poodles." He branded the colonial lobby "criminally stupid" and full of "idle chatter." "Finally, we cease with the colonial and commercial policy of the pre-war period," he wrote, "and proceed with the land policy of the future." Germany's need for territory, he insisted, "cannot be fulfilled in the Cameroon but almost exclusively in Europe."[1]

Hitler promised that Germany would focus on "living space" in Eastern Europe.[2] The bourgeoisie that had lobbied for colonies was a failure and "does not possess a single creative political idea for the future," he complained. He explained in a 1931 note: "As long as Germany itself is a tributary colony, to be exploited by foreigners

201

and international high finance, colonial efforts must take a back seat." German colonialism had been based on a false premise, Hitler argued, because it failed to maintain a "geographical connection with the motherland." The liberal and free capitalism of the German colonial era would be replaced by a managed war economy under "national socialism." The German colonial experience had been an "escapade" that had fortunately ended at Versailles.[3] Hitler was the fulfillment of naval-captain-turned-journalist Count Reventlow's hopes that anti-colonial rancor "might be turned to good account" for a splendid little war on Europe.

As late as 1938, the British prime minister Neville Chamberlain offered the Nazis a return of Cameroon and East Africa to prevent their European incursions. But the British appeasers soon learned that Hitler detested the very idea of colonies. What he craved was a free hand in Europe. "I would not waste a single day fighting for a colony," he pledged.[4] As proof, after Hitler signed an alliance with Japan in 1940, he did not demand a return of the 1,400-odd islands of former German New Guinea.

Hitler rejected not just colonialism in general, but German colonialism in particular. The German model of colonialism was particularly noxious to Hitler because of its emphasis on local legitimacy, the protection and documentation of local cultures, and the globalization of German national identity. The successful alloy of classical liberalism and conservative patriotism that had forged what one scholar called the unique "transculturality" of German colonialism was explicitly rejected by Hitler.[5] As the University of Hamburg historian Birthe Kundrus wrote: "The Nazi leadership positioned itself unequivocally in a state of discontinuity with respect to classic colonialism."[6]

There was an additional revulsion to colonialism: the Jews had their fingerprints all over it. The two men who headed the Colonial

Office in Berlin from 1890 to 1910, Paul Kayser and Bernhard Dernburg, both had Jewish parents and were seen as Jewish by their peers. The legendary colonial adventurer Eduard Schnitzer, who became the governor of an Ottoman province in Egypt and changed his name to Emin Pasha, was born a German Jew as well. "Dernburg and Emin Pasha even became heroes to the procolonial public, lauded as champions of colonialism," noted American scholar Christian Davis.[7]

The most vocal colonial advocate after World War I in the moderate Social Democratic Party was Max Cohen-Reuss, whose group in the party advocated a return to the Spirit of Berlin as mutually beneficial and legitimate overseas rule they called "colonialism without imperialism."[8] Cohen-Reuss fled the Nazis in 1934 and survived the war by hiding in a mountain barn in Switzerland.

Dr. Robert Koch, meanwhile, was a protégé of bacteria specialist Ferdinand Cohn and was mentored by the research doctor Paul Ehrlich as well as other Jews. As outsiders in German society, they saw Koch's brilliance when the German scientific establishment did not. Koch planned to hand over his lab to another Jew who unfortunately became too ill for the task. The Nazis could not celebrate German colonial achievements in the realm of medicine, much less any other sphere, because they were accomplished by Germany's storied Jewish community.[9] A return to colonialism would undermine the anti-Semitism on which Nazi power depended. "By providing the public with such prominent examples of 'Jewish' German patriots," wrote Davis, "colonialism seemed to undermine—in a most public way—racial antisemitism's basic principle of a diametrical opposition between 'Jews' and 'Germans.'" As such, "colonialism helped weaken the imagined racial divide within the German body politic that mattered most to antisemites."[10]

Thus for anti-colonialists, anti-Semitism was the natural position. The bitterly anti-Semitic Count Reventlow wrote of how *Völkisch* national identity stripped of its cosmopolitan and Jewish features would make Germany a world power. This *Völkisch* spirit should be taken up by other oppressed peoples, like the nationalists of India, he assayed.[11] Like many Nazis, Reventlow saw communism in Moscow as a natural ally of this effort under his concept of "ethno-communist unification." He formed the core of the socialist bloc within the Nazi party pushing for alliance with Moscow.[12]

The Jews had been central to defining an outward-oriented and confident Germany that was every bit as patriotic as it was cosmopolitan. The "world politics" or *Weltpolitik* of overseas trade and governance under the Spirit of Berlin was countered by a new idea of "nearby living space" or *Lebensraum* pushed by the likes of Count Reventlow. The fundamental dissonance between the colonial project and fascism could not be more evident.

• • •

Anti-colonial forces beyond Europe were quick to recognize kindred spirits in the Nazis. Of course, the Nazis had to explain with contorted logic that their domestic race laws implied only differences, not a hierarchy, of races. This was enough to satisfy the growing ranks of race chauvinists in East Asia, India, Africa, and the Middle East whose anti-white racism now rivalled the anti-Semitic racism of the Nazis. Parochialism, racism, and illiberalism were after all the *natural* positions for all anti-colonialists. Hitler referred to nationalists in India like Gandhi as his "natural allies."[13]

Strangely, the contemporary academy is completely silent on the fascist origins of anti-colonialism. As one scholar writes: "Historians have consistently ignored the question whether there was any profound interplay between fascism and certain strands of anti-colonial nationalism." As he notes, progressive academics consciously ignore evidence of Nazi sympathies in anti-colonial circles even when that evidence stares them in the face.[14] They simply do not want to admit that the anti-colonial movements they admire are rooted in fascist ideas and connections.

In Latin America, the Nazi doctrine of reclaiming national glory resounded with embittered politicians in Guatemala clamoring to "retake" the neighboring colony of British Honduras. Suddenly, every irredentist claiming "lost territories" was cheered on by the Nazis.

Asian nationalists too were smitten with the romantic anti-modernization impulses of the Nazis. Nationalists in Burma swooned to Nazi race-purity doctrines as the basis for their campaigns. "One blood, one voice, one leader" was the official slogan of the chauvinistic Burmese government created by the Japanese.

Indonesian anti-colonialists at the funeral for a party leader in 1941. *Royal Netherlands Institute of Southeast Asian and Caribbean Studies.*

The British provided arms and supplies to Burma's Anti-Fascist Organization during the Second World War.[15]

The most extensive fascist borrowing in Asia was by nationalists in Indonesia.[16] In 1936, the explicitly fascist Great Indonesia Party was created. Its youth wing, the Sun of Heroes, lined up the kids each morning to offer a Nazi salute. A top party official urged Indonesians to learn from "great" Europeans such as Hitler and Mussolini. He called for a "period of sacrifice" to rid the country of colonial rule and restore national greatness.[17] By the time the Japanese fascists landed in 1942 to accelerate the romance, fascim was already well entrenched in the Indonesian nationalist movement. Not surprisingly, the only pro-colonial party in Indonesia of the 1930s was hostile to fascist ideas.

Nazi fascism was particularly attractive to anti-colonialists in India. The Congress Party leader Subhas Chandra Bose enlisted the support of fascists in Germany and Japan against British rule. Once the war began, Bose founded a Free India Centre in Berlin that cooperated with the Nazi Foreign Office to persuade Indians in Europe and South Asia to fight for the Nazis.[18] Bose raised a three thousand-man Indian Legion of the Nazi military from among Indian POWs in Germany. They were joined by British Indians who had been captured by General Rommel in Libya.

The Indian nationalist leader Mohandas Gandhi, a darling of Moscow, wrote kind letters to Hitler during the war, addressing Hitler as "dear friend," and offering a sympathetic ear to the madman for his "struggles." In 1942, the day after Churchill visited British forces in Egypt that had suffered 13,500 casualties (and would suffer the same again protecting India's economic lifeline of the Suez Canal from Nazi control), Gandhi callously issued a demand for independence from Britain.

In private, Hitler expressed puzzlement about why the British did not "just shoot" Gandhi. Liberal colonial rule was a complete mystery

Indian anti-colonialist Subhas Chandra Bose touring Nazi field forces in Germany, n.d. *Author's collection*

to the Führer. But in public, Hitler kindly listened to the arrogant, homespun-clad lawyer and applauded his quixotic recommendation to the British to lay down arms.[19] After the war, Gandhi's political heir, the future Indian prime minister Jawaharlal Nehru, another darling of Moscow, acted as defense attorney for the leaders of Bose's fascist Indian National Army in court. The fascist flirtations of Gandhi and Nehru alarmed India's Muslim population, which had prospered under British colonialism. The threat of a Hindu-fascist movement replacing colonial rule led to history's bloodiest breakup in Partition.

● ● ●

The love affair between the Nazis and Arab nationalists was first noticed by communist researchers who had access to captured Nazi documents, although Moscow was loathe to publicize the fact for fear of embarrassing its Arab client states.[20] Of course, the anti-Semitic depravity of the Nazis made them an obvious partner for Arab nationalists.[21] But the attraction was more far-reaching. Arab movements borrowed from fascism to create an "amalgam of militarism, authoritarian visions of social and political order, fantasies about the 'new man,' anti-Jewish resentment, radical ethnic nationalism . . . and a hostility towards liberalism, which was associated with Western imperial domination," noted one reviewer of the literature on the subject.[22]

In Syria and Lebanon, nationalist leaders of the 1930s expressly styled themselves after the Nazis, condemning the "old colonial elites" as corrupt and feckless whereas they represented a vigorous and youthful new nationalism that would rescue the national identity. "These organizations adopted fascist-inspired practices, patterns of organization, modes of operation, and worldviews," wrote one expert on the subject.[23]

In Iraq, fascist forces led by the local translator of *Mein Kampf* attempted a coup against the British-backed government in 1941. After this, the Nazis formed a German-Arab Training Unit to recruit more Iraqis to the Nazi cause. Hitler ordered his staff to cultivate "the Arab freedom movement" since it was a "natural ally against England." The basic idea, he insisted, was that "the victory of the Axis will liberate the Middle East from the British yoke." In addition to the joys of decolonization, this would open the way for anti-Jewish pogroms.[24]

North African nationalists also rallied to the Nazi cause. They joined the French Vichy governments of the region and in 1944 formed a Second Brigade Nord-Africaine with the help of the pro-Nazi French Gestapo to fight against the Free French colonies in Africa. The organization, which included about three hundred Arabs and Berbers, was led by the pro-Nazi Algerian Mohammed El-Maadi. Hitler later wished he had forced Vichy France to grant independence to all its colonies since this would have unleashed a native fury against the remaining European colonies in the continent.[25]

In Egypt, General Rommel's invasion of the country in 1942 and the Nazi conquest of the strategic town of El Alamein were welcomed by nationalists as a liberating force. Several officers in the Egyptian army defected to Rommel's camp amidst widespread pro-Nazi sentiment. Nazi calls to replace the decadent ruling class of old elites with a vigorous youth was particularly welcome in countries with youthful populations like Egypt. Young Egypt, the movement that spawned the bombastic independence leader Gamal Nasser, "promoted secular Egyptian chauvinism under the direct influence and imitation of Italian fascism and German Nazism," in the words of the key work on the subject.[26] After the war, Egyptian anti-colonialists living in

Palestinian cleric Amin al-Husseini meeting Hitler in Berlin, 1941. *Author's collection*

Germany expressed support for the German retaking of Upper Silesia and the Rhineland. They believed that Hitler would support their right to Sudan as their own "living space." After the war, a young recruit in the Egyptian army wrote a glowing letter to Hitler (presumed to be in Heaven) praising his attacks on Western colonial powers. This man, Anwar Sadat, would become Egypt's president.[27]

● ● ●

The most notorious Arab leader who took up the Nazi banner was the Palestinian cleric Amin al-Husseini. The British and French had become imperial rulers in the Near East thanks to the collapse of the Ottoman Empire and the nimble diplomacy of Lawrence of Arabia. Colonial rule brought a wave of Jewish settlers fleeing pogroms in the Soviet Union and elsewhere. In Palestine, they faced attacks from Arab groups. In Jerusalem, these were encouraged by al-Husseini, better known as the "Mufti of Jerusalem" in reference to his lordly Sunni sinecure in the holy city.[28] Fearing arrest by the British, he fled to French Lebanon in 1937.

Under French protection, al-Husseini sought Nazi support and revived the Berlin Islamic Central Institute, originally founded in 1927, as a venue for his pro-Nazi, anti-colonial propaganda. Winston Churchill, with his characteristic moral clarity, told the House of the Commons in 1939 that the Mufti's efforts were "ceaselessly inflamed by Nazi and by fascist propaganda" and that if Britain were to cower before them "we shall find ourselves relieved of many overseas responsibilities other than those comprised within the Palestine Mandate."

In a highly publicized event in Berlin in 1941, the Mufti met Hitler. The pair looked like interchangeable lunatics raging at European civilization. "Once Germany has forced open the road to Iran and Iraq," Hitler promised of his campaign through southern Russia, "it will be the beginning of the end of the British Empire."[29] The Mufti listened in rapt attention. He hoped to emerge as the Arab leader of an ethnically cleansed Middle East where the Jews who had escaped Hitler's death camps would be driven into the sea. Anti-colonialists everywhere took it as given that "liberation" from the shackles of colonialism, with its nonsense about human rights and plural societies, would be an opportunity to settle scores with ancient rivals.

The following year the Nazis and Italian fascists offered all Arab groups "aid in their fight for liberation."[30] The Nazis positioned themselves "as a champion of secular anti-imperialism, especially against Britain," noted one scholar. Arabs saw fascist Germany as "a model to emulate of a nation that had been humiliated yet had recovered its independence and unity."[31]

In exile, the Mufti spent the war years stirring anti-colonial revolts in the Middle East. From 1942, he led the Arabic Information Bureau, a pro-Nazi colonial successor to the League Against Imperialism. He also worked with Heinrich Himmler to create Muslim units of the Waffen SS. "Himmler dreamt of establishing huge Muslim military units," noted one French expert on the rise of Islamofascism. "The Waffen SS created an Islamic Study Institution and designed their own uniforms and special nutrition for the Muslim recruits of the SS."[32]

The most noxious moment came in 1943 when the Mufti toured a Nazi labor camp with a clutch of Third World nationalists. The camp was part of a larger concentration-camp system where Jews were murdered. The men were there for a Nazi "training course" on how to liquidate Jewish populations. A year later, Himmler wished the Mufti "warm wishes for the continuation of your battle until the big victory" against "the Jewish invaders."[33]

After the war, the Mufti relocated to Egypt where he was greeted as a national hero. In his memoirs, he dismissed rumors that he had visited the Nazi camps as "a smear campaign" by Jews. Alas, a series of photographs of the visit surfaced in an estate sale in Jerusalem in 2017.[34]

"The basic challenge of honest history-writing is to place the greater problem of [the Mufti's] partnership with Nazi Germany on the agenda," wrote the scholar Joel Fishman, one of the few academics who calls out the contemporary academy's silence on the close relationship between the Arabs and the Nazis. "This subject represents 'inconvenient information.' It is inconvenient for many because of its direct connection with the present."[35] While Fishman's concern is to highlight the shared anti-Semitism of the Nazis and Arabs, this should be put in the larger context of their shared anti-colonialism.

While the Mufti was the most famous Third World leader smitten with Hitler, he was representative of post-colonial leaders. One book on the subject opens with the aptly titled chapter "More than the Mufti."[36] The fact that post-colonial leaders like Idi Amin, who expelled Israelis from Uganda, or Gamal Nasser, who hired two thousand ex-Nazis and wrote a love letter to Hitler, styled themselves as tropical fascists is written off as naughty behavior by otherwise virtuous liberators. After all, the scholars insist, these leaders were opponents of colonialism, and, as we all know, colonialism was the *true* fascism! Thus when a post-colonial critic like the Zimbabwean Tendai Ruben Mbofana notes "the resurgence of Nazi-like propaganda jingles on the state broadcaster" in Zimbabwe as the ruling party resurrects its earlier fascist persona, the parallels wash off academic minds like water off the back of a duck.[37] See no evil, hear no evil, speak no evil.

If Samuel Maherero had lived to see the rise of Hitler, he too, no doubt, would have written love letters to the Führer and fished for an invitation to Berlin. The Mufti's armchair pulled up close to Hitler would still be warm when Maherero sat down to take his lessons in demagoguery and ethnic purification from the master. Surely, the

Wahehe and Ngoni warlords who had been subdued by German colonialism would have lined up in the wings for meetings as well. Come to think of it, there are very few enemies of German colonialism who would not have jumped at the opportunity to meet and learn from Hitler. The brotherhood between Nazi Germany and anti-colonial agitators involved far more than the Mufti.

• • •

Most research on the Arab-Nazi love affair centers on either their shared anti-Semitism or its significance to contemporary Islamic extremism. A more useful framework would center on their shared anti-colonialism. As we have seen, the Nazis grew out the failure of liberalism in Germany and that country's loss of colonies. In Arab lands too, the embrace of fascism was a direct reaction by nationalist elites against liberalism, which was embodied in European colonial rule. The seminal work on the Nazi enchantment in Egypt opens with a chapter entitled "The Failure of Liberalism and the Reaction against Europe," which might well serve as the opening chapter to the history of Nazi Germany as well.[38]

Some revisionists have insisted that mainstream opinion in places like Egypt remained liberal and democratic. "The voices of democracy's champions were louder than those of its critics who were fascinated by the *Führer* and the *Duce*," wrote one revisionist historian. "Most of them ... remained dedicated to the democratic idea."[39] Gershoni too suggests that because the colonial powers enjoyed robust support from Arab publics in their war efforts, the appeal of fascism must have been limited.[40]

These revisionists forget the important distinction between elite and mass opinion. No doubt, Arab publics were far from smitten with the racist Hitler and his promises to "liberate" them into the hands of post-colonial despots. But Arab elites were different, metropolitan intellectuals who knew how to work the levers of the colonial system and get themselves declared "representatives of the people" despite their fascist ideals. The "decolonization" they envisaged would be a process of handing over power from reforming, liberal, colonial systems to reactionary fascist ones where they would receive the salutes from a podium.

"Liberalism" in the Middle East circa 1939 was embodied in the hopes and plans of colonial rulers, not in some magical, future, liberal democracy sprouting from the dry soil of Arab society. While the Arab Street fought nobly for the Allies, it was also vulnerable to the siren calls of anti-colonialism sounded by Arab elites taking their cues from the Nazis. The litmus test for Arab public opinion was not just whether Arabs fought *for* colonial rulers but whether they fought *against* the Young Egypt–types who would replace them with fascist national transformation. The fact that later events led willy-nilly to similar transformations suggests that Arab nationalism and Nazi fascism share a more fundamental consanguinity. Arab nationalism was basically illiberal and fascist, not liberal and democratic, despite what today's voices may say on the topic.

Faced with the evidence, scholars retreat to the "blame colonialism" line. The only reason that Nazi and more general fascist ideas spread like wildfire among the anti-colonial movements in the Middle East, they write, is that otherwise liberal elites had no choice in the face of the grinding oppression of colonialism. "The reluctance of France to grant independence and sovereignty" to its mandates in Syria and Lebanon, despite those mandates being barely a decade old, insisted one scholar, "shaped local responses to Nazism."[41] Not really their fault, you see, more the fault of the colonialists.

But the crisis of liberalism in the 1920s and 1930s was caused not by colonialism but by attacks on colonialism, including ironically the attacks of Britain and France on German colonialism that contributed to the rise of the Nazis. The fascist movements in the Arab world rejected colonialism *because* it was liberal, not in spite of its liberalism.

Anti-colonialism a strand of fascist ideology? "Surely not!" insist the academics. We have been fanning the flames of a racist and reactionary ideology with our post-colonial research programs? "How dare you!" they clamor. The calamities of contemporary Third World states run by fanatical despots are best compared to the calamities thrust upon Germany by the Nazis? "Outrageous!" Yes: outrageous, preposterous, and true.

• • •

Between 1935 and 1943, Hitler occasionally threatened to march into the Third World grabbing new colonies. After all, fascists in

The German Colonial Society, now under Nazi control, continues to agitate for a return of colonies, n.d. *Author's collection*

Africa, the Middle East, and Asia were already replicating Nazi organization. Why not bring the Third Reich directly to their doorstep
for more "training courses"?

What precisely a "Nazi colony" would have looked like is anyone's
guess, given Hitler's loathing for colonialism. The most likely scenario
would have been a reign of terror run by an autocratic chauvinists,
much like the situations that emerged after decolonization in places
like Uganda under Idi Amin or Egypt under Gamal Nasser. One
thing was clear: Nazi colonialism would have represented a clear
break from the German colonial past.

Fascist Italy's occupation of Ethiopia from 1936 to 1941 offers a
brief clue to this alternate reality. Fascism was popular among Arab
nationalists, and many welcomed the Italian invasion of the medieval
Christian kingdom. Styling himself as an Arab liberator and as sympathetic to Islamism, Mussolini promised to use the country as a base
to wage war on the British and French empires. The Egyptians sent
two retired Ottoman generals and three medical teams to support
the Italian invasion. The Saudi king sold camels to Mussolini's army.[42]
At first, Arab writers could barely contain their enthusiasm for the
Italian governor and his promises to create an Islamic state, oust
non-Islamic bureaucrats, build mosques, spread Arabic, and imple-
ment sharia law. Mussolini visited in 1937 promising to brandish "the
sword of Islam." This bolstered Ethiopia's long-standing reputation
as a bastion of resistance to Western colonialism, a resistance now
waged by good Muslims allied with fascist forces.

Hitler's threats to create similar fascist colonies were empty,
however. Hitler simply wanted to exact more concessions from the
British and French in Europe, as the definitive work by the British
historian Andrew Crozier showed.[43] British experts understood that
Hitler was an anti-colonial monster who had made common cause
with the empire's enemies, not some revenant German colonialist.[44]

This is why the Nazis never took *any* concrete steps to begin a colonization drive. As Wempe concludes: "Whereas the [old] German colonial movement placed primacy on colonial restitution and the creation of a new colonial policy for Germany, overseas possessions were more of an afterthought for the Nazis."[45]

The Free University of Berlin historian Karsten Linne shows that the amount of detail and ambition that the old colonial lobby put into its plans was in inverse proportion to their political significance.[46] The historian Christian Hartmann calls Nazi colonial talk "marginal" to their purpose.[47] The Third Reich's Colonial Office, for instance, had no executive powers. It was prohibited from engaging in any advertisements for German settlement in the former colonies. The energetic activities of the old colonial lobby, wrote the American historian Willeke Sandler, "were met with a mix of occasional support, ambivalence, or even outright opposition from some Nazi officials, who privileged the Nazi regime's European territorial goals over colonialists' overseas goals."[48] *Ostpolitik* was serious. *Kolonialpolitik* was not. Since there was *no chance* that the Nazis would ever build an empire in Africa, there were no constraints on the fantasy empire building that took place inside the old colonial lobby, which was really a bunch of retired officials sitting in a retirement home playing a glorified board game.

Heinrich Schnee noted as early as 1935 that the colonial question was "not at the forefront of the domestic political situation."[49] Schnee, who had joined the Nazis in 1933 hoping to revive colonial claims, was "repeatedly ignored" by the Nazis and finally told that *any* discussion of German colonization outside of Eastern Europe was forbidden.[50] The old colonial lobby refused to cease its dissent, and finally in 1943 the Nazis "used the simple expedient of cutting the paper ration of the intransigent Africanists, who were still claiming that not to mention Africa represented 'a betrayal of our ideals and mission.'"[51] Wempe calls the brief Nazi humoring of the lobby a "bad romance" noting that "imperial internationalism was fundamentally at odds with Nazi philosophies of imperialism, which relished nationalist competition."[52]

The lobby soon discovered that the Nazis were not just insincere in their colonial claims but also fundamentally antagonistic to the Spirit of Berlin. The feminist journalist and bush pilot Louise Diel flew solo around Africa in 1938 to drum up support for a return to classic German colonialism. Diel's book *The Colonies Are Waiting!*, written after she flew herself to Cameroon, Namibia, Tanzania, and Togo, is nothing if not a testament to the energies of the old colonial lobby.[53] A self-described "girl in a pith helmet,"[54] Diel even toured Mussolini's Ethiopia, which she hoped might spark a renewed colonial lobby in Africa. Perhaps this would subvert the Nazi menace at home by reigniting the civilizing two-way conversation that Seitz and Bismarck had hoped would emerge from Germany's colonial era.[55]

But Hitler was not interested in colonial exploits, especially those advocated by a loud-mouthed woman who was also an Anglophile admirer of the British Empire. Diel was eventually targeted by the Nazis as unreliable—too many Jewish and Catholic friends, too much emphasis on female freedom, too much love of the non-German world.[56] Contemporary German scholars studiously ignore Diel's persecution by the Nazis because they are desperate to hold together the myth that her colonial agitation was a fascist project.

Another "colonial" advocate persecuted by the Nazis was the German artist Ernst Ludwig Kirchner, who drew upon the large collections of "looted" art from the colonies to forge a new German modernism. Kirchner was labelled by the Nazis as a source of "degenerate" art. Impressively, twenty-five of his works were shown in the Nazi's Degenerate Art Exhibition of 1937. The Nazi persecution of artists like Kirchner, who committed suicide in 1938, puts modern-day scolds in a ticklish situation because they too assail such "colonial" artists for their offensive cultural borrowing. In a 2021 exhibition of German modernist artists at the Los Angeles County Museum, the curators charged Kirchner with "encountering [the collections from the colonies] removed from their original context." That is of course so true a statement as to be banal. Elsewhere, the Woke curators of Los Angeles insisted that all European artists saw African cultures "through a colonialist lens," which again is either nonsense (they were not colonial officials) or a truism (the contact resulted from colonialism, so how else could they have encountered them?). The more we delve into these latter-day Woke critiques, the more they sound like the Nazi charges of creating "impure" and "degenerate" art, with all the anti-intellectualism and imbecilities that this implies.

Another "colonial" critic of the Nazis was the director of the decaying Colonial School, founded in 1899. "Those who really belonged to Hitler's movement," he declared "lacked . . . the [innate] qualifications to be members" of the school. Only about 20 percent of the student body were Nazi members even during the Nazi era. The fundamental conflict between Nazism and colonialism was too great to paper over. At first, the director, as well as the director of a parallel school for women, "interpreted instances of obstruction by Nazi officials as logistical rather than ideological blocks." One director was spurned because his daughter had married a Greek. The other faced a revolt from his Nazi students for clinging tenaciously to the aim of sending graduates to Africa rather than to work for the Reich in Eastern Europe. When one female student was found dancing with a black staff member at the women's school, the director brushed it off as insignificant, which one scholar calls "astonishing" because it was "clearly out of synch with the reality of life in Nazi Germany."[57]

The Potemkin village of Nazi-era colonial claims collapsed at the Battle of Stalingrad. "Colonial policy thus became for the Nazis an instrument of domestic politics, rather than foreign policy," wrote the Canadian historian of Germany Martin Kitchen. "Suddenly in 1943 an order from [Hitler's close aide Martin] Bormann caused the empire to collapse like a house of cards."[58] Hitler's threat to make war for former colonies was strategic, not ideological (to use the terms of Brückenhaus), and he reverted quickly to his anti-colonial default position in his final two years.

• • •

In 1935, Otto Arendt, a Jewish friend of the East African adventurer Carl Peters, wrote a letter to the Nazi foreign minister seeking an official pardon for the deceased colonial hero. "In a certain sense Peters is a precursor to Hitler," Arendt wrote in a sentence that became music to the ears of later critics of German colonialism.[59] Hitler signed the pardon in 1937, and Peters' widow was given a state pension.

Fourteen years later, another Jew surnamed Arendt put an academic sheen on the so-called "continuity thesis" that saw a direct line of descent from classical German colonialism to modern Nazi terror. This time, however, the comparison was not meant as flattering. "African colonial possessions became the most fertile soil for the flowering of what later was to become the Nazi elite," wrote philosopher Hannah Arendt in another sentence beloved of later critics.[60] As we have seen, Nazi leader Hermann Göring, the man who assumed command of the defunct East Africa Protectorate Force, was the son of the first commissioner of German Southwest Africa, the man who "did not tire of extracting cannon balls and sewing up wounds" of Herero and Nama men injured in their constant tribal conflicts. Hermann was probably conceived by his parents in Windhoek before being born in Germany, in this telling a kind of horror child infected with colonial evil. For Hannah Arendt—and legions of scholars who have toiled to stand up her "continuity thesis" ever since—German colonialism and German fascism were like father and son.

Despite Hitler's explicit anti-colonialism and his phony threats to retake the former German colonies, scholars still insist that the Nazis were a continuation of German colonialism in new guise. These scholars are candid about their *desperate* need to equate nineteenth-century German colonialism with twentieth-century German fascism. As Stanford historian Russell Berman wrote: "To argue a continuity between nineteenth-century imperialism and twentieth-century Nazism . . . would not irritate standard value judgments: one evil, colonialism, is hypothetically set in relation to another evil, Nazi Germany."[61] The American historian Shelley Baranowski writes: "Because Nazi crimes loom large in the history of Germany, finding similarities between Imperial colonial warfare and Nazi ethnic cleansing and genocide later seems irresistible."[62] But just because something is "irresistible" or comports with the "standard value judgements" in the faculty lounge does not make it true. Indeed, given the politicized nature of the contemporary academy, it is more likely to suggest that it is false.

The strategy for these savants is to find some idea, practice, or personality from the classical colonial era and then to find some parallel to it in the Nazi era. Presto! The former *caused* the latter. Lacking any scientific validation of the proposition, the bookworms use fudge words like "entanglements" and "complications" to lull the reader into submission.

Take one example. Under the Spirit of Berlin, it was assumed (correctly) that liberal European states had something to share with the rest of humanity. "Aha!" cry the critics, the Nazis also insisted that they had something to share with the hapless peoples of Eastern Europe. *Therefore* Nazi imperialism and classical colonial imperialism grew from the same roots, namely "racism." As two dons elaborate: "Colonial racism nevertheless dovetailed with Nazi perceptions of fundamental biological characteristics, and may reveal the extent to which the Nazi *Weltanschauung* (world view) and older German colonial perspectives blended together during the Third Reich." How so? "Both held a Eurocentric perception of the world in which 'civilization' was linked to 'whiteness', and the role of the European/German was in some sense to civilize the non-white world."[63]

This is academic ideology run amok. To accuse classical German colonialism of "Eurocentrism" is to state the obvious: how could it *not* be Eurocentric given that Germans were Europeans? And the "civilization" they shared, like life-saving health interventions and job alternatives to slave raiding, was deeply valued by colonial peoples, as we have seen. Moreover, if nineteenth-century Germans "linked" their national achievements to their race, that made them no different than others, including the Chinese, Samoans, and Herero. It is a massive leap from a liberal project to improve the lives of others with their consent to a fascist war on Europe to eliminate liberalism and purify German culture. The desperate academic need to slander colonialism by linking it to fascism leads academics to distort the historical record.

Take another example. The German historian Sarah Ehlers charges that *because* some Nazi-era scientists working in tropical medicine began their careers in the colonial era, *therefore* colonial medical research begat Nazi science. Rather than establishing a causal link or showing how one led to the other, Ehlers talks of "entanglements," academic jargon that should immediately alert the reader that he is in the realm of scholarly mendacity.[64] In a similar vein, two other German professors argue that colonial medicine was "deeply involved in the Nazi crimes against humanity" because

Gerhard Rose, a Polish German scientist who was a key figure in the Koch sleeping-sickness research of the 1920s, went on to head a Nazi research institute.[65] This is like saying that flight-training schools were responsible for the 9/11 attacks.

Christian Davis, the American historian who wrote a whole book showing how Jewish participation in German colonialism was a powerful vehicle for social inclusion and the combatting of anti-Semitism, *nonetheless* insists that colonialism led to Nazi rule. (Fixed ideas die hard in the academy.) By digging around feverishly for examples of anti-Semitic individuals or periodicals that supported German colonialism, he insists that "the evidence" shows the two were "deeply intertwined."[66] Again, such words should alert the reader that they are in the realm of scholarly nonsense.

Other scholars make dark reference to the fact that both the German colonialists and the Nazis sought to expand globally, and when one adds a few "entanglements" showing how the outward orientation of colonialism resembled the outward gaze of Nazism, *voila!* It is proven that the one begat the other.[67]

Beyond such sophistry, scholars revel in the Potemkin village of Nazi propaganda threatening to retake former German colonies. The fact that the Nazis took over *every* social organization in Germany, not just the old colonial ones, under their policy of "coordination" (*Gleichschaltung*), goes unremarked. One might as well argue that postage stamps caused fascism because philately clubs came under Nazi command.

The feverish but foolish endeavor of blaming colonialism for fascism has been pursued in respectable history departments in the West for half a century. Yet it fails because of the fundamental discord between classical German colonialism and the fascists' own statements on the colonies. As the eminent American historian Henry Cord Meyer wrote way back in 1965, it "blurs the characteristics of colonial . . . agitation during the Weimar era, when the movement stood on a non-Nazi, conservative-national platform." By blurring this distinction, he continued, scholars cannot explain how the classical colonial drive for liberal overseas empire was replaced by the Nazi drive for illiberal continental empire, or, as he put it "how a *bona fide* conservative-national issue was cajoled, twisted, or compromised into a fascist-racist policy."[68]

● ● ●

An equally urgent question is why some members of the old colonial lobby found themselves parading around Berlin in swastikas. Initially, as one researcher found, some members of the lobby plumped for the Nazi party "when it appeared to take a more uncompromising stand against the Versailles settlement than any other political group and was therefore most likely to raise the colonial claim."[69] It was, as he suggests, a tactical choice. Here we might appropriate Brückenhaus's mistaken language about the friendship between the Nazis and the anti-colonialists and apply it more suitably to this forced marriage of the colonial lobby to the Nazis: it was "based on strategic considerations, rather than any kind of ideological conviction."[70]

Another reason is simple prudence. In a totalitarian setting, it is costly to refrain from supporting the ruling party. Scolding someone like Heinrich Schnee for joining the Nazi party is like scolding Aleksandr Solzhenitsyn for joining the Communist Party of the Soviet Union. Schnee served in the Reichstag as a representative of the German People's Party from 1924 to 1932 before the Nazi takeover and then became a member of the Nazi parliament. Those who have studied his behavior find that Schnee was *never* a loyal Nazi and that he secretly worked with anti-Nazi movements even as he served in their parliament.[71] His wife was an orphan and part-time actress whom the Nazi elite despised for her uncertain bloodlines. Schnee refused to join the Nazi's Colonial league (*Reichskolonial-bund*) because, as he noted, "it turned out that the Nazi Party was overwhelmingly opposed to the settlement of Germans outside of Europe," and "winning back the German colonies was the least of their concerns."[72] One of his former colleagues, the last governor of German Samoa, Wilhelm Solf, was an outspoken critic of the Nazis. Solf died in 1936, and his wife and adopted Samoan daughter were sent to a Nazi concentration camp.

Another colonial figure alleged to have taken up the Nazi cause was the tropical disease expert Ernst Rodenwaldt, who as we saw invented the concept of "medical geography" from his studies in German Togo. After the colonies were seized, the Dutch hired him as the director of public health for East Java, where he spent the 1920s. Like others, he was intrigued by Hitler's occasional threats to retake the colonies and returned to Germany in 1934. He became head of the Tropical Medicine Institute in 1940. He refused to participate in any of the Nazi race and eugenics research, but he was aware of the work and was branded a "minor offender" after the war by the U.S. administration. He appealed the charge, citing his research done in the Dutch East Indies that favorably evaluated the racially mixed peoples of East Timor and made fun of the "devoted and gullible enthusiasts" of German fascism. He won reinstatement as a professor in 1948.[73] Whatever the degree of sincerity or opportunism with which Rodenwaldt bowed before Nazi doctrine, one thing is clear: it required him to explicitly *disavow* his earlier "colonial" work that saw positive results from the racial mixing under colonialism.

More generally, many in the colonial lobby opposed the Nazi cause, and most of them simply slunk into silence. "Although there was a significant amount of mutual flirtation between the Nazi regime and some opportunistic Colonial Germans who continued the pursuit of colonial restitution by any means," noted Wempe, "there were a fair number of Colonial Germans who did not find the Nazi Party appealing."[74]

In practice, the Nazis proved every bit as anti-colonial as their billing. Their "entanglement" with anti-colonialists in the Third World, to borrow a term, was an institutionalized and meaningful relationship grounded in a shared ideology. The "entanglement" with the colonial lobby was not. The illiberal empire of the Third Reich was precisely the obstacle to a renewed liberal empire of German colonialism. It may be "irresistible" for contemporary academics to equate colonialism with Nazism, but it is factually wrong.

• • •

The most extreme version of the "continuity thesis" asserts a *monocausal* and *deterministic* link from German colonialism to the Holocaust. Those toiling to stand up this audacious pretense must backcast *everything* in German colonial history as an overture to Nazi genocide.[75] The alleged "colonial crimes" of Germany are reexamined with an eye to finding logical or fanciful ways to tap them as the hidden bogeymen of Auschwitz.

The "colonial origins of the Holocaust" thesis was first elaborated by East Germany's communist-propaganda machine in the 1960s as it churned away to discredit the colonial past by making the most lurid assertions.[76] It then spread to the West German academy in the 1970s, which saw itself as taking up the progressive cause of "memory politics" in its research on the German past.[77] By the twenty-first century, it had become something of an article of faith. It found its fullest expression in Woke god-king Jürgen Zimmerer's pinning the blame for the Holocaust on the counterinsurgency campaigns against

the Herero and Nama—"Windhoek to Auschwitz" as he billed it.[78]
The epithet brought Zimmerer such acclaim that the original question mark he used in the German book title was removed in the
English version.[79] In his most extreme mood, Zimmerer has asserted
that absent the bungling efforts of Lothar von Trotha and his parched
soldiers, there would have been no Holocaust at all. Indeed, those
events in German Southwest Africa were "a decisive link to the
crimes of the National Socialists."[80] Apparently, every shot fired by
the haggard and thirsty German forces in the deserts of Southwest
Africa in 1904 led—via some twitching of butterfly wings—to the
greatest calamity of twentieth-century Europe.

Following Zimmerer, an entire industry of "Windhoek to Auschwitz"
scholars has emerged to repeat the holy mantra.[81] Their labors are taken
up by others to make even more audacious claims that *all* of European
colonialism was *wholly* genocidal and resulted in wholly genocidal
modern Western countries. As with most research on German colonialism, the thesis is so untethered from reality that it has moved into
the hands of literary theorists, philosophers, and artists. A book by the
American historian Elizabeth Baer, for instance, proposes that a 2005
art installation that mashes up the Holocaust and German Southwest
Africa "functions to further validate the idea of connections across
decades among genocides." In other words, a radical artist takes up the
"Windhoek to Auschwitz" theme, and his work provides "evidence"
of its historical validity. Despite this cozy little arrangement between
radical activists and scholars, educated people in free societies have a
troubling tendency, in Baer's view, to reject the dogma: "Wholesale
acceptance by historians of the continuity thesis has yet to arrive."[82]
Perhaps a few more didactic art installations would do the job! Something about the "imperial gaze" of aerial filming techniques perhaps.

The "Windhoek to Auschwitz" postulate has been subject to
withering critique from scholars who base their theories on historical

reality rather than ideology. We have already shown that there *was no* genocide in German Southwest Africa, not even close. Nor do any of the other alleged "colonial crimes" of Germany like the Maji Maji or the Sokehs counterinsurgency campaigns fit that description. So, *by definition*, there cannot be any causal link to the Holocaust.

Radical scholars hate to be reminded about the logical and empirical problems of the "Windhoek to Auschwitz" claim, and thus they fall back upon terms of abuse like "apologist" and "denier" to discredit the recalcitrant, another good indicator that one is in the realm of academic foolery. "This preoccupation with the denial of [colonial] genocide merges with denialism in relation to the Holocaust," writes a German sociologist in full smear mode.[83] In other words, since the Holocaust happened, and since the Nazis *must* have emerged from colonialism, therefore colonial genocide in German Southwest Africa *must* have happened as well. Along with twenty-first century art installations, we now have chronological reversal as a further methodological aid to "validate" the continuity thesis.

Others try stand up the "Windhoek to Auschwitz" thesis with reference to German counterinsurgency methods. The journalist Klaus Bachmann, for instance, exonerated Trotha from the charge of genocide but still insisted that the "bureaucratic racism" hatched in German Southwest Africa gave rise to the Holocaust.[84] But as Marie Muschalek of the University of Freiburg notes, "the forms of colonial violence Bachmann discusses here . . . were committed or induced by the settler community and not the colonial military," and thus it is difficult to see how this is "bureaucratic" or was somehow energized by formal German rule given the constant conflicts between colonial authorities and the settlers.[85] As Indiana University scholars Roberta Pergher and Mark Roseman wrote: "When we turn to the Holocaust, the colonial stamp of imperial Germany is so faint as to be barely legible. The continuities in personnel and governmental structures were minimal; the resonances in institutional reflexes or societal norms, hard to ascertain."[86] Those directly involved in Nazi genocide were mostly from borderlands lost after World War I, not from colonial families in the German heartland.[87]

An equally forceful rebuttal was offered by the University of Dublin scholar Robert Gerwarth and Stephan Malinowski of the Freiburg Institute for Advanced Studies. German colonial peacekeeping and stabilization operations—including the counterinsurgency against the Herero and Nama rebellions—were no different than those of other European colonies, they note. German officials and their native allies in Africa did not seek to eliminate groups but to eliminate security threats. Colonial operations were formulated on the ground and implemented in contingent ways. Communications with ministry officials in Berlin took weeks. There was no "German colonial model" of counterinsurgency and no systemic tendency in German colonialism towards an excessive use of force. Once again, there cannot *by definition* be a link to the Holocaust from something, in this case a "model of counterinsurgency," that did not exist.

The path from "Windhoek to Auschwitz," then, is mainly about *disconnection*: "National Socialism and the [Holocaust] constituted a *break* with European traditions of colonialism rather than a continuation," conclude Gerwarth and Malinowski. While such an interpretation is less satisfying to radical scholars, they note with schoolmasterly tone, "such an interpretation would have an important advantage: the advantage of being empirically sound."[88]

There is a simpler fact: if the Nazi *génocidaires* modeled themselves on Lothar von Trotha's handiwork, why did not a single Nazi or Nazi-policy document *ever* mention it? Wouldn't we have evidence that they had studied it or at least referred to it? Yet there is no such reference. The Nazis after all wanted nothing to do with the German colonial era. If they thought about that era, it would have been to cite the "wars of liberation" of the Herero and Nama as the sorts of things they believed in.

Let's put the point more strongly: Adolph Hitler more closely resembles Samuel Maherero or Hendrick Witbooi than Lothar von Trotha. All three were anti-colonial fascists and race purists. Maherero's "Kill All Germans!" became Hitler's "Kill All Jews!" Both were fanatics trying to purify and create a national myth and a homeland freed of alien, cosmopolitan, liberal influences. Today, the intellectual heirs to Maherero and Hitler dominate the contemporary university, raging against liberal civilization, Jews (in the polite form of Israel), and the market economy.

The great, hidden truth that emerges here, then, is this: If there is *any* causal link between the Holocaust and Germany's colonial legacies, it came from German *anti-colonialism*. Hitler and the Nazis were anti-colonial through and through. The anti-colonial constituency they cultivated on Friedrichstrasse was a key part of the collapse of German liberalism, seeking favor equally among communists and fascists. The dangers of this illiberal movement should have been immediately clear from the consequences of the Russian Revolution, where anti-colonialism quickly translated into domestic pogroms and the Gulag. The sidelining of the colonial project in Germany contributed—how much we need not speculate—to the rise of the Nazis and to their horrific policies. If there is a pathway to Auschwitz, it came not from Windhoek but from Friedrichstrasse, where the League Against Imperialism headquarters was located. The book that mainstream scholars do not want written would have the title: *From Friedrichstrasse to Auschwitz: On the Relationship Between Anti-Colonialism and the Holocaust.*

CHAPTER 13

*Communist Anti-Colonialism
and the Division of Europe*

G ermany did not experience a "messy end of empire" during
the global decolonization wave of the postwar decades
because abrupt decolonization had occurred thirty years
earlier. There was no roiling debate on empire, and no anti-German
resentments festered in the Third World, where German investors
found a ready welcome. In the former colonies, the last natives to
remember "the kind German uncle"[1] were entering old age, and the
sprouts of nostalgic Germanophilia were apparent. Germany's messy
end of empire had consumed the country from 1933 to 1945. Now, the
colonial issue was past.

The last vestige of pro-colonial sentiments in Germany were
found in the hearts of the young men who shipped out to fight for
declining empires elsewhere. Approximately 35,000 Germans served
in the French Foreign Legion in Indochina until the French defeat
1954. Another 12,000 fought for French rule in Algeria from 1954 to
1962. Such colonial pursuits were largely passé in postwar Germany.
Heinrich Schnee was barred from holding any government position
by a postwar denazification tribunal and died in an auto accident in

1949. When his family published his memoirs in 1964, the German public received them with stony indifference.[2]

In the smoldering remains of the Nazi movement in Germany, anti-colonialism continued to rage. A former Arab organizer for the Nazis, Johann von Leers, took up a position as advisor to Gamal Nasser's bombastic anti-Western government in Cairo in 1955. There, "he combined his geopolitical ideas with the emerging Third-Worldism of the time" and wrote a book entitled *The World Fight against Imperialism and Colonialism*.[3] He was one of two thousand former Nazis who lived in Egypt and worked for its anti-Western government after the war. They directed Cairo's support for Algeria's rebellion against French rule. In the words of scholar Joel Fishman, von Leers "saw an opportunity in the 'wars of liberation' of the time and positioned his antisemitism within the context of Third-Worldism." Leers encouraged Nasser to seize the Suez Canal in 1956, fulfilling Hitler's dream of driving a dagger into the heart of the British Empire. More generally, as Fishman wrote, the Islamofascist von Leers provided Arab leaders with "a coherent geopolitical vision, which had its roots in German and Nazi traditions." These traditions, he continues, included, "spreading political antisemitism and anti-Zionism to the Third-World and bringing about the Islamization of Europe by encouraging mass migration in order to change its demographics and to undermine its Christian traditions and culture."[4]

The most enduring Nazi influences were in the Algerian insurgency against French rule that erupted in 1954. The struggle would claim 350,000 lives. While progressive academics who admire the insurgency tend to emphasize its borrowings from totalitarians on the left like Lenin or Samir Amin, the movement borrowed just as much from the totalitarian right. Hitler's *Völkisch* rejection of liberal society was music to the ears of the ethno-nationalists in the colonies. Like the later French author and white ethno-nationalist Alain de

Benoist, these Third World anti-colonialists would always say when asked if they were "racists" that, no, in fact, they were great "anti-racists" because they were preserving their distinctive races against the intrusions of liberal society.[5]

The troubadour of the Algerian insurgency was the black psychiatrist Frantz Fanon, a native of French Martinique in the Caribbean. The German scholar Egon Flaig refers to "the fascist anti-colonialism" of Fanon with his explicit borrowing of Nazi themes.[6] Fanon's 1961 *The Wretched of the Earth* was "a brilliant counter-enlightenment manifesto," according to Flaig, because of its explicit rejection of liberal universalism in favor of pre-Enlightenment medievalism. Fanon praises the Nazis for resolving Germany's border issues by force and points out that likewise Algeria had "lost patience" with the peaceful resolution of political problems. "When the Algerians reject any method which does not include violence, this is proof that something has happened or is in the process of happening. The colonized peoples, these slaves of modern times, have run out of patience." He echoes a widely heard but apocryphal claim by Hermann Göring that "when I hear culture, I unholster my Browning" by writing "when the colonized hear a speech on Western culture, they pull out their machetes."[7] Fanon was not intelligent enough to understand the delicious irony of his misquotation. To make a point about the evils of Western culture, he misquotes the son of a former German colonial governor who "did not seem to tire of extracting cannon balls and sewing up wounds" of Africans injured in incessant tribal warfare. Fanon's glorification of the "curative" or "therapeutic" role of violence in bringing out a genuine freedom is straight out of *Mein Kampf.* "Why, one might ask, do Fanon's sentences read . . . like Nazi ideology?" asks Flaig. The reason is obvious: both approach racial questions as "politically unbounded," questions to be resolved not in the legislature but on the battlefield.

• • •

Not to be outdone by the dregs of the Nazis still fomenting anti-colonial revolutions from Cairo, the German far left picked up its game. German communists worked feverishly to offer their own support for the insurgency in Algeria. Any attempt by the West German government in Bonn to aid the counterinsurgency efforts of France and Portugal in their colonies was met with furious denunciations. Eventually, Bonn caved into the German far left and offered the German communist Winfried Müller and other Algerian terrorists political asylum.[8]

Campus activists, meanwhile, slowly strangled any deviations from the new anti-colonial orthodoxy. The acme of the campus movement came when students at the University of Hamburg in 1968

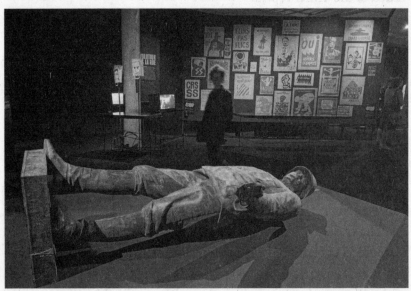

A statue of Herman von Wissmann, governor of German East Africa, toppled by German students in 1968. *DPA Picture Alliance / Alamy*

toppled an eight-foot bronze statue of Hermann von Wissmann, the colonial explorer, military head, and governor of German East Africa who was remembered chiefly for the number of slaves he had freed. The students did not topple the statue in the name of Western-liberal values. Quite the opposite. It was because von Wissmann represented Western-liberal values that they toppled it. "In the context of the debate about liberation movements in the Third World, Germany's colonial past was an excellent example to demonstrate the 'evil machinations' of capitalism," noted one approving scholar. "From the Cuban revolution to the Vietnam War and the Cultural Revolution in China, the Third World appeared to be breaking its chains and emancipating itself from the rule of its former colonial masters." The act of vandalism "heralded the rapid decline of capitalism," the professor swooned. The ardent hope of the students and their radical professors was to send Germany back into a totalitarian nightmare along with much of the Third World.[9]

• • •

The former German colonies all suffered various degrees of collapse and chaos after being "freed" from European governance. The German colonial lobby's predictions that these colonies would fail as independent countries were fully borne out.

Qingdao was swallowed up by Chinese communist takeover in 1949 and promptly looted for its wealth by the ruling party. Its brewery survived in the 1960s only by exporting to colonial Hong Kong.[10]

The three African mandates that became Tanzania, Togo, and Cameroon experienced various forms of calamity and collapse. Tanzania was fortunate to be governed by the British, who continued much of the German development program. The skull of the Wahehe rebel leader that the Germans were supposed to return to East Africa under the terms of Versailles was finally sent back in 1954. The British had ignored the odd issue until it became clear that independence would soon be forced upon the country. In a bid to shore up support for the last push to establish a stable government, the governor, Sir Edward Twining, made use of a home leave in 1953 to visit the anthropological museum of Bremen where he found the skull. It was returned with much pomp and ceremony.[11]

Over time, the Wahehe erected a vast epic around the resistance of their despotic and murderous leader. But as a British scholar wrote, this was mainly because colonial authorities themselves celebrated and institutionalized them as a group: "The respect which many Germans acquired for the [Wa]Hehe and the way in which the British administration dealt with them has been one of the most important factors in creating a sense of unity among the [Wa]Hehe."[12] One of the Wahehe leader's cousins became speaker of the national parliament after independence.

Independence, however, was a bitter pill. President Julius Nyerere's experiment in one-party rule and socialist economics led to the forced displacement of eleven million people into collective "*ujamaa* villages" and was soon followed by famines in 1974 and 1981. A 1,860-kilometer "freedom railway" to Zambia completed in 1975 by Maoist China displaced villagers and became an instrument of state despotism in both countries. It carried only about a quarter of its capacity, was frequently out of service due to poor engineering, and had to be retrofitted with new train engines in 1981. The new engines came from Germany.[13] Nyerere finally admitted failure and resigned in 1985, leaving the failing country to pick up the pieces.

Togo and Cameroon became petty dictatorships, but not before giving their former German colonial masters a warm vote of thanks. The last German governor of Togo was the guest of honor at independence in 1960, where the Germans were received with warmth.

Shortly thereafter, President Sylvanus Olympio was gunned down by rivals while fleeing to the American embassy in 1963. A military general and his son have ruled since 1967.

In Cameroon, a series of one-party regimes dominated politics from the get-go. President Paul Biya seized power in 1982 and moved into the former German governor's residence, where he has resided ever since. The independence of Papua New Guinea in 1975 and Namibia in 1990 did not go much better; these countries were burdened with such a pervasive mythology of colonial victimization that they did not bother to take responsibility for their own fates and overlooked misgovernance as a "legacy of colonialism." As two German scholars observed: "Given the existence of failed states, ethnic cleansing, and the perpetuation of aged and more or less totalitarian rulers in today's Africa, European imperialists seemed, by comparison, less self-seeking and exploitative."[14]

• • •

The main institutional base of German anti-colonialism after World War II was the German Democratic Republic (or East Germany). As a puppet state of the Leninist empire to the East, the GDR was predictably and formulaically anti-colonial. Mainstream scholars today fawn over the agitprop produced by East German scholars because, in the words of one, it continued a glorious tradition "of German socialist and communist thinking that called for solidarity with colonized subjects as a global community of proletarians united against imperialism."[15] These East German efforts are continually portrayed by contemporary academics as well-meaning and progressive, even if coming up a bit short in terms of valid results with any grounding in fact.

The key event that shaped later historiography on German colonialism was the seizure of the colonial archives by Soviet troops when they entered Berlin in 1945. After being sent to Moscow, the records were returned to the GDR's archives at Potsdam. There, they became fodder for state-directed propagandists to crank out books on the evils of German colonialism. Commissars assigned a team of GDR and Soviet academics to each former German colony with a mandate, in the admiring words of the American historian Dennis Laumann, to "dismantle" any notions that German colonialism had been legitimate or beneficial. "The works of these scholars based in the USSR and its allied countries were informed by the theories of imperialism and neo-colonialism articulated by respectively, Lenin and [Ghanaian dictator Kwame] Nkrumah," Laumann enthuses.[16] Most significantly, as mentioned above, the first assay of the "Windhoek to Auschwitz" theory came from the East German propaganda machine in a 1966 book.[17]

The Leninist scholar-workers toiling away to "dismantle" objective history were less enthusiastic than later admirers. Their duty, in the words of one team member, Ulrich van der Heyden, was "to refute the traditional euphemistic apologetics about the colonial past of Germany through thorough research." The scholars were instructed to sever "traditional ties to bourgeois knowledge systems" and replace them with ties to Marxist, Leninist, and Maoist knowledge systems. All positive references to German colonial achievements were airbrushed like an inconvenient politburo member in a staged photograph. It was not social science but "policy advocacy" for the Soviet bloc, van der Heyden recalled. "The historians of Africa were forced to adapt their research projects to [propaganda] guidelines . . . if they wanted to justify their existence." The ideological rigidity of their marching orders reflected the ideological rigidity of the communist systems themselves, he noted, which explained why global communism eventually collapsed, a delicious "dialectical" result.[18]

A two-volume history of German Cameroon done by a team at the GDR's Humboldt University in the 1960s aimed to describe the emergence of a "proletariat" and "working class consciousness" in the jungles of Africa.[19] Chief Ndumbe Bell's son, who succeeded him on the Duala throne, was attacked by the Leninist scholars for his unwillingness to create a "militant mass movement." The book ended with an ode to the convicted Soviet spy Rosa Luxemburg. In a review of the volumes, the storied female economist and political scientist Charlotte Leubuscher, who fled Nazi Germany for Britain, bemoaned that they add "nothing to our knowledge of the subject; the serious scholar will find little of interest in it, except that it shows how history is at present being taught at the university that once counted Niebuhr, Ranke, Mommsen and other illustrious historians among its teachers."[20]

As Lewis Gann explained: "East Germany, calling itself the first German workers' and peasants' state, became the first legatee of a former colonial power whose official policy obliged contemporary historians to condemn the record of all preceding governments. East Germany's colonial historiography derived from Lenin more than Marx. . . . Lenin's revisionist approach, however, stripped colonialism of all progressive functions. Lenin's ideological heirs in the German Democratic Republic could not help but follow suit."[21]

This meant not only that the colonial past was treated as a prisoner to be tortured in line with the contemporary ideology of power—something not even the Nazis had bothered to do—but also that there was a constant striving towards a "final" understanding in which no more intellectual work was required because history had now been correctly told. West German scholars eagerly absorbed the communist propaganda published by Progress Verlag, the West German arm of the Soviet propaganda machine. San Francisco State professor Volker Langbehn applauded that machine's "anti-imperialist, revisionist view of German history which focused on the exploitative and brutal character of Germany's colonial past."[22] By the mid-1970s, East German research on German colonialism ceased because, in the words of one scholar, "it was already considered to have been comprehensively researched according to the Marxist understanding of history."[23]

• • •

While circulating vapid critiques of Germany's colonial past, the GDR was at the same time imposing ruthless tyrannies on black and brown people everywhere. In South Yemen, a Marxist movement supported by Egypt and the Soviet Union ended the successful and mild rule of the British in 1967. Abetted by the former Nazis in Cairo, the GDR helped to install a cruel communist regime on the hapless Arabs of the region. East Germany was given the responsibility by Moscow of overseeing the domestic revolution. At its peak, there were two thousand East German functionaries in South Yemen instituting

East German party chief Erich Honecker tours communist farms created in anti-colonial Yemen that brought mass starvation, 1979. *Bundesarchiv*

systems of mass repression and starvation. Systems of police, kinder-gartens, theater, and television were imported from the GDR. The East German secret police ferreted out 250 Yemeni military officers deemed disloyal to the new regime and slayed them. What had been a prosperous and cosmopolitan British protectorate based at Aden was reduced to rubble thanks to East German anti-colonialism.[24] One third of the workforce fled to the Gulf states and Saudi Arabia (despite the regime declaring it illegal), bringing in 60–70 percent of foreign exchange earnings. Per capita income had fallen by half to $450 by 1982.[25] Land collectivization caused peasants to flee to cities where they became beggars.

Despite the calamity of German communist rule in Yemen, there is no industry of German scholars writing the truth about this sorry episode. The disastrous confluence of ex-Nazis in Cairo and contem-porary Marxists in East Berlin imposing vast human suffering on brown people in the name of anti-colonialism is politely swept under the carpet as a progressive vision that encountered some unfortunate technical difficulties. Most of those problems, in the delusional words of one admirer, were "unresolved issues inherited from" . . . wait for it . . . "colonialism."[26] The twenty to thirty million people of Yemen have never recovered.

The other major instance of catastrophic East German anti-colonialism was in the former German Southwest Africa.[27] For progressive scholars, GDR support for the revolutionary militants who launched terrorist attacks on South Africa's post-1914 stewards of the country was justified as payback for the crimes of Lothar von Trotha. The organization they backed, the South West Africa People's Organiza-tion, or SWAPO, was founded to defend the rights of the majority Ovambo group, not the Herero or Nama who were their historical ene-mies. (Black and brown people are essentially interchangeable for progres-sive whites.) For most of the 1960s through 1980s, the Herero and Nama opposed the SWAPO insurgency and supported rule by the apartheid government in South Africa. At independence most Herero and Nama were part of the anti-SWAPO Democratic Turnhalle Alliance.

For advanced Marxist thinkers, East German communist agitation provided the people of Southwest Africa with the blessings of social revolution and economic collapse.[28] The GDR secret police also had a community outreach program here that helped SWAPO root out "traitors."[29] With GDR and Soviet funding, SWAPO murdered at least 700 of its own members in the 1980s during its anti-colonial crusade operating out of Angola. Another 4,200 people who disappeared from its prison camps are still referred to as "missing."[30]

Today, anti-colonial scholars excuse the misrule and oppression of SWAPO as reflecting the "structurally embedded inequality and injustice" of . . . wait for it . . . German colonialism! Colonialism provides an ever-ready excuse for every folly and foible of post-colonial rulers in Namibia and their former communist overlords in East Berlin. "Today's commercial agrarian sector in Namibia remains heavily associated with . . . [colonial] land theft," asserts the former SWAPO militant and modern-day "genocide scholar" Henning Melber. "The current distribution of land in private ownership is a constant reminder that colonialism did not end with independence."[31]

To the contrary, serious economists believe that Namibia's land and other economic problems are a result of the mismanagement and corruption of SWAPO inspired by the GDR.[32] Even Melber has shyly admitted that attempts to "decolonize" land ownership in Namibia have been a disaster.[33] After a successful cut-flower farm was expropriated by SWAPO cadres, "production collapsed and the infrastructure deteriorated." After the country's biggest farm in the south was taken over by the state, "the resettled residents were dependent on food aid." A central farm with a profitable tourist lodge and six thousand fruit-bearing olive trees was given to the intelligence agency, never to be used again. All the olive trees died. The blame, of course, must lie with the "structurally embedded inequality" and the "unresolved issues" caused by colonialism!

Melber, like other former radicals of the left, stumbles away from the chaos agog, not sure who or what to blame: The "beneficiaries" of state-led land theft, he ventures, "were often not able to utilize the land efficiently due to a lack of capital and know-how."[34] The case for colonialism was centrally about exactly those two things, broadly understood: capital and know-how. A lack of them is not mere technical detail, but the very heart of the matter. What is the point of decolonization if it makes people worse off, aside from lining the pockets of regime cronies and stirring the cooing of anti-colonial scholars living in comfort somewhere else? Assertions by anti-colonial scholars like Melber allow contemporary Germans to luxuriate in narcissistic colonial guilt. The people of Namibia would no doubt prefer some contemporary accountability from their rulers. But for the likes of Melber, the mundane issues of governance in contemporary Namibia pale compared to the urgent need for "more intensive" guilt by Germans about the colonial past.[35]

Elsewhere, academics regularly criticize the pre-1914 German mission schools in Africa and Asia that provided basic literacy. But they extol the benefits of the GDR indoctrination schools in Africa for, in the words of one admirer, having "opened new horizons" of socialist thinking for Africans.[36] The East German regime and its academic fan base used high-sounding slogans about "solidarity" with brown people to "distinguish the 'anti-colonial' GDR from the 'neo-colonial' [West Germany]," observed one historian. Millions were dying from the tender ministrations of East German comrades, but since their hearts were in the right place, this was a mere technical difficulty, easily attributed to colonialism if anyone asked. In the gallows humor of that same historian, the GDR emphasized "solidarity between peoples at the cost of the solidarity between people."[37]

It is no wonder that when the German government in 2000 agreed to fund a documentary research center on SWAPO's "anti-colonial resistance and liberation struggle" it set the official cut-off date as 1966, before all the SWAPO atrocities and misrule began.[38] The "wall of silence" about East German-funded anti-colonial horrors was torn down by a German missionary in 1995, but few people noticed. German and other Western academics were too busy congratulating themselves for their historical contortions to notice their complicity in fascism and post-colonial human disasters.[39]

The GDR also imposed grave human suffering on other African peoples by funding anti-colonial and pro-communist insurgencies. The GDR-funded overthrow of Portuguese colonialism in Angola and Mozambique continues to bedevil those countries. "Kalashnikovs, Not Coca-Cola, Bring Self-Determination to Angola," went one slogan celebrating East German military aid to what contemporary scholars atavistically refer to as "liberation movements."[40] The criminal organizations calling themselves Marxist liberators funded by East Germany ran terror campaigns against black populations that killed millions. When East German leader Erich Honecker declared in 1980 that his country had "broken with the German imperial past once and for all," it was as true a statement as has ever been said. Whereas the German imperial past of economic uplift and the rule of law had been a startling success enjoying broad native support, the East German imperial present of socialism and thought policing was grotesquely illiberal and illegitimate.[41]

The GDR also supplied tanks and small arms to the genocidal Mengistu regime in Ethiopia (in power from 1977 to 1991) that killed between one and two million Ethiopians. As one scholar of the tainted alliance summarizes: "By the end of the 1980s, the GDR leadership had one ideological goal left in Africa: to keep repressive, 'socialist' regimes in power, notably that headed by Haile Mariam Mengistu, regardless of the hatred felt towards it by most ordinary Ethiopians."[42] A book of joyful reminiscences by former GDR functionaries in these African countries published in 2005 carried the gaspingly ironic title: "We Left Our Mark!"[43]

The common refrain from the GDR's state-leashed scholars in the 1960s was that it was West German aid for good governance in Africa that caused harm, not East German support for insurgencies.[44] They criticized the Social Democrats who held power in West Germany from 1969 to 1982 for a cautious attitude towards decolonization.[45] The quality of their criticisms was so poor, one British scholar noted wryly, that "one cannot help feeling that many Communist propagandists are not really earning their keep."[46] Today, not much has changed, except that the academic critics are on the payroll of a unified Germany rather than an East German Leninist-agitprop outfit.

The GDR clearly won the Cold War as far as German scholarship on colonialism is concerned. Radicals continue to extoll the progressive visions of the GDR, while "conservatives" are at best allowed to assert the moral equivalence of East and West Germany.[47] Only American "cold warriors" such as the political scientist Melvin Croan can state the obvious: the anti-colonial GDR, like the anti-colonial Ngoni of the Maji Maji Rebellion, did not intend to "liberate" anyone but to put them more firmly under the thumb of their system of terror. West Germany's pro-capitalist and pro-democracy policies were the only progressive vision available.[48] Those policies were "colonial" in the best sense of the word. But by the end of the century, which began with the "shabby annexations" of Versailles, Germany had suffered a second shabby annexation: the annexation of its intellectual life by Woke warriors whose anti-Western ideological agenda turned German colonialism into a term of abuse.

CHAPTER 14

Woke Anti-Colonialism and the Hollowing of Europe

G ermany was once the heart of Europe. It serenaded the world with Bach and Beethoven; expanded its horizons with Gutenberg and Kepler; enlightened it with Einstein and Weber; challenged it with Kant and Nietzsche; healed it with Koch and Pilates; and moved it from place to place with Diesel and Daimler. At the high tide of the European colonial encounter, it was Germany—not Britain—that convened the world's powers to set guidelines for civilized behavior when ruling alien peoples. That impulse was both patriotic as well as cosmopolitan. It could not have been otherwise. Only nations with a strong sense of confidence in their national cultures and institutions have the ability to attract international support to lead in global affairs.

German leadership in colonial affairs was tragically terminated at the peace of Versailles, despite every indication prior to the war that the Germany colonial record deserved praise. The loss of colonies, combined with other factors, doomed German liberalism and gave rise to a toxic politics of extreme left and right. After World War II, West Germany at least was restored as a liberal and democratic country. The reckoning with the Nazi period and then, after

1989, the communist period was necessary and thorough. But rather than return to its pre-1933 trajectory, Germany succumbed to an all-embracing and debilitating "guilt politics" that cast its flourishing era of liberal internationalism—forged by a patriotic alliance of conservative and social-democratic parties—as an unbroken tale of oppression. The result was a gaping hole at the heart of Europe, and more generally in the fabric of the West.

Searching for the origin story of Nazi evil, contemporary radicals have fixated on the colonial era. Like all governance systems, that era had its share of failures and abuses. Yet these were in no way endemic to the enterprise, nor did they ever rise to a level that discredited German colonial rule. Quite the opposite, as we have seen. German colonial rule was a startling success, and it responded to its failures with alacrity and integrity. It was the unfair attacks on that record, beginning at Versailles, that gave comfort to Moscow stooges, Nazi madmen, East German Leninists, Third World tyrants, and, of course, contemporary Woke warriors. All those groups have played their part in hollowing out this great nation, and all of them have done so in part by casting aspersions on the German colonial past. The defense of German colonialism with reference to empirical facts is important in the ongoing defense of the West itself. Its enemies, most of whom live in splendor in the West itself, would like nothing more than to see a collapsed civilization of state-dependent serfs looking for guidance from arrogant elites telling them how guilty they should feel.

Rather than showing up the dangers of illiberalism and a loss of faith in the West, this anti-colonial activism has fueled ever more illiberal and cynical movements. The misrepresentation of the German colonial era must stand as a central exhibit in the ravages of illiberal politics in the West. By appropriating "guilt politics" with respect to the Nazi era and backcasting it onto the colonial era, the movement trivialized the former and distorted the latter. This country, which above all countries should have emerged from the Cold War as the unrivalled bastion of the Western-liberal and capitalist tradition, became instead a self-doubting wreck of a country that dared not speak its own name. Every proposal from Berlin about, say, protecting the integrity of European borders or maintaining the fiscal sustainability of Europe was invariably met with charges of revenant *kraut* evil— "filming out of the back of an airplane" and so on.

If there is a defensible "guilt politics" to be had, it should concern how the illiberal forces of the West denuded and destroyed the foundations of human flourishing that were being built in colonial areas, not least in German colonial areas. If there are apologies to be offered, they should be to the hapless natives from the anti-colonial activists who whipsawed countless lives and livelihoods with their "progressive" visions.

The hollowing out of Europe via the hollowing out of Germany was best exemplified in the post–Cold War era by the startling promotion of Joschka Fischer to foreign minister and state vice chancellor from 1998 to 2005. Fischer had been active in kidnappings, firebombings, murders, and other civic engagements in the West Germany of the 1960s and 1970s. Reborn as a Green Party politician, he became Germany's foreign minister. During a trip to South Africa in 2001, Fischer decried the "exploitation by colonialism" of the continent and called on all Germans to feel guilty and handover large sums of cash as indulgence money.[1] Nothing was said about the East German communist "marks" on the continent much less of the postwar Nazi cells operating out of Cairo and Algeria to foment anti-colonial insurgencies. It was a performative act, and it was not clear what he was apologizing for or why. In a sense, those pesky details did not matter. Under the constant barrage of anti-colonialists, the average German had only a dim understanding of that past. Beginning with the unfair cavils of Socialist Party legislators in the colonial period, critics of colonialism had leapt effortlessly like circus riders from the Moscow-run League Against Imperialism to the Nazi party to the GDR and, finally, to the contemporary university. German scholars today are under pressure to embrace "a brown and black perspective" when writing about German colonial history—as if all non-white people think alike and as if they are a subhuman species that need to be studied outside of conventional scientific norms. And so Woke academics stumble like drunkards from one ideological snifter to the next.[2]

Introducing a manual on how to care for museum objects "plundered" during colonial days, a German government agency in 2021 stated: "They bear witness to a value system in which, on the basis of an assumed superiority, colonial powers placed themselves above other states and their populations or parts of the population, exploiting and oppressing them." The instructions are accompanied by a background essay by ideologue-in-chief Jürgen Zimmerer that defines colonialism as "a relationship marked by domination, in which the colonised are limited in their self-determination, are subject to heteronomy, and forced to adapt to the needs and interests of the colonisers, especially as far as politics and economic aspects are concerned."[3]

Every word in that definition is false, so much so that we could repurpose it to define colonialism as follows: *Colonialism is a relationship marked by shared governance and liberation from native domination in which the colonized are given unprecedented opportunities to develop the capacities and practices of self-determination, are subject as equals to laws and rules that provide a degree of self-organization and autonomy unprecedented in their histories, and for the first time are able to articulate as equals the needs and interests of their communities, especially as far as politics and economic aspects are concerned.*

Imagine how much different the contemporary management of museums would look if this more historically accurate description of colonialism informed their practice. Curators would not be constantly blindsided by claims from mobilized activists backed by angry professors. The collections would actually attract visitors, since they would not be didactically designed as a perp-walk for guilty Germans. Provenance research would be serious, historical inquiry instead of performative exculpation. And perhaps, though perhaps too hopeful a prediction, everyday Germans might take an interest in other parts of the world, an interest now virulently prevented by pervasive charges of racism.

German anti-colonialism asphyxiates the classical liberal heritage and the European Enlightenment itself, and thus the heart of the West. The intellectuals whose works the faculty espouse today are not interested in a liberal society based on human rights and freedom. Rather, as the University of Rostick's Egon Flaig noted, they rally to odious intellectuals such as the black race-chauvinist Frantz Fanon who advocated fascist ideas about "national liberation."[4] As the German colonial era fades further into the background, Flaig noted, debates on "history" are being replaced by "memory politics" in which activists use German colonial history to advance their contemporary political projects.[5] German scholars of colonialism move like a herd of water buffalo from one conference to the next where they grunt and heave as one, quenching their intellects at the latest "Windhoek to Auschwitz" or "racism in the colonies" watering hole. The idea of history as an objective set of facts that one could accurately describe and explain has been replaced by a postmodern idea: "history" is now a progressive narrative forced upon the past in order to advance contemporary political projects, whether social restructuring or banning fossil fuels. Only naïve people still think of history as anything else.

Today, it is an article of faith among academics that the German public, in the arrogant words of Reinhart Kossler, suffers from amnesia and "widespread isolation from the grim realities of colonialism."⁶ Kossler does not explain on what basis he summarizes 366 million people-years of German colonialism as a "grim reality." Given that most German academics think that life in present-day Germany is also a "grim reality," it may say more about their own psychologies than anything useful about the past.

In 2019, a long-time German journalist in Africa, Bartholomäus Grill, published a fierce denunciation of German colonial history with the subtitle *Our Racist Heritage*.⁷ In his own words, the purpose of the book was to seek out any evidence of the "violence, exploitation, arbitrariness and racism" of German colonialism. This "firm point of view," which he took with him on his travels, he tells the reader, was learned by reading such tribunes of Third World radicalism as "Frantz Fanon, Edward Said, and Aimé Césaire." The result, noted one review in *Frankfurter Allgemeine Zeitung*, is that "wherever Grill wants to appear particularly anti-racist and post-colonial, his tone becomes shrill and his prose preaching."⁸ The contemporary German public is being instructed in its "racist heritage" by Woke elites like Grill who make no attempt to conceal the fact that their ideological project draws directly from the likes of Said and Fanon, authors motivated more by sadistic dreams of the destruction of the West than altruistic desires to lift up their countrymen.

The same year, dozens of German academics contributed to a volume entitled *The Colonialism Debate*.⁹ An uninformed outsider might be excused for expecting the book to contain contributions about the successes and failures, benefits and harms, and moral and immoral acts of the German colonial era. In other words, foolish people expect a book with the word "debate" in the title to contain a debate. But no. Every single essay in the "debate" took a rigidly anti-colonial position. The only "debate" was whether German colonialism was terrible and awful or *really* terrible and awful. In either case, the scholars in the "debate" agreed that Germany should immediately and unconditionally hand over billions of euros, denounce itself before those it previously oppressed, and empty its museums and libraries of any offensive works. The only permissible "conservative" view was whether these necessary acts of penance should be done a little more slowly with more care to ensure they achieve the desired self-loathing and liquidation of the German nation. This was like a "debate" in Maoist China about whether capitalist-roaders and right-deviationists should be summarily executed or merely turned into slaves of state factories.

By the 2020s, the "decolonize" movement in Germany had become a well-organized industry of lobbyists, scholars, and politicians, all engaged in the cult of colonial crimes. The epistemic community no longer questioned but simply repeated its dominant principles: Germany should be ashamed of its colonial record—it caused harms, was illegitimate, and left harmful legacies; Germans should grovel and seek forgiveness; Germans should pay vast sums of money to former colonial areas (and to anti-colonial scholars and activists); and Germans need to open their borders as penance for the crimes of colonialism. As one scholar writes enthusiastically about how the anti-colonial ideology can be continually deployed for contemporary political activism: "The 'postcolonial project' in German literature is certainly not finished, not in terms of critically retracing and rereading the ramifications of colonial history, nor in terms of the postcolonial critique of contemporary German society and its global resonances."[10] God forbid that historians should continue to engage in actual research on German colonialism that might upend the firmly-entrenched anti-colonial conclusions of the academy, as that might put in jeopardy the deployment of that ideology in contemporary political activism, the ultimate aim of which is the complete destruction of this most important Western country.

The revered symbol of membership in this cult is to show that you "know" that German colonialism was just a warm-up act for the Great Satan, namely U.S. global domination. "The question can be asked," wrote Zimmerer "as to whether the policy of Washington and NATO after September 11, 2001 moved in neo-colonial traditions."[11] There is very little distinction at this point between today's utterances of the German academy and other Woke warriors who write and speak on German colonialism and yesterday's virulent attacks on Germany's liberal heritage from East German party hacks and Nazi ideologues.

• • •

In 2019, state-culture ministers in Germany met to discuss the question of the official attitude toward colonialism. The Greens want colonialism officially designated a "crime against humanity" (which for a group that advocates socialism is rather ironic) and directly compared to the Holocaust (which would trigger a lot of government money and processes). All others except the Alternative for Germany (AfD) insisted that it be classified as a negative or harmful episode in German history.

The left wants all cultural artifacts "repatriated" including the Pillar of Cape Cross, erected in today's Namibia in 1486 by Portuguese Christians. The "return" of museum collections is a scandal on many levels. The Berlin art historian Horst Bredekamp speaks of a "grotesquely simple-minded picture of history" that pervades the returns movement and "refuses to accept the diversity and contradictions of history." A "rigor of interpretation" has arisen "that tries to mentally try to get rid of everything that is contrary."[12]

Street renaming is also in fashion. In 2018, the Berlin city government renamed Peters Street (named after Carl Peters) as Maji Maji Street. Whatever we think of Peters the person, he is clearly a seminal figure in German colonial history who deserves recognition. Having air-brushed him like editors at *Pravda*, city officials put in his place a shopping avenue named after a criminal organization of misogynistic warlords and slave traders. Like the GDR terrorists in Africa, those Berlin city councilors will be able in future to sit back as they smoke Cuban cigars and proclaim, "We Left Our Mark!"

By the 2020s, the anti-colonial lobby in Germany had been transformed into a straightforward extortion racket. In *Colonial Repercussions: The Case of Namibia*, a human rights group insists that "neither former colonial powers like the United Kingdom, France and Germany, nor the successors of the private companies involved in colonization have yet fully acknowledged, apologized or paid reparations for the crimes committed during European colonialism."[13] It is comical to see *Berliner Zeitung* run a story about "descendants of victims of the genocide" demanding cash where most of the people in an accompanying photo holding up the banner "Genocide will not be forgotten" are white Germans.[14]

At an event entitled "Crimes Committed by Colonial Germany Against the Herero and Nama" put on by the Academy of Arts in Berlin in 2018, the former deputy minister for land reform in Namibia called Germany "Satan" and "the Devil." Another Namibian who leads the extortion efforts in U.S. courts said, "I am from the victim community" and that Namibia was poor "as a result of 1904 to 1908."[15] In other words, the Namibian people have had no responsibility for their lives for over one hundred years. They are like children who never moved out of their parent's basement but still blame their parents for their failures. White liberals in Germany refuse to allow the Herrero and Nama to become free human beings, treated not as slaves on the liberal plantation of colonial crimes but as equals. Whatever one's conclusions about German negligence and war crimes during the Herero and Nama conflicts, there is no legal basis for any

Herero and Nama individuals protest in Berlin in 2016 for more money and handouts over an alleged "genocide" more than a century before. *Joachim Zeller/ Flickr Commons*

restitution.[16] There is only a wobbly moral case, and even that is gravely mistaken because tracing harms from individuals in the colonial era to individuals today is virtually impossible (and would have to include atrocities committed by Herero and Nama against Germans as well as each other). Also, if the point is to "make whole," there is no evidence that such historical shakedowns do anything except further harm the "beneficiaries" while lining the pockets of their lawyers and activists.

One might point out, for instance, that Namibia has yet to account for its role in the Great World War of Africa that began with the Rwanda genocide of 1994 in the Congo. President Sam Nujoma sent Namibian troops to the DRC in 1998. Six million people died in that conflict involving ten African countries. Where are the protestors in the streets of Windhoek demanding justice for the victims of

Namibian war crimes of ten years ago? They are all in Berlin pro-testing General von Trotha of one hundred years ago! After all, Berlin has money, Windhoek does not. Anti-colonial advocates are rational rent-seekers if nothing else.

In Namibia, the three hundred thousand descendants of the Herero and Nama have continued to spend their time demanding reparations in U.S. courts and at learned conferences in Germany presided over by radical white professors. In this way, the histories of the Herero and Nama are forever centered on the white man and his quest for moral superiority. They exist to stimulate white guilt. For Woke anti-colonial professors the "lasting structural consequences of the atrocities"[17] of one hundred years ago matter more than recent events. In other words, nothing that Namibians have done for over one hundred years is of any interest or importance. Meanwhile, the Namibians are reduced to acting like a cargo cult hoping that repara-tions will fall from the sky from the German Bundestag to magically transform their country into a modern society. This is the essentially racist element of the contemporary anti-colonial agenda.

When the German government said it would only deal with the Namibian government, the Herero and Nama were horrified because they realized that the German guilt cash would end up in the pockets of SWAPO cadres (most of whom belong to the dominant Ovambo group). They quickly created their own organizations to lobby the German government. Not to be outdone, SWAPO created its own "genocide committee" to sideline the genocide committees of the Herero and Nama angling for direct cash payments. The issues of history and development are now distant afterthoughts as the various cadres and chiefs scramble for ascendancy in the cargo cult of German cash drops.

In 2021, Germany's foreign minister in Namibia formally apolo-gized for a genocide that, as we have seen, never happened, and he handed over a check for $1.34 billion to the three hundred thousand people who claim to be descendants of the Herero and Nama, the equivalent of $4,500 per person, not a bad day's work and worth half a year's gross domestic product. The leaders of the Herero-Nama extortion racket immediately demanded $582 *billion* instead, but suggested they would be willing to negotiate for, say, a few hundred billion. "This is not about money. It is about the restoration of human dignity," Reuters quoted one Nama woman born in 1969 as saying.[18] Apparently, she has no human dignity because of something that happened two generations before she was born, and the grubby spectacle of black Africans fighting each other in pursuit of their share of German cash restores it to her.

In effect, the Woke anti-colonial professoriate in Germany wishes to transform all former German colonies into reparation cargo cults. It is not just that this denial of the agency of these peoples in favor of "lasting structural legacies" of the Germans is racist. It is also economically and socially illiterate. A society cannot modernize through charitable donations, much less lies about its past. So much of this error of historical scholarship on colonialism reflects the vague socialist ideals of the contemporary academy that have been proven disasters for human well-being time and again. Keeping former colonial peoples in permanent thrall to anti-colonial ideology is the most damaging form of alien rule of all.

The claims by professors that they struggle under constant attacks from right-wing political forces to write their truthful accounts that "unmask" the dark secrets of colonialism are a farce. The only struggles they face are struggles to gain stature in the anti-colonial cult of contemporary Germany. These are struggles to outdo one's peers in denouncing colonial evils. The attacks, such as they are, come from within their own ranks when someone fails to adopt a sufficiently anti-Western "healthy point of departure" or a properly anti-colonial "moral framework." Even the federal archive on German colonialism drips with cynicism, distortion, and censure, as if the main point of scholarship and debate on the past is competition for who can offer the most over-the-top moral condemnation, a rhetorical Olympics of a sort. "Violence, whether subtle or spontaneously, was used by the German colonial administration in all of the areas it subjugated," the overview written by former Stalinist scholar for East German communists Ulrich van der Heyden insists.[19]

It seemed only a matter of time before politicians scrambling amidst the moral panic of "colonial crimes" decided to put German colonial history on the same pedestal as the Holocaust. In 2019, the left faction demanded an official policy for "dealing with, reparations, and education" about colonial crimes, as if there was no doubt about the premises, only questions about how to respond to them.[20] This reflected a coalition government that had put "dealing with colonial history" alongside dealing with the Nazi period as part of its agenda in 2018. "The injustice that happened must not be forgotten, it is part of our historical responsibility." The resulting coalition agreement named "the coming to terms with German colonial history as part of the basic democratic consensus."[21] Thus, the German government officially slammed the door on historical debate, institutionalizing a false narrative in which the distorted history told by anti-colonial activists and scholars became laurels of achievement.

There are occasional "scandals" in the German academy when someone dares to publish something that suggests that German colonial rule was not a "grim reality." One early dissent came from the German-descended Namibian Brigitte Lau who pointed out that German academics were so intent on calling themselves evil oppressors with Superman abilities to shape the destinies of other people that they had become little more than white supremacists who refused to believe that black and brown people could bear responsibility for their own destinies.[22] The odd result was that it was unconventional scholars such as Lau and others like Hinrich Schneider-Waterberg[23] who began "writing back to the center" with their pro-colonial dissents.

It is faintly comical every time an establishment German scholar publishes yet another piece of anti-colonial agitprop with book-jacket declarations that their work "pierces amnesia" about the topic and "challenges the myth of benevolent colonialism." The claim of a great act of intellectual daring is a farce. For sixty years, the German academic establishment has published *nothing more* than such books. It is like Zhou Enlai claiming a great act of intellectual courage by publishing a new edition of the collected works of Chairman Mao.

When those dissident amateurs challenge the establishment, the professors do not like it one bit. The former director of Germany's National Archive responsible for Namibia, Werner Hillebrecht, a self-described Maoist, charged in response to Lau's book: "Why did a historian and archivist with *progressive credentials* and a record of painstaking and ground-breaking research allow herself to write and maintain such a shoddy piece of biased non-research which would make her the crown witness of an unsavory array of unrepentant colonialists and neo-Nazis?" Note the smear tactics as well as the disappointed tone in writing about someone whose "progressive credentials" should have guided them to the approved ideological conclusion. The GDR had nothing on the contemporary academy in terms of rigid guidelines for approved research.

The threat to the German academic anti-colonial cult is clear: if you dare to deny items of belief such as "the basic truth that German [colonial] 'development' . . . was colonial underdevelopment based on fundamental injustice to the indigenous population,"[24] you will be called a Holocaust denier and closet Nazi. This is what Germany's great intellectual tradition has become.

Indeed, the anti-colonial establishment is increasingly turning its energies towards this emergent pushback. In the operatic words of one scholar, referring to this author's presentation to the AfD faction in 2019 that was the basis of this book, "With Nazi-sympathizers even in their highest party ranks, the new right-wing white supremacist reincarnations of megalomaniac thoughts and claims of Empire have arrived in Germany with full force."[25] The academy must be in panic if such sentences pass muster in a peer-reviewed publication.

Now that the debate on German colonialism has been explicitly linked to a range of contemporary public-policy issues, the stakes have become much greater. With historical distortions now being used to justify a range of policy positions on issues like immigration, foreign aid, trade policies, climate change, defense policy, global public health, public education, political systems, and global governance, the need to recover a truthful account of German colonialism is more important than ever. If Germans do not refute the distortions about their colonial past, Germany as well as the broader West will pay the price for decades to come.

Notes

Preface: Black Berliners and Their White Supporters

1. Sven Felix Kellerhoff, "Wie verrechnet man versklavte Menschen mit Brunnen?" [How do you balance slavery against water wells?], *Die Welt*, December 1, 2019.
2. Oliver Georgi, "AfD und deutsche Kolonialzeit: Danke für die Unterdrückung!" [The AfD and German colonial era: Thanks for the oppression!], *Frankfurter Allgemeine Zeitung*, November 28, 2019.

Chapter 1: Laying the Prussian Lash on German Colonial History

1. The petition can be found at: "Petitions to German Authorities (1919), Wayback Machine," https://web.archive.org/web/20200101090448/https://blackcentraleurope.com/sources/1914-1945/petitions-to-german-authorities-1919/; see also Daniel Pelz, "100 Jahre Dibobe-Petition: Der vergessene Kolonialismus-Protest" [The Dibobe petition at 100: A forgotten colonial protest], *Deutsche Welle*, July 25, 2019.
2. "Petitions to German Authorities."
3. Bruce Gilley, "Contributions of Western Colonialism to Human Flourishing: A Research Bibliography (Version 3.0)," ResearchGate.Net, November 2020, https://www.researchgate.net/publication/346401531_Contributions_of_Western_Colonialism_to_Human_Flourishing_A_Research_Bibliography_Version_30.
4. Arlette-Louise Ndakoze, "Das Erinnern an Kolonialismus-Verbrechen wirkt allmählich" [The slow work of remembering colonial crimes], *Deutschlandfunk Kultur*, March 28, 2018.
5. William Rogers Louis, *Great Britain and Germany's Lost Colonies, 1914–1919* (1967), 3.
6. Africanus, *The Prussian Lash in Africa: The Story of German Rule in Africa* (1918), 29.
7. William Harbutt Dawson, introduction to *German Colonization: Past and Future*, by Heinrich Schnee (1926).

8. Harry Rudin, *Germans in the Cameroons, 1884–1914: A Case Study in Modern Imperialism* (1938), 419.

9. Lewis Gann and Peter Duignan, *The Rulers of German Africa, 1884–1914* (1977).

10. Michael Perraudin and Jürgen Zimmerer, eds., introduction to *German Colonialism and National Identity* (2010), 1.

11. Bruce Gilley, "The Case for Colonialism: A Response to My Critics," *Academic Questions* (2022).

12. Sara Friedrichsmeyer, Sara Lennox, and Susanne Zantop, eds., *The Imperialist Imagination: German Colonialism and Its Legacy* (1998).

13. Frank Biess, "Moral Panic in Postwar Germany: The Abduction of Young Germans into the Foreign Legion and French Colonialism in the 1950s," *Journal of Modern History* (2012): 824.

14. Uwe Klußmann and Dietmar Pieper, "Konzept des rassistischen Terrors: Ist die koloniale Vergangenheit wirklich vergangen?" [The concept of racist terror: Has the colonial past really passed?], *Der Spiegel*, March 6, 2016.

15. Horst Gründer and Hermann Hiery, eds., *Die Deutschen und ihre Kolonien: Ein Überblick* [The Germans and their colonies: An overview] (2017).

16. George Kibala Bauer, "Germany's Crimes," AfricaIsACountry.com, January 3, 2018, https://africasacountry.com/2018/03/what-are-the-politics-of-colonial-memory-in-germany.

17. Gisela Graichen and Horst Gründer, *Deutsche Kolonien: Traum und Trauma* [German colonies: dreams and nightmares] (2005); Jürgen Zimmerer, "Menschenfresser und barbusige Mädchen: Eine ZDF-Serie und ein Buch verkitschen und verharmlosen den deutschen Kolonialismus [Cannibals and bare-breasted girls: A ZDF series and a book are messing up and playing down German colonialism]," *Süddeutsche Zeitung*, November 24, 2005.

18. Heiko Wegmann, "Zwei Schritte vorwärts und einen zurück—Anmerkungen zur aktuellen Debatte um den Maji-Maji-Krieg in Deutsch-Ostafrika" [Two steps forward and one step back: Comments on the current debate about the Maji Maji War in German East Africa], *Freiburg Postkolonial*, November 1, 2005.

19. "Liberalism: Old and New," *Public Opinion*, 1899, 683.

20. Bouda Etemad, *Possessing the World: Taking the Measurements of Colonisation from the 18th to the 20th Century* (2007), chapter 10.

21. Gilley, "Contributions of Western Colonialism to Human Flourishing."

22. Lora Wildenthal, *German Women for Empire, 1884–1945* (2001), 46.

23. Victor LeVine, *The Cameroons: From Mandate to Independence* (1964), 26.

24. Arthur Knoll and Hermann Hiery, eds., *The German Colonial Experience: Select Documents on German Rule in Africa, China, and the Pacific 1884–1914* (2010), 93.

25. Gustav Noske, *Kolonialpolitik und Sozialdemokratie* [Colonialism and social democracy] (1914), 74.

26. David Simo, "The Legal Foundation of the Colonial Enterprise: A Case Study of German Colonization in Cameroon," in *Germany's Colonial Pasts*, ed. Eric Ames, Marcia Klotz, and Lora Wildenthal (2005), 105.

27. James Feyrer and Bruce Sacerdote, "Colonialism and Modern Income: Islands as Natural Experiments," *Review of Economics and Statistics* (2009).

28. Joan Robinson, *Economic Philosophy* (1962), 46.

29. Carl Gotthilf Buttner, *Anthologie aus der Suaheli-Litteratur [Anthology of Swahili Literature]* (1894), 196

30. Ola Olsson, "On the Democratic Legacy of Colonialism," *Journal of Comparative Economics* (2009).

31. Ibid., 540.

32. Jacob Hariri, "The Autocratic Legacy of Early Statehood," *American Political Science Review* (2012).

33. Ronald Robinson, "Non-European Foundations of European Imperialism: Sketch for a Theory of Collaboration," in *Studies in the Theory of Imperialism*, ed. Roger Owen and Bob Sutcliffe (1975).

34. Etemad, *Possessing the World*, 47–48, 206.

35. Martin Meredith, *The Fate of Africa: A History of the Continent Since Independence* (2011), 5.

36. Allen Isaacman and Barbara Isaacman, "Resistance and Collaboration in Southern and Central Africa, c. 1850–1920," *International Journal of African Historical Studies* (1977), 56.

37. Knoll and Hiery, *German Colonial Experience*, 495, vii.

38. Ibid., xi.

39. Hilde Lemke, *Die Suaheli-Zeitungen und- Zeitschriften in Deutsch-Ostafrika* [Swahili newspapers and magazines in German East Africa] (1929).

40. Katrin Bromber, "German Colonial Administrators, Swahili Lecturers and the Promotion of Swahili at the Seminar Für Orientalische Sprachen in Berlin," *Language in Africa* (2004).

41. Charles Pike, "History and Imagination: Swahili Literature and Resistance to German Language Imperialism in Tanzania, 1885–1910," *International Journal of African Historical Studies* (1986), 215, 217.

42. Ibid., 220.

43. Anonymous, "Review of Ann Brumfit, *The Rise and Development of a Language Policy in German East Africa*," *Bulletin of Tanzanian Affairs* (1981), 12.

44. Knoll and Hiery, *German Colonial Experience*, x.

Chapter 2: The Spirit of Berlin

1. Edward Said, *Orientalism* (1978), 123, 18.

2. Ibid., 18–19.

3. Ibn Warraq, *Defending the West: A Critique of Edward Said's Orientalism* (2007), 44.

4. Albert Hopman, *Das Logbuch eines deutschen Seeoffiziers* [Logbook of a German naval officer] (1924), 138.
5. Steven Press, *Rogue Empires: Contracts and Conmen in Europe's Scramble for Africa* (2017), 153, 159.
6. Ibid., 201.
7. "General Act of the Conference of Berlin Concerning the Congo," *American Journal of International Law* (1909).
8. Thomas Pakenham, *The Scramble for Africa, 1876–1912* (1991), 254.
9. Great Britain, National Archives, PRO30/29, "Malet to Granville," February 21, 1885.
10. Geoffrey de Courcel, "The Berlin Act," in *Bismarck, Europe and Africa: The Berlin Africa Conference, 1884–1885, and the Onset of Partition,* ed. Stig Forster, Wolfgang Mommsen, and Ronald Robinson (1988), 255.
11. Imanual Geiss, "Free Trade, Internationalization of the Congo Basin, and the Principle of Effective Occupation," in *Bismarck, Europe and Africa,* 271.
12. Ulrike Lindner, *Koloniale Begegnungen: Deutschland und Großbritannien als Imperialmächte in Afrika, 1880–1914* [Colonial encounters: Germany and Great Britain as imperial powers in Africa, 1880–1914] (2011).
13. Hesketh Bell, *Glimpses of a Governor's Life, from Diaries, Letters and Memoranda* (1946), 207.
14. Hermann Hiery, *Fa'a Siamani: Germany in Micronesia, New Guinea, and Samoa 1884–1914* (2020), 144.
15. Camille Lefebvre, *Frontières de Sable, Frontières de Papier: Histoire de Territoires et de Frontières, du Jihad de Sokoto à la Colonisation Française du Niger, Xixe-Xxe Siècles* [Sand borders, paper borders: History of territories and borders, from the jihad of Sokoto to the French colonization of Niger, 19th–20th centuries] (2015).
16. Camille Lefebvre, "We Have Tailored Africa: French Colonialism and the 'Artificiality' of Africa's Borders in the Interwar Period," *Journal of Historical Geography* (2011): 199, 201.
17. "Nigeria-Cameroons Boundary," *The Times* (London), April 15, 1913.
18. Ibid.
19. Philipp Lehmann, "Review of *Koloniale Begegnungen,*" *German History* (2012): 607.
20. Jörg Fisch, "Africa as *Terra Nullius*: The Berlin Conference and International Law," in *Bismarck, Europe and Africa,* 360.
21. Tom Flanagan, *First Nations? Second Thoughts* (2000), 35.
22. Jake Spidle, "Colonial Studies in Imperial Germany," *History of Education Quarterly* (1973): 244.
23. Suzanne Miers, "Humanitarianism at Berlin: Myth or Reality?" in *Bismarck, Europe and Africa,* 341.
24. Lewis Gann and Peter Duignan, *Burden of Empire: An Appraisal of Western Colonialism in Africa South of the Sahara* (1967).

25. John Van der Veer, "Germany and Her Lost Colonies," *The Times* (London), June 9, 1919.
26. Félicien Cattier, *Étude sur la situation de l'État indépendant du Congo* [A study of the situation of the Congo Free State] (1906), 341.
27. Edmund Morel, *The African Problem and the Peace Settlement* (1917), 28.
28. Arthur Keith, *The Belgian Congo and the Berlin Act* (1918), 65.
29. Joseph Conrad, *Heart of Darkness* (2007), 9.
30. Arthur Dix, *Was Deutschland an seinen Kolonien verlor* [What Germany lost in its colonies] (1926), 14.

Chapter 3: Who Shot Off My Thumb?

1. Gregor Dobler, "Boundary Drawing and the Notion of Territoriality in Pre-Colonial and Early Colonial Ovamboland," *Journal of Namibian Studies* (2008).
2. Michael Bollig and Jan-Bart Gewald, eds., *People, Cattle and Land: Transformations of a Pastoral Society in Southwestern Africa* (2000).
3. Paul Rohrbach, *Deutsche Kolonialwirtschaft. Band 1, Südwest-Afrika* [The German colonial economy. volume 1. Southwest Africa] (1907), 20.
4. Bruce Biber, *Intertribal War in Pre-Colonial Namibia* (1989), 238.
5. Rohrbach, *Deutsche Kolonialwirtschaft*, 236.
6. Nikolai Mossolow, *Waterberg, Beitrag zur Geschichte der Missionsstation Otjozondjupa, des Kambazembi-Stammes und des Hererolandes* [Waterberg: A contribution to the history of the Mission Station Otjozondjupa, the Kambazembi Tribe and the Hereroland] (1992), 10.
7. Eginald Mihanjo and Oswald Masebo, "Maji Maji War, Ngoni Warlords and Militarism in Southern Tanzania: A Revisionist View of Nationalist History," *Journal of African Military History* (2017): 70.
8. Dag Henrichsen, "Ozombambuse and Ovasolondate: Everyday Military Life and African Service Personnel in German South West Africa," in *Hues Between Black and White: Historical Photography from Colonial Namibia 1860s to 1915*, ed. Wolfram Hartmann (2004).
9. Arthur Knoll and Hermann Hiery, eds., *The German Colonial Experience: Select Documents on German Rule in Africa, China, and the Pacific 1884–1914* (2010), 120, 119.
10. Kurd Schwabe, *Mit Schwert und Pflug in Deutsch-Südwestafrika: vier Kriegs- und Wanderjahre* [With sword and plough in German Southwest Africa: Four years of war and wandering] (1899).
11. Alex Haenicke, "Wie Deutschland Kolonialmacht wurde" [How Germany became a colonial power], in *Das Buch der deutschen Kolonien* [The book of German colonies], ed. Heinrich Schnee (1937).
12. Adam A. Blackler, "From Boondoggle to Settlement Colony: Hendrik Witbooi and the Evolution of Germany's Imperial Project in Southwest Africa, 1884–1894," *Central European History* (2017): 456–57.

13. Dag Henrichsen, "Pastoral Modernity, Territoriality and Colonial Transformations in Central Namibia, 1860s–1904," in *Grappling With the Beast: Indigenous Southern African Responses to Colonialism, 1840–1930*, ed. Peter Limb, Norman Etherington, and Peter Midgley (2010).

14. Paul Leutwein, *Theodor Leutwein, der Eroberer Deutsch-Südwestafrikas* [Theodor Leutwein: The conqueror of Southwest Africa] (1934), 537.

15. Klaus Lorenz, *Die Rolle der Kaiserlichen Schutztruppe als Herrschaftsinstrument in Südwestafrika* [The role of the Imperial Protection Force as an instrument of rule in Southwest Africa] (1999), section VI:2.

16. Amanda Kay McVety, "Rinderpest and the Origins of International Cooperation for Disease Control," in *The Rinderpest Campaigns: A Virus, Its Vaccines, and Global Development in the Twentieth Century* (2018), chapter 1.

17. Jan-Bart Gewald, *Towards Redemption: A Socio-Political History of the Herero of Namibia between 1890 and 1923* (1996), 168.

18. Jan-Bart Gewald, *Herero Heroes: A Socio-Political History of the Herero of Namibia, 1890–1923* (1999), 125–28.

19. Daniel Lerner, *The Passing of Traditional Society: Modernizing the Middle East* (1958).

20. Leutwein, *Theodor Leutwein*, 541.

21. Knoll and Hiery, eds., *German Colonial Experience*, 464–65.

22. German General Staff War History Department, *Die Kämpfe der deutschen Truppen in Südwestafrika* [The fighting of the German troops in Southwest Africa] (1906), 5–6.

23. Lukas Grawe, "The Prusso-German General Staff and the Herero Genocide," *Central European History* (2019): 598.

24. Susanne Kuss, *German Colonial Wars and the Context of Military Violence*, trans. Andrew Smith (2017), 42.

25. Grawe, "The Prusso-German General," 604–5.

26. Frank Robert Vivelo, "The Entry of the Herero into Botswana," *Botswana Notes and Records* (1976): 40.

27. Woodruff Smith, *German Colonial Empire* (1978), 54.

28. Mark Kettler, "What did Paul Rohrbach Actually Learn in Africa?" *German History* (2020): 243.

29. Gunter Spraul, "Der Völkermord an den Herero: Untersuchungen zu einer neuen Kontinuitätstheorie" [The genocide of the Herero: Explorations in a New Continuity Theory], in *Geschichte in Wissenschaft und Unterricht* [History in science and teaching] (1988), 739.

30. Hartmut Lang, "The Population Development of the Rehoboth Basters," *Anthropos* (1998): 384.

31. Heinrich Schnee, *German Colonization Past and Future: The Truth about the German Colonies* (1926), 117 (italics in original).

32. Kuss, *German Colonial Wars*, 74, 47.

33. Lorenz, *Die Rolle der Kaiserlichen Schutztruppe*, section VII:3.

34. Ibid.

35. Paul Rohrbach, *Der deutsche Gedanke in der Welt* [German thought in the world] (1912), 141.

36. Rohrbach, *Deutsche Kolonialwirtschaft*, 358–60.

37. Smith, *German Colonial Empire*, 45.

38. William Otto Henderson, *The German Colonial Empire, 1884–1919* (1993), 114.

39. Robert Gerwarth and Stephan Malinowski, "Hannah Arendt's Ghosts: Reflections on the Disputable Path from Windhoek to Auschwitz," *Central European History* (2009).

40. Uwe Klußmann and Dietmar Pieper, "Konzept des rassistischen Terrors: Ist die koloniale Vergangenheit wirklich vergangen?" [The concept of racist terror: Has the colonial past really passed?], *Der Spiegel*, March 6, 2016.

41. Klaus Bachmann, *Genocidal Empires: German Colonialism in Africa and the Third Reich* (2018), 311.

42. Hinrich Schneider-Waterberg, *Der Wahrheit eine Gasse: Anmerkungen zum Kolonialkrieg in Deutsch-Südwestafrika 1904* [A path to truth: Notes on the colonial war in German Southwest Africa 1904] (2008); Andreas Eckl, *"S'ist ein übles Land hier": zur Historiographie eines umstrittenen Kolonialkrieges* ["It's a bad country here": On the historiography of a controversial colonial war] (2005); Claus Nordbruch, *Völkermord an den Herero in Deutsch-Südwestafrika?: Widerlegung einer Lüge* [Genocide of the Herero in German Southwest Africa? Refuting a lie], (2006).

43. Brigitte Lau, *History and Historiography: 4 Essays in Reprint* (1995).

44. Reinhart Kössler, "Entangled History and Politics: Negotiating the Past Between Namibia and Germany," *Journal of Contemporary African Studies* (2008): 322.

45. Oliver Georgi, "AfD und deutsche Kolonialzeit: Danke für die Unterdrückung!" [The AfD and German colonialism: Thanks for the oppression!], *Frankfurter Allgemeine Zeitung*, November 28, 2019.

Chapter 4: The Culturally Competent Krauts

1. Theodore Roosevelt, *African Game Trails: An Account of the African Wanderings of an American Hunter-Naturalist* (1910), 5.

2. Thaddeus Sunseri, "Statist Narratives and Maji Maji Ellipses," *International Journal of African Historical Studies* (2000): 567.

3. Helmuth Stoecker, "The Annexations of 1884–1885," in *German Imperialism in Africa*, ed. Helmuth Stoecker (1986), 29.

4. Fritz Ferdinand Müller, *Deutschland-Zanzibar-Ostafrika. Geschichte einer deutschen Kolonialeroberung 1884–1890* [Germany-Zanzibar-East Africa: A history of the German colonial conquest 1884–1890] (1959), 222.

5. Charles Thomas, "Abushiri Revolt" in *Encyclopedia of African Colonial Conflicts*, vol. 1, ed. Timothy Stapleton (2017).

6. Bradford Martin, "Muslim Politics and Resistance to Colonial Rule: Shaykh Uways B. Muhammad Al-Barāwī and the Qādirīya Brotherhood in East Africa," *Journal of African History* (1969): 480.

7. Arthur Knoll and Hermann Hiery, eds., *The German Colonial Experience: Select Documents on German Rule in Africa, China, and the Pacific 1884–1914* (2010), 67.

8. Gilbert Gwassa, "The German Intervention and African Resistance in Tanzania," in *A History of Tanzania*, ed. Isaria Kimambo and Arnold Temu (1969), 98.

9. Knoll and Hiery, *German Colonial Experience*, 470–71.

10. Alison Redmayne, "Mkwawa and the Hehe Wars," *Journal of African History* (1968): 433.

11. Edgar Winans, "The Head of the King: Museums and the Path to Resistance," *Comparative Studies in Society and History* (1994): 233.

12. Jan Pierskalla, Alexander De Juan, and Max Montgomery, "The Territorial Expansion of the Colonial State: Evidence from German East Africa 1890–1909," *British Journal of Political Science* (2019).

13. Heinrich Schnee, *German Colonization: Past and Future* (1926), 113.

14. Arne Perras, *Carl Peters and German Imperialism 1856–1918: A Political Biography* (2004), 186.

15. Christian Davis, *Colonialism, Antisemitism, and Germans of Jewish Descent in Imperial Germany* (2012), 70.

16. Martin Reuss, "The Disgrace and Fall of Carl Peters: Morality, Politics, and *Staatsräson* in the Time of Wilhelm II," *Central European History* (1981), 123.

17. Sean Andrew Wempe, *Revenants of the German Empire: Colonial Germans, Imperialism, and the League of Nations* (2019), 10–11.

18. Davis, *Colonialism, Antisemitism, and Germans of Jewish Descent*, 70.

19. Perras, *Carl Peters and German Imperialism*, 238, 223.

20. "There are Judges at Berlin," *The Times* (London), April 26, 1897.

21. Reuss, "The Disgrace and Fall of Carl Peters," 141.

22. Brian Hoyle, "Gillman of Tanganyika, 1882–1946: Pioneer Geographer," *Geographical Journal* (1986).

23. Hans Meyer, *Das Deutsche Kolonialreich: eine Landerkunde der Deutschen Schutzgebiete: Ostafrika und Kamerun* [The German colonial empire: A geography of the German protected areas: East Africa and Cameroon] (1909).

24. Bernhard Gissibl, *The Nature of German Imperialism: Conservation and the Politics of Wildlife in Colonial East Africa* (2016).

25. Vinzenz Hediger, "Das Tier auf unserer Seite: Zur Politik des Filmtiers am Beispiel von 'Serengeti darf nicht sterben'" [The animal on our side: On the politics of the film animal, using the example of 'Serengeti shall not die']," *Politische Zoolgie* (2007).

26. Tobias Boes, "Political Animals: 'Serengeti Shall Not Die' and the Cultural Heritage of Mankind," *German Studies Review* (2013): 51.

27. Thomas Jesse Jones, *Education in East Africa: A Study of East, Central and South Africa by the Second African Education Commission* (1924), 178.

28. Marcia Wright, "Local Roots of Policy in German East Africa," *Journal of African History* (1968): 629, 628.

29. Mary Evelyn Townsend, *The Rise and Fall of Germany's Colonial Empire, 1884–1918* (1966), 269.

30. Ralph Austen, *Northwest Tanzania Under German and British Rule: Colonial Policy and Tribal Politics, 1889–1939* (1968), 93–100.

31. Wright, "Local Roots of Policy," 628–29.

32. "Bericht des Lieutenants Sigl über den Sklavenhandel" [Lieutenant Sigl's report on the slave trade], *Deutsches Kolonialblatt*, December 1, 1891; see also Jan-Georg Deutsche, *Emancipation Without Abolition in* German East Africa, c. *1884–1914* (2006).

33. Heinrich Brode, *British and German East Africa: Their Economic and Commercial Relations* (1911), 71.

34. Thaddeus Sunseri, "Slave Ransoming in German East Africa, 1885–1922," *International Journal of African Historical Studies (1993):* 490, 495.

35. John Iliffe, *Tanganyika Under German Rule, 1905–1912* (1969), 27.

36. Eginald Mihanjo and Oswald Masebo, "Maji Maji War, Ngoni Warlords and Militarism in Southern Tanzania: A Revisionist View of Nationalist History," *Journal of African Military History* (2017), 63.

37. Germany, Reichstag, Legislative Term 13, Session 1, Appendices 304, no. 1421 (1914).

38. Woodruff Smith, *The German Colonial Empire* (1978), 159.

39. Lewis Gann, "Marginal Colonialism: The German Case," in *Germans in the Tropics: Essays in German Colonial History*, ed. Arthur Knoll and Lewis Gann (1987), 15.

40. Andreas Eckert, *Herrschen und Verwalten: Afrikanische Bürokraten, staatliche Ordnung und Politik in Tanzania, 1920–1970* [Rule and administration: African bureaucrats, state order and politics in Tanzania, 1920–1970] (2007).

41. Eva Bischoff, "Acting Cannibal: Intersecting Strategies, Conflicting Interests, and the Ambiguities of Cultural Resistance in Iringa, German East Africa," in *German Colonialism Revisited: African, Asian, and Oceanic Experiences*, ed. Nina Berman, Klaus Mühlhahn, and Patrice Nganang (2014), 214.

42. Wempe, *Revenants of the German Empire*, 87–88.

43. Steven Fabian, "Curing the Cancer of the Colony: Bagamoyo, Dar es Salaam, and Socioeconomic Struggle in German East Africa," *International Journal of African Historical Studies* (2007): 444, 466–67.

44. Ibid., 467.

45. Daniel Walther, "Sex, Race and Empire: White Male Sexuality and the 'Other' in Germany's Colonies, 1894–1914," *German Studies Review* (2010): 45, 52, 46.

46. Jürgen Zimmerer, "Expansion und Herrschaft: Geschichte des europäischen und deutschen Kolonialismus [Expansion and domination: History of

European and German colonialism]," *Bundeszentrale für politische Bildung*
(October 23, 2012).

47. Frank Schubert, "Das Erbe des Kolonialismus—oder: warum es in Afrika
     keine Nationen gibt" [The legacy of colonialism—or why there are no nations
     in Africa], Zeitgeschichte-Online, June 1, 2010.

48. George Ayittey, *Indigenous African Institutions* (2006).

49. Richard Reid, "Mutesa and Mirambo: Thoughts on East African Warfare and
     Diplomacy in the Nineteenth Century," *International Journal of African
     Historical Studies* (1998).

50. Alice Werner, "The Native Races of German East Africa," *Journal of the Royal
     African Society* (1910): 60–61.

51. Max Weiss, Die Völkerstämme im Norden Deutsch-Ostafrikas [The ethnic
     groups of Northern German East Africa] (1910).

52. Woodruff Smith, *German Colonial Empire* (1978), 163.

53. Michael Pesek, "The Boma and the Peripatetic Ruler: Mapping Colonial Rule
     in German East Africa, 1889–1903," *Western Folklore* (2007): 251–52, 236.

54. Lewis Gann and Peter Duignan, *The Rulers of German Africa, 1884–1914* (1977),
     146.

55. Juhani Koponen, *Development for Exploitation: German Colonial Policies in
     Mainland Tanzania, 1884–1914* (1995), 352.

56. Sebastian Conrad, *German Colonialism: A Short History*, trans. Sorcha
     O'Hagan (2012), 73.

57. Paolo Giordani, *The German Colonial Empire: Its Beginning and Ending* (1916),
     156.

58. Bouda Etemad, *Possessing the World: Taking the Measurements of Colonisation
     from the 18th to the 20th Century* (2007), 47.

59. Fritz Ferdinand Müller, *Kolonien unter der Peitsche: Eine Dokumentation*
     [Colonies under the whip: A documentation] (1962), 114.

60. Bischoff, "Acting Cannibal," 222, 213.

61. Michelle Moyd, "Bomani: African Soldiers as Colonial Intermediaries in
     German East Africa, 1890–1914," in *German Colonialism Revisited*, 102.

62. Nina Berman, Klaus Mühlhahn, and Patrice Nganang, introduction in
     German Colonialism Revisited, 7.

63. Walter Nuhn, *Flammen über Deutschost. Der Maji-Maji-Aufstand in Deutsch-
     Ostafrika 1905–1906, die erste gemeinsame Erhebung schwarzafrikanischer
     Völker gegen weiße Kolonialherrschaft* [Flames over the German East: The Maji
     Maji Uprising in German East Africa 1905–1906, The first joint uprising by
     black African peoples against white colonial rule] (1998).

64. Heike Schmidt, "(Re)Negotiating Marginality: The Maji Maji War and Its
     Aftermath in Southwestern Tanzania, ca. 1905–1916," *International Journal of
     African Historical Studies* (2010): 29.

65. Alexander De Juan, "State Extraction and Anti-Colonial Rebellion:
     Quantitative Evidence from the Former German East Africa," GIGA Working
     Papers, April 15, 2015.

66. Eginald Mihanjo and Oswald Masebo, "Maji Maji War, Ngoni Warlords, and Militarism in Southern Tanzania: A Revisionist View of Nationalist History," *Journal of African Military History* (2017), 63.

67. Susanne Kuss, *Deutsches Militär auf kolonialen Kriegsschauplätzen: Eskalation von Gewalt zu Beginn des 20. Jahrhunderts* [The German military in colonial theaters of war: The escalation of violence at the beginning of the 20th century] (2010).

68. Schnee, *German Colonization*, 117; Robin Neillands, *The Dervish Wars: Gordon and Kitchener in the Sudan, 1880–1898* (1996).

69. Iliffe, *Tanganyika Under German Rule*, 6.

70. Thaddeus Sunseri, "Statist Narratives and Maji Maji Ellipses," *International Journal of African Historical Studies* (2000).

71. John Iliffe, "The Organization of the Maji Maji Rebellion," *Journal of African History* (1967): 512.

72. Heiko Wegmann, "Zwei Schritte vorwärts und einen zurück—Anmerkungen zur aktuellen Debatte um den Maji-Maji-Krieg in 'Deutsch-Ostafrika'" [Two steps forward and one back—Comments on the current debate about the Maji Maji War in German East Africa], *Freiburg-Postkolonial*, November 15, 2005.

Chapter 5: Rafting the Sanaga in Wicker Baskets

1. Ralph Austen and Jonathan Derrick, *Middlemen of the Cameroon Rivers: The Duala and Their Hinterland, c.1600–c.1960* (1999), 89, 103.

2. Ralph Austen, "The Metamorphoses of Middlemen: The Duala, Europeans, and the Cameroon Hinterland, ca. 1800–ca. 1960," *International Journal of African Historical Studies* (1983): 11, 13.

3. Heinrich Norden, *Als Urwalddoktor in Kamerun: Ein Arzt-Missionar erlebt Afrika* [Jungle doctor in Cameroon: A doctor-missionary experiences Africa] (1940).

4. Harry Rudin, *Germans in the Cameroons, 1884–1914: A Case Study in Modern Imperialism* (1938), 420.

5. Theodor Seitz, "Notwendigkeit deutscher Kolonialpolitik" [The need for a German colonial policy], in *Das Buch der deutschen Kolonien*, ed. Heinrich Schnee [The book of German colonies] (1937).

6. Heinrich Schnee, *Die deutschen Kolonien vor, in und nach dem Weltkrieg* [The German colonies before, during, and after the First World War] (1935), chapter 1, section 4.

7. Kurt Hassert, "Vorläufiger Bericht über einige Ergebnisse der Kamerun-Expedition 1907/8 des Reichs Kolonialamtes" [Preliminary report on some of the results of the 1907/8 Cameroon Expedition of the Reich Colonial Office], *Geographische Zeitschrift* (1908): 628.

8. Helmut Schroeter and Roel Ramaer, *Die Eisenbahnen in den einst deutschen Schutzgebieten Ostafrika, Südwestafrika, Kamerun, Togo und die Schantung-Eisenbahn: damals und heute* [Railways in the former German colonies of East

Africa, Southwest Africa, Cameroon, Togo and the Shandong Railway: Then and now] (1993).

9. Arthur Knoll and Hermann Hiery, eds., *The German Colonial Experience: Select Documents on German Rule in Africa, China, and the Pacific 1884–1914* (2010), 231.

10. Richard Goodridge, "'In the Most Effective Manner'?: Britain and the Disposal of the Cameroons Plantations, 1914–1924," *International Journal of African Historical Studies* (1996): 253–54.

11. Bongfen Chem-Langhëë, *The Paradoxes of Self-determination in the Cameroons under United Kingdom Administration: The Search for Identity, Well-Being, and Continuity* (2004).

12. Rudin, *Germans in the Cameroon*, 306.

13. Heinrich Schnee, *German Colonization Past and Future: The Truth about the German Colonies* (1926), 141.

14. William Otto Henderson, *Studies in German Colonial History* (1962), 38.

15. Rudin, *Germans in the Cameroon*, 195.

16. The petition can be found at: "Petitions to German Authorities (1919), Wayback Machine," https://web.archive.org/web/20200101090448/https:// blackcentraleurope.com/sources/1914-1945/petitions-to-german-authorities -1919/.

17. Ricardo Márquez Garcia, "Johny Baleng (c. 1890–1964): A Colonial Broker from the Cameroon Grassfields," *Cultural Dynamics* (2021): 365, 378.

18. Hans Dominik, *Vom Atlantik zum Tschadsee: Kreigs- und Forschungsfahrten in Kamerun* [From the Atlantic to Lake Chad; War and research trips in Cameroon] (1908); *Kamerun Sechs Kriegs- und Friedensjahre in deutschen Tropen* [Cameroon: Six years of war and peace in the German tropics] (1901).

19. Philippe Laburthe-Tola, "Charles Atangana (c. 1882–1943) : un chef Camerounais entre deux colonisations" [Charles Atangana (c. 1882–1943), A Cameroonian chief during two colonizations], *Mondes et Cultures* (1998).

20. Frederick Quinn, "Charles Atangana of Yaounde," *Journal of African History* (1980): 488.

21. "The German Colonial Scandals," *The Times* (London), December 5, 1906.

22. Schnee, *German Colonization*, 105.

23. Heiko Möhle, Branntwein, *Bibeln und Bananen: der deutsche Kolonialismus in Afrika: eine Spurensuche* [Brandy, Bibles, and bananas: German colonialism in Africa: A search for traces] (1999).

24. "The German Colonial Scandals," *The Times* (London), April 26, 1907.

25. Jens-Uwe Guettel, "The Myth of the Pro-Colonialist SPD: German Social Democracy and Imperialism before World War I," *Central European History* (2012).

26. Brynjolf Hovde, "Socialistic Theories of Imperialism Prior to the Great War," *Journal of Political Economy* (1928).

27. William Harbutt Dawson, introduction in *German Colonization Past and Future: The Truth about the German Colonies*, by Heinrich Schnee (1926), 17.

28. Roger Fletcher, "A Revisionist Looks at Imperialism: Eduard Bernstein's Critique of Imperialism and *Kolonialpolitik*, 1900–14," *Central European History* (1979): 246.

29. Eduard Bernstein, "Der Sozialismus und die Kolonialfrage" [Socialism and the colonial question], *Sozialistische Monatshefte* (1900): 550–51, 559.

30. "German Colonial Policy: Lord Milner on Treatment of Natives," *The Times* (London), January 14, 1914.

Chapter 6: How Do You Say Class Conflict in Ewe?

1. Arthur Knoll and Hermann Hiery, eds., *The German Colonial Experience: Select Documents on German Rule in Africa, China, and the Pacific 1884–1914* (2010), 40, 35.

2. Johann Karl Vietor, *Geschichtliche und kulturelle Entwickelung unserer Schutzgebiete* [The historical and cultural development of our protected areas] (1913).

3. Joseph Udimal Kachim, "African Resistance to Colonial Conquest: The Case of Konkomba Resistance to German Occupation of Northern Togoland, 1896–1901," *Asian Journal of Humanities and Social Studies* (2013).

4. William Crabtree, "Togoland," *Journal of the Royal African Society* (1915): 172.

5. Otto Stammermann, *Maßnahmen einer Kolonialmacht zur Festigung ihrer Herrschaft: Am Beispiel der togolesischen Bevölkerung während der deutschen Kolonialzeit* [Consolidating colonial rule: The case of Togoland in the German colonial era] (2019).

6. Alex Haenicke, "Das kleine Togo" [Little Togo], in *Das Buch der deutschen Kolonien* [The book of German colonies], ed. Heinrich Schnee (1937).

7. Donna Maier, "Slave Labor and Wage Labor in German Togo, 1885–1914," in *Germans in the Tropics: Essays in German Colonial History*, ed. Arthur Knoll and Lewis Gann (1987).

8. D. E. K. Amenumey, "German Administration in Southern Togo," *Journal of African History* (1969): 637.

9. Peter Sebald, *Malam musa—Gottlob Adolf Krause, 1850–1938: Forscher—Wissenschaftler—Humanist. Leben und Lebenswerk eines antikolonial gesinnten Afrika-Wissenschaftlers unter den Bedingungen des Kolonialismus* [Malam Musa: Gottlob Adolf Krause, 1850–1938: Researcher, scientist, humanist: The life and work of an anti-colonial scientist in Africa during colonialism] (1966).

10. Peter Markov and John Sebald, "Gottlob Adolph Krause," *Journal of the Historical Society of Nigeria* (1963).

11. D. E. K. Amenumey, "German Administration in Southern Togo," *Journal of African History* (1969): 632.

12. Andrew Zimmerman, *Alabama in Africa: Booker T. Washington, the German Empire, and the Globalization of the New South* (2010).
13. Guenter Rutkowski, *Die deutsche Medizin erobert Togo: Beispiel des Nachtigal-Krankenhauses in Klein-Popo (Anecho), 1884–1914* [German medicine conquers Togo: the case of the Nachtigal Hospital in Klein-Popo (Anecho), 1884–1914] (2012).
14. Albert Calvert, *The German African Empire* (1916), 215.
15. Ralph Erbar, *Ein Platz an der Sonne? Die Verwaltungs- und Wirtschaftsgeschichte der deutschen Kolonie Togo 1884–1914* [A place in the sun? The administrative and economic history of German Togo, 1884–1914] (1991).
16. Michael Ehret, *Die Bildungspolitik in der deutschen "Musterkolonie" Togo. Nachhaltige Entwicklung oder Optimierung der Ausbeutung?* [Education policy in the German "model colony" Togo: Sustainable development or optimization of exploitation?] (2018).
17. Ralph Austen, "Review of *'Ein Platz an der Sonne'?*" [A place in the sun?], *Journal of African History* (1992): 337.
18. Bernhard Olpen, *Johann Karl Vietor (1861–1934): Ein deutscher Unternehmer zwischen Kolonialismus, sozialer Frage und Christentum* [Johann Karl Vietor (1861–1934): A German entrepreneur between colonialism, social issues, and Christianity] (2014).
19. Bettina Zurstrassen, *Ein Stück deutscher Erde schaffen: Koloniale Beamte in Togo 1884–1914* [Creating German soil: colonial officials in Togo 1884–1914] (2008).
20. Amenumey, "German Administration in Southern Togo," 630.
21. Markus Seemann, *Julius Graf Zech: Ein deutscher Kolonialbeamter in Togo* [Julius Graf Zech: A German colonial official in Togo] (2012).
22. Lewis Gann and Peter Duignan, *The Rulers of German Africa, 1884–1914* (1977), 82.
23. Knoll and Hiery, *German Colonial Experience*, 113.
24. Ernst Bürgi, *Geographie des Ewelandes* [The Geography of Eweland] (1892); *Kurzgefasste Grammatik der Ewesprache* [A brief Ewe grammar] (1897).
25. Benjamin Nicholas Lawrance, "Most Obedient Servants: The Politics of Language in German Colonial Togo," *Cahiers d'Études Africaines* (2000): 514.
26. Heinrich Klose, *Togo unter deutscher Flagge: Reisebilder und Betrachtungen von Heinrich Klose* [Togo under the German flag: Travel pictures and observations by Heinrich Klose] (1899).
27. Valentin Massow, *Die Eroberung von Nordtogo 1896–1899: Tagebücher und Briefe* [The conquest of North Togo 1896–1899: Diaries and letters] (2014).
28. Lawrance, "Most Obedient Servants," 492.
29. "Ewe Union Opposed by French, British," *New York Times*, December 10, 1947.
30. Rainer Gepperth and Hanns-Seidel-Stiftung, eds., *Hundert Jahre deutsch-togolesische Beziehungen/ Les cent ans des relations germano-togolaises* [A century of German-Togo relations] (1984), 30.

31. Têtêvi Godwin Tété-Adjalogo, *De la colonisation allemande au Deutsche-Togo Bund* [From the German colonial era to the German-Togo League] (1998), 10.

32. Dennis Laumann, "Narratives of a 'Model Colony': German Togoland in Written and Oral Histories," in *German Colonialism and National Identity*, ed. Michael Perraudin and Jürgen Zimmerer (2010), 287.

33. Oskar Fritz Metzger, *Unsere alte Kolonie Togo* [Our former colony Togo] (1941), 30–31, 285.

34. Oliver Georgi, "AfD und deutsche Kolonialzeit: Danke für die Unterdrückung! [The AfD and German Colonialism: Thanks for the oppression!]" *Frankfurter Allgemeine Zeitung,* November 28, 2019.

35. Rebekka Habermas and Ulrike Lindner, "Kunst der Kolonialzeit: Rückgabe— und mehr!" [Colonial art: Return and do more!], ZeitOnline, December 15, 2018.

36. Rebekka Habermas, *Skandal in Togo: ein Kapitel deutscher Kolonialherrschaft* [Scandal in Togo: An episode of German colonial rule] (2016).

37. Felix Ohene, "The Gruner Map is 100 Years (1913–2013)," *Modern Ghana*, June 21, 2013.

38. Hans Gruner, *Vormarsch zum Niger: Die Memoiren des Leiters der Togo-Hinterland-Expedition 1894/95* [Advance to Niger: The memoirs of the head of the Togo Hinterland Expedition 1894/95] (1997).

39. Ohene, "The Gruner Map."

40. A. R. Alhassan, "Ghana History: Alhaji Umaru Karachi," *Accra Mail,* September 23, 2000.

41. Peter Sebald, *Togo 1884–1914: eine Geschichte der deutschen "Musterkolonie" auf der Grundlage amtlicher Quellen* [Togo 1884–1914: A history of the German "model colony" using official sources] (1988).

42. Peter Sebald, *Die deutsche Kolonie Togo 1884–1914: Auswirkungen einer Fremdherrschaft* [German Togo 1884–1914: The legacies of foreign rule] (2013).

43. Hans Peter Hahn, Review of *Die deutsche Kolonie Togo 1884–1914* [German Togo 1884–1914], *Anthropos* (2014): 742.

44. Dennis Laumann, "A Historiography of German Togoland, or the Rise and Fall of a 'Model Colony,'" *History in Africa* (2003): 204, 208, 211.

45. Ibid., 208.

46. Ibid., 211.

47. Ibid.

48. David Thiele, "La mémoire de la colonisation allemande au Togo : enjeux et construction du 'centenaire de l'amitié germano-togolaise'" [The memory of German colonization in Togo: Challenges and construction of the 'Centenary of the German-Togolese friendship'], *HAL Archive Ouverte* (2020), 4.

49. Christine de Gemeaux, "La République fédérale d'Allemagne et le Togo: Prendre pied sur le continent africain?" [The Federal Republic of Germany and Togo: Gaining a foothold on the African continent?], *Allemagne d'Aujourd'Hui* (2016): 159.

Chapter 7: *The Suspicious Dr. Koch*

1. Moritz von Brescius, *German Science in the Age of Empire: Enterprise, Opportunity and the Schlagintweit Brothers* (2019).
2. Ian Maudlin, "African Trypanosomiasis," *Annals of Tropical Medicine and Parasitology* (2006).
3. Hesketh Bell, *Glimpses of a Governor's Life* (1946), 112–13.
4. Adam Hochschild, *King Leopold's Ghost* (1998), 231.
5. Robert Koch, *Über meine Schlafkrankheits-Expedition: Vortrag* [My sleeping sickness expedition] (1908), 21.
6. Wolfgang Eckart, "The Colony as Laboratory: German Sleeping Sickness Campaigns in German East Africa and in Togo, 1900–1914," *History and Philosophy of the Life Sciences* (2002): 78.
7. Mari Webel, "Medical Auxiliaries and the Negotiation of Public Health in Colonial North-Western Tanzania," *Journal of African History* (2013): 407.
8. Mari Webel, "Ziba Politics and the German Sleeping Sickness Camp at Kigarama, Tanzania, 1907–14," *International Journal of African Historical Studies* (2014): 399–423.
9. Webel, "Medical Auxiliaries," 414.
10. Robert Koch, *Gesammelte Werke* [Collected works] (1912).
11. Mary Evelyn Townsend, *The Rise and Fall of Germany's Colonial Empire, 1884–1918* (1966), 296.
12. Orhan Pamuk, *Istanbul: Memories and the City* (2006), 291.
13. Hanan Kholoussy, "Monitoring and Medicalising Male Sexuality in Semi-Colonial Egypt," *Gender & History* (2010): 681.
14. Daniel Walther, *Sex and Control: Venereal Disease, Colonial Physicians, and Indigenous Agency in German Colonialism, 1884–1914* (2015), 2.
15. Bradley Naranch, "German Colonialism Made Simple," in *German Colonialism in a Global Age*, ed. Bradley Naranch and Geoff Eley (2014), 12.
16. Sarah Ehlers, *Europa und die Schlafkrankheit: koloniale Seuchenbekämpfung, europäische Identitäten und moderne medizin 1890–1950* [Europe and sleeping sickness: Colonial disease control, European identities, and modern medicine 1890–1950] (2019).
17. Ulrich-Dietmar Madeja and Ulrike Schroeder, "From Colonial Research Spirit to Global Commitment: Bayer and African Sleeping Sickness in the Mirror of History," *Tropical Medicince and Infectious Disease* (2020): 164.
18. Webel, "Medical Auxiliaries," 398.
19. Guillaume Lachenal, *The Lomidine Files : The Untold Story of a Medical Disaster in Colonial Africa* (2017), 21.
20. Ibid., 7 (italics mine).
21. Christoph Gradmann, *Krankheit im Labor: Robert Koch und die medizinische Bakteriologie* [Illness in the laboratory: Robert Koch and medical bacteriology] (2005).

22. Christoph Gradmann, "'Das Robert Koch-Institut hat genau den richtigen Namen'" [The Robert Koch Institute has exactly the right name], *Deutschlandfunk Kultur,* May 27, 2020.

23. Lachenal, *Lomidine Files,* 16, 149.

24. Isaac Brako and Seth Frimpong, "German Colonialism in West Africa: A Legacy of Mixed Results," in *Germany and Its West African Colonies,* ed. Wazi Apoh and Bea Lundt (2013), 226, 229.

Chapter 8: *The Dancing and Feasting Continued by Torchlight for Two Nights*

1. Hermann Hiery, *Fa'a Siamani: Germany in Micronesia, New Guinea and Samoa 1884–1914* (2020), 54.

2. Ibid., 11.

3. Ibid., 117.

4. Richard Parkinson, *Dreissig Jahre in der Südsee: Land und Leute, Sitten und Gebräuche im Bismarckarchipel und auf den deutschen Salomoinseln* [Thirty years in the South Seas: Country and people, customs and traditions in the Bismarck Archipelago and on the German Solomon Islands] (1907).

5. Hiery, *Fa'a Siamani,* 155.

6. Ibid., 156.

7. Nancy Viviani, *Nauru: Phosphate and Political Progress* (1970), 15, 22–23.

8. Hiery, *Fa'a Siamani,* 74.

9. Francis Hezel, *Strangers in Their Own Land: A Century of Colonial Rule in the Caroline and Marshall Islands* (1995), 98.

10. Paul Mark Ehrlich, "The Clothes of Men: Ponape Island and German Colonial Rule, 1899–1914" (1978), 220.

11. Hiery, *Fa'a Siamani,* 147.

12. Dirk Spennemann, "Trial and Error: The Introduction of Plants and Animals to German Micronesia 1885–1914," *Journal of Pacific History* (2019): 521–22.

13. Simon Haberberger, *Kolonialismus und Kannibalismus: Fälle aus Deutsch-Neuguinea und Britisch-Neuguinea 1884–1914* [Colonialism and cannibalism: Cases from German New Guinea and British New Guinea, 1884–1914] (2007).

14. Heinrich Schnee, *German Colonization, Past and Future* (1926), 115.

15. Richard Thurnwald, "Nachrichten aus Nissan und von den Karolinen" [News from Nissan and the Carolines], *Zeitschrift für Ethnologie* (1908).

16. Richard Thurnwald, "The Price of the White Man's Peace," *Pacific Affairs* (1936): 349.

17. Hiery, *Fa'a Siamani,* 52.

18. Ibid., 88.

19. Bernd Leicht, "Kannibalen in Deutsch-Neuguinea: der 'Andere' im kolonialzeitlichen Diskurs," [Cannibals in German New Guinea: The "other" in colonial discourse] (2000).

20. Shirley Lindenbaum, "Thinking about Cannibalism," *Annual Review of Anthropology* (2004).

21. Jaap Timmer, "Review of *Kolonialismus und Kannibalismus*," *Bijdragen tot de Taal-, Land- en Volkenkunde* (2009): 586.

22. Arthur Knoll and Hermann Hiery, eds., *The German Colonial Experience* (2010), 439–40.

23. Paul Hambruch, *Ponape: Ergebnisse der Südsee-Expedition 1908–1910* [Ponape: Results of the South Seas Expedition 1908–1910] (1932).

24. M. L. Berg, "'The Wandering Life among Unreliable Islanders': The Hamburg Südsee-Expedition in Micronesia," *Journal of Pacific History* (1988): 101.

25. Glenn Petersen, "Hambruch's Colonial Narrative: Pohnpei, German Culture Theory, and the Hamburg Expedition Ethnography of 1908–10," *Journal of Pacific History* (2007): 329, 327.

26. Glenn Petersen, *Traditional Micronesian Societies: Adaptation, Integration, and Political Organization* (2009), 148–56, 1.

27. Hiery, *Fa'a Siamani*, 82–83.

28. Ira Bashkow, "The Dynamics of Rapport in a Colonial Situation," in *Colonial Situations: Essays on the Contextualization of Ethnographic Knowledge*, ed. George Stocking (1991), 192–93, 195.

29. Arno Senfft, "Ethnographische Beitrage iiber die Karolineninsel Yap" [Ethnographic Contributions on the Caroline Island of Yap], *Dr. A. Petermanns Mitteilungen aus Justus Perthes Geographischer Anstalt* (1903); Arno Senfft, *Wörterverzeichnis der Sprachen der Marshall-Insulaner* [Dictionary of the languages of the Marshall Islanders] (1900).

30. Hezel, *Strangers in Their Own Land*, 107.

31. Hiery, *Fa'a Siamani*, 189.

32. Albert Hahl, *Zur Geschichte der kolonialen Betätigung der europäischen Völker* [On the history of the colonial activities of the European peoples] (1924).

33. Albert Hahl, "Deutschlands Schutzgebiete in der Südsee" [Germany's protected areas in the South Seas], in *Das Buch der deutschen Kolonien* [The book of German colonies], ed. Heinrich Schnee (1937).

34. Richard Deeken, "Die Deutschen Kolonien in der Sudsee" [German colonies in the South Seas], in *Dreißig Jahre deutsche Kolonialpolitik mit weltpolitischen Vergleichen und Ausblicken* [Thirty years of German colonial policy: With global political comparisons and perspectives], ed. Paul Leutwein (1913), 220.

35. Dirk Spennemann, *An Officer, Yes; But a Gentleman? A Biographical Sketch of Eugen Brandeis, Military Adviser, Imperial Judge and Administrator in the German Colonial Service in the South Pacific* (1998).

36. Hiery, *Fa'a Siamani*, 56, 68.

37. Peter Hempenstall, *Pacific Islanders under German Rule: A Study in the Meaning of Colonial Resistance* (1978), 117–18.

38. Albert Hahl, *Gouverneursjahre in Neuguinea* [Governor of New Guinea] (1937); also Albert Hahl, *Deutsche Kolonien in der Südsee* [German colonies in the South Seas] (1938).
39. Nigel Oram, "Review of Albert Hahl, *Governor of New Guinea*," *Journal of the Polynesian Society* (1982): 153.
40. Margarete Brüll, "Die deutschen Kolonien in der Südsee" [German colonies in the South Seas], freiburg-postkolonial.de, 1995, 6, 7, 15.
41. Hiery, *Fa'a Siamani*, 120
42. Ibid., 143
43. Ibid., 20.
44. Carl Eduard Michaelis, "Offenen Brief an den Pflanzerverein von Samoa [An open letter to the Samoa Planters' Association]," *Samoanische Zeitung*, April 1, 1911.
45. Matthew Fitzpatrick, "The Samoan Women's Revolt: Race, Intermarriage and Imperial Hierarchy in German Samoa," *German History* (2017).
46. Ian Campbell, "Resistance and Colonial Government: A Comparative Study of Samoa," *Journal of Pacific History* (2005): 52.
47. Arthur Knoll and Hermann Hiery, eds., *The German Colonial Experience: Select Documents on German Rule in Africa, China, and the Pacific 1884–1914* (2010), 103.
48. Hempenstall, *Pacific Islanders Under German Rule*, 25.
49. Hiery, *Fa'a Siamani*, 124.
50. Holger Droessler, "Copra World: Coconuts, Plantations and Cooperatives in German Samoa," *Journal of Pacific History* (2018).
51. Richard Scaglion, "Multiple Voices, Multiple Truths: Labour Recruitment in the Sepik Foothills of German New Guinea," *Journal of Pacific History* (2007): 351.
52. Commonwealth of Australia, *Report to the League of Nations on the Administration of the Territory of New Guinea, 1 July 1921 to 30 June 1922* (1923), 52.
53. Stewart Firth, *New Guinea under the Germans* (1983).
54. Hiery, *Fa'a Siamani*, 77, 150, 75.
55. Peter Sack, "A History of German New Guinea: A Debate about Evidence and Judgement," *Journal of Pacific History* (1985): 92, 94.
56. Judith Bennett, *Wealth of the Solomons: A History of a Pacific Archipelago, 1800–1978* (1987)
57. Peter Sack, "Who Wants to Know What 'Really' Happened? 'King' Gorai and the Population Decline in the Shortland Islands," *Journal of Pacific History* (2005).
58. Hiery, *Fa'a Siamani*, 101.
59. Götz Aly, *Das Prachtboot: Wie Deutsche die Kunstschätze der Südsee raubten* [The magnificent boat: How Germans stole the art treasures of the South Seas] (2021)

60. Günther Wessel, "Ein Diebstahl unter vielen? [One theft among many?]," *Deutschlandfunk Kultur,* May 25, 2021.

61. Rautenstrauch-Joest-Museum, "RESIST! Conversations: Götz Aly in Conversation with Stefan Koldehoff," RESIST!, June 11, 2021.

62. Ibid.

63. Hermann Hiery, *Das Deutsche Reich in der Südsee (1900–1921): Ein Annäherung an die Erfahrungen Verschiedener Kulturen* [The German empire in the South Seas (1900–1921): An approach to the experiences of different cultures] (1995).

64. Hermann Hiery, *The Neglected War: The German South Pacific and the Influence of World War I* (1995).

65. Peter Overlack, "Review of *Das Deutsche Reich in der Südsee*," Journal of Military History (2001): 810.

66. Hermann Hiery, "The Madang Revolt of 1904: A Chimera," *Small Wars and Insurgencies* (1993).

67. Hiery, *Fa'a Siamani*, 186, 168.

68. Klaus Neumann, "The Stench of the Past: Revisionism in Pacific Islands and Australian History," *Contemporary Pacific* (1998).

69. "Zehnjahresprogramm des Gouverneurs Solf, 1907," in *Handbuch der deutschen Südsee* 1884–1914 [Handbook of the German South Seas 1884–1914], ed. Hermann Hiery (1998), 663.

70. Corinna Erckenbrecht, "Die wissenschaftliche Aufarbeitung der deutschen Kolonialzeit in der Südsee. Kritische Bemerkungen zum Handbuch 'Die deutsche Südsee, 1884–1914'" [The scientific treatment of the German colonial era in the South Seas: Critical comments on the manual 'The German South Seas, 1884–1914'], *Anthropos* (2002): 178.

71. Gabriele Richter, "'Zake The Papuan Chief': An Alliance with a German Missionary in Colonial Kaiser-Wilhelmsland," in *German Colonialism Revisited: African, Asian, and Oceanic Experiences*, ed. Nina Berman, Klaus Mühlhahn, and Patrice Nganang, (2014).

72. Christian Keyßer, *Zake, der Papuahäuptling* [Zake the Papua chief] (1934).

73. Paul Hambruch, *Ponape: Ergebnisse der Südsee-Expedition 1908–1910* [Ponape: Results of the South Seas Expedition 1908–1910], vol. 1 (1932), 206.

74. Peter Hempenstall, *Pacific Islanders Under German Rule: A Study in the Meaning of Colonial Resistance* (1978), 221.

75. Ehrlich, "The Clothes of Men," 223.

76. Hiery, *Fa'a Siamani*, 196.

77. Thomas Morlang, *Rebellion in der Südsee: der Aufstand auf Ponape gegen die deutschen Kolonialherren 1910/11* [Rebellion in the South Seas: The uprising on Ponape against the German colonial rulers in 1910/11] (2010).

78. Pohnpei State Division of Historic Preservation and Cultural Affairs, *The Rehabilitation of the German Bell Tower: Final Project Report* (2000), 28.

Chapter 9: Ganbei! *How the Chinese Colonized Qingdao*

1. Baron Ferdinand von Richthofen, *Schantung und Seine Eingangspforte Kiautschou* [Shandong and its gateway Jiaozhou] (1898); "Germany and China: How Kiao-Chau Was Selected," *The Times* (London), December 11, 1907.

2. Qingdao was originally spelled Tsingtau or Tsingtao. The area of Jiaozhou was originally spelled Kiautschou or Kiaochow.

3. Heinrich Schmitthenner, "Kiautschau," *Geographische Zeitschrift* (1914): 664.

4. Fion Wai Ling So, *Germany's Colony in China: Colonialism, Protection and Economic Development in Qingdao and Shandong, 1898–1914* (2019), 12.

5. Annette Biener, *Das deutsche Pachtgebiet Tsingtau in Schantung, 1897–1914: Institutioneller Wandel durch Kolonialisierung* [German Qingdao, 1897–1914: Institutional change through colonization] (2001).

6. Wilhelm Schrameier, *Die deutsch-chinesischen Handelsbeziehungen* [Sino-German trade relations] (1917), 25–26.

7. Georg Crusen, "Die rechtliche Stellung der Chinesen in Kiautschou" [The legal status of the Chinese in Jiaozhou], *Zeitschrift für Kolonialrecht* (1913); "Moderne Gedanken im Chinesenstrafrecht des Kiautschougebietes" [Modern thoughts on the Chinese criminal law of Jiaozhou], *Mitteilungen der Internationalen Kriminalistischen Vereinigung* (1914).

8. Schmitthenner, "Kiautschau," 662; Heinrich Schmitthenner, *Chinesische Landschaften und Städte* [Chinese landscapes and cities] (1925); and Heinrich Schmitthenner, *China im Profil* [A profile of China] (1934).

9. Klaus Mühlhahn, *Herrschaft und Widerstand in der "Musterkolonie" Kiautschou: Interaktionen zwischen China und Deutschland, 1897–1914* [Rule and resistance in the "Model Colony" Jiaozhou: Interactions between China and Germany 1897–1914] (2000), 268–80.

10. George Steinmetz, *The Devil's Handwriting: Precoloniality and the German Colonial State in Qingdao, Samoa, and Southwest Africa* (2007), 442, 507.

11. The "Memorial of Zhou Fu to the Grand Council" of December 31, 1902, is held at the Institute for Modern History of the Academia Sinica in Taiwan.

12. Klaus Mühlhahn, "Mapping Colonial Space: The Planning and Building of Qingdao by German Colonial Authorities, 1897–1914," in *Harbin to Hanoi: Colonial Built Environment in Asia, 1840 to 1940*, ed. Laura Victoir and Victor Zatsepine (2013), 119.

13. Arthur Knoll and Hermann Hiery, eds., *The German Colonial Experience: Select Documents on German Rule in Africa, China, and the Pacific 1884–1914* (2010), 170.

14. Lina Mintzlaff, *Die Musterkolonie Kiautschou von 1897 bis 1914* [The model colony of Jiaozhou from 1897 to 1914] (2020).

15. So, *Germany's Colony in China*, 9, 12.

16. Sun Lixin, "The Formation of the Chinese Business Association in Qingdao under German Rule," *Provincial China* (2009).

17. Klaus Muhlhahn, "A New Imperial Vision? The Limits of German
     Colonialism in China," in *German Colonialism in a Golden Age*, ed. Bradley
     Naranch and Geoff Eley (2014), 146.

18. Jianjun Zhu, "Nationalism and Pragmatism: The Revolutionists in German
     Qingdao (1897–1914)," in *German Colonialism Revisited: African, Asian, and
     Oceanic Experiences*, ed. Nina Berman, Klaus Mühlhahn, and Patrice
     Nganang (2014), 190.

19. Wilhelm Schrameier, *Kiautschou: Seine Entwicklung und Bedeutung; Ein
     Rückblick* [Jiaozhou: Its development and significance: A review] (1915);
     Wilhelm Schrameier, *Hafenbetrieb und Hafenverwaltung Zu Tsingtau* [The
     port and port authority of Qingdao] (1904); Wilhelm Schrameier, *Aus
     Kiautschous Verwaltung* [On the administration of Jiaozhou] (1914).

20. Michael Silagi, "Land Reform in Kiaochow, China: From 1898 to 1914 the
     Menace of Disatrous Land Speculation Was Averted by Taxation," trans. Susan
     N. Faulkner, *American Journal of Economics and Sociology* (1984): 171.

21. Hal Schiffrin, "Sun Yat-sen's Early Land Policy," *Journal of Asian Studies* (1956),
     561.

Chapter 10: The "Shabby Annexations" of Versailles

1.   Vladimir Illych Lenin, *Imperialism: The Highest Stage of Capitalism* (1916), 123,
     77, 144.

2.   Comte de Pouvourville, "Deutsch-Franzoesische Beziehungen" [Franco-
     German relations], *Deutsche Kolonialzeitung* (1905), 302.

3.   Jens-Uwe Guettel, "Between Us and the French There Are No Profound
     Differences': Colonialism and the Possibilities of a Franco-German
     Rapprochement before 1914," *Historical Reflections* (2014).

4.   "German Colonial Policy," *The Times* (London), January 14, 1914.

5.   Victor Rothwell, *British War Aims and Peace Diplomacy, 1914–1918* (1971), 47, 72,
     74.

6.   Reinhard Klein-Arendt and Peter Sebald, *Kamina-des Kaisers Großfunkstation
     in Afrika Telefunken in der deutschen Kolonie Togo 1911–1914* [Kamina: The
     emperor's large radio station in Africa: Telefunken in German Togo, 1911–1914]
     (2019).

7.   Jacqueline de Vries, "Cameroonian Schutztruppe Soldiers in Spanish-Ruled
     Fernando Po During the First World War: A 'Menace to the Peace'?," *War &
     Society* (2018)

8.   Hans Poeschel, *Die Koloniale Frage im Frieden von Versailles* [Colonial
     questions at Versailles] (1920), 242–43.

9.   Heinrich Schnee, *Die deutschen Kolonien vor, in und nach dem Weltkrieg* [The
     German colonies before, during and after the Great War] (1935), chapter 1,
     section 5.

10. Woodruff Smith, *The German Colonial Empire* (1978), 163.

11. Michael Pesek, "Colonial Heroes: German Colonial Identities in Wartime, 1914–18," in *German Colonialism and National Identity*, ed. Jürgen Zimmerer and Michael Perraudin (2011), 128.
12. Schnee, *Die deutschen*, chapter 1, section 5.
13. Heinrich Schnee, *Deutsch-Ostafrika im Weltkriege: Wie wir lebten und kämpften* [German East Africa in the world war: How we lived and fought] (1919); see also Katharina Abermeth, *Heinrich Schnee: Karrierewege und Erfahrungswelten eines deutschen Kolonialbeamten* [Heinrich Schnee: Career paths and experiences of a German colonial official] (2017).
14. Heinrich Schnee, *German Colonization Past and Future: The Truth about the German Colonies* (1926), 168.
15. Rémy Porte, "La Défense des Colonies Allemandes Avant 1914: Entre Mythe et Réalités" [The defense of German colonies before 1914: Between myth and reality], *Revue Historique des Armées* (2013).
16. Schnee, *Die deutschen Kolonien*, chapter 1, section 6.
17. Victor Rothwell, *British War Aims and Peace Diplomacy, 1914–18* (1971), 69.
18. Otto von Gottberg, *Die Helden von Tsingtau* [The Heroes of Quingdao] (1915).
19. Frank John Maclean, *Germany's Colonial Failure: Her Rule in Africa Condemned on German Evidence* (1918).
20. David Fieldhouse, *The Colonial Empires: A Comparative Survey from the Eighteenth Century* (1966), 235, 371.
21. William Crabtree, "Togoland," *Journal of the Royal African Society* (1915): 176.
22. William D'Avenant, *The Cruelty of the Spaniards in Peru: A Masque in Six Entries* (1658); Janet Clare, "The Production and Reception of Davenant's 'Cruelty of the Spaniards in Peru,'" *Modern Language Review* (1994).
23. René Puaux, *La Question des Colonies Allemandes* [The issue of German colonies] (1918).
24. Hugh Clifford, *German Colonies: A Plea for the Native Races* (1918), 113.
25. Great Britain, Public Records Office, PRO CO 537/1–17, "Telegram from Mr. Long to Australia, New Zealand and South Africa," January 4, 1918.
26. Charles Dundas, *A History of German East Africa* (1923).
27. Charles Fletcher, *Stevenson's Germany: The Case Against Germany in the Pacific* (1920), viii.
28. Great Britain, House of Parliament, *Correspondence Relating to the Wishes of the Natives of the German Colonies As to Their Future Government* (1918), 25, 26, 57, 24.
29. Great Britain, House of Parliament, *Treatment of Natives in the German Colonies* (1919).
30. William Harbutt Dawson, introduction in *German Colonization: Past and Future*, ed. Heinrich Schnee (1926), 20.
31. Ibid., 68.
32. Great Britain, Foreign Office, *Report on the Natives of South West Africa and their Treatment by Germany* (1918).

33. Edmund Morel, *The Black Man's Burden: The White Man in Africa from the Fifteenth Century to World War I* (1920), 56–57.
34. Reich Colonial Office, *Die Behandlung der einheimischen Bevölkerung in den kolonialen Besitzungen Deutschlands und Englands. Eine Erwiderung auf das englische Blaubuch vom August 1918* [The treatment of the native populations in the colonies of Germany and Britain: A reply to the British Blue Book of August 1918] (1919).
35. Schnee, *German Colonization*, 175–76.
36. Dawson, introduction in *German Colonization*, 31, 25, 27.
37. Office of the Historian, "The Covenant of the League of Nations (Art. 1 to 26)," 1919, article 22, https://history.state.gov/historicaldocuments/frus1919Parisv13/ch10subch1.
38. Arthur Dix, *Was Deutschland an seinen Kolonien verlor* [What Germany lost in its colonies] (1926), 14; Arthur Dix, *Schluss mit "Europa"!: Ein Wegweiser durch Weltgeschichte zu Weltpolitik* [The end of "Europe": A guide through world history and politics] (1928).

Chapter 11: Why the Loss of Colonies Doomed German Liberalism

1. Great Britain, Public Records Office, FO 800/256, Lugard to Chamberlain, November 29, 1924.
2. William Harbutt Dawson, introduction in *German Colonization Past and Future: The Truth about the German Colonies*, ed. Heinrich Schnee (1926), 31, 25, 27.
3. William Shirer, *The Rise and Fall of the Third Reich* (1960), 89.
4. Dirk Schumann, "Europa, der Erste Weltkrieg und die Nachkriegszeit. Eine Kontinuität der Gewalt?" [Europe, the First World War, and the postwar period: A continuity of violence?], *Journal of Modern European History* (2003).
5. "The Future Of Kiao-Chau," *The Times* (London), August 12, 1907; see also Ernst Count Reventlow, *Weltfrieden oder Weltkrieg! Wohin geht Deutschlands Weg?* [World peace or world war! Where is Germany going?] (1907).
6. Heinrich Schnee, *Deutsches Kolonial-Lexikon* [Lexicon of German colonialism] (1920).
7. Erich Schultz-Ewerth and Leonhard Adam, *Das Eingeborenenrecht: Sitten und Gewohnheitsrechte der Eingeborenen der ehemaligen deutschen Kolonien in Afrika und in der Südsee* [Indigenous law: Customs and customary rights of the natives of the former German colonies in Africa and the South Seas] (1929).
8. David Thomas Murphy, *The Heroic Earth: Geopolitical Thought in Weimar Germany, 1918–1933* (1997), 92.
9. Ibid., 95.
10. Hermann Hiery, *Das Deutsche Reich in der Südsee (1900–1921): Eine Annäherung an die Erfahrungen Verschiedener Kulturen* [The German empire in the South Seas (1900–1921): An approach to the experiences of different cultures] (1995), 312.

11. Heinrich Schnee, *Die deutschen Kolonien vor, in und nach dem Weltkrieg* [The German colonies before, during and after the Great War] (1935), chapter 2, section 6.

12. Heinrich Schnee, *Die koloniale Schuldlüge* [The myth of colonial guilt] (1924).

13. "German Claim to Colonies," *The Times* (London), June 28, 1926.

14. George Padmore, *Pan-Africanism or Communism? The Coming Struggle for Africa* (1956).

15. Fredrik Petersson, *Willi Münzenberg, the League against Imperialism, and the Comintern, 1925–1933,* vol. 2 (2013), 973, 974, 976.

16. Theodore Draper, *American Communism and Soviet Russia* (1960), 321.

17. Mary Grabar, *Debunking Howard Zinn* (2019), 169.

18. Petersson, *Willi Münzenberg,* 238.

19. Ibid., 251–52, 245.

20. Sean McMeekin, *The Red Millionaire: A Political Biography of Willi Münzenberg, Moscow's Secret Propaganda Tsar in the West* (2005), 194.

21. Fredrik Petersson, "Hub of the Anti-Imperialist Movement: The League against Imperialism and Berlin, 1927–1933," *Interventions: The International Journal of Postcolonial Studies* (2014): 58.

22. Michele Louro, *Comrades Against Imperialism: Nehru, India, and Interwar Internationalism* (2018), 1.

23. Sean Andrew Wempe, *Revenants of the German Empire: Colonial Germans, Imperialism, and the League of Nations* (2019),184, 162, 183.

24. Schnee, *Die deutschen Kolonien,* chapter 3.

25. Konstanty Gilwicki and Erhard Jansen, *Die Enteignung des Deutschen Kolonialbesitzes* [The expropriation of German colonial property] (1937); Harro Brenner, *Wem hat Deutschland seine Kolonien aufgrund des Versailles Diktats überlassen?* [Who did Germany leave its colonies to under the dictates of Versailles?] (1938); Lotar Kühne, *Das Kolonialverbrechen von Versailles* [The colonial crime of Versailles] (1939).

26. Daniel Gorman, "Ecumenical Internationalism: Willoughby Dickinson, the League of Nations and the World Alliance for Promoting International Friendship Through the Churches," *Journal of Contemporary History* (2010).

27. Wempe, *Revenants of the German Empire,* 17.

28. Ibid., 211, 210.

29. McMeekin, *The Red Millionaire,* 1.

30. Daniel Brückenhaus, *Policing Transnational Protest: Liberal Imperialism and the Surveillance of Anticolonialists in Europe, 1905–1945* (2017), 204, 194.

31. Ibid., 170, 217.

32. "German Claim for Colonies," *The Times* (London), June 17, 1933.

33. Richard Evans, *The Coming of the Third Reich* (2003), 372.

34. "A Strange Contribution," *The Times* (London), June 19, 1933.

35. "German Claim to Colonies," *The Times* (London), May 30, 1934.

36. Schnee, *Die deutschen Kolonien,* chapter 3.

37. Lewis Gann, "Marginal Colonialism: The German Case," in *Germans in the Tropics: Essays in German Colonial History*, ed. Arthur Knoll and Lewis Gann (1987), 15.

38. William Harbutt Dawson, "The Future of Germany," *The Times* (London), March 7, 1944.

39. Isabel Hull, *Absolute Destruction: Military Culture and the Practices of War in Imperial Germany* (2013), 332.

40. Heinrich Schnee, ed., *Das Buch der deutschen Kolonien* [The big book of German colonies] (1933, 1936, 1937, 1938).

41. Theodor Seitz, "Notwendigkeit deutscher Kolonialpolitik" [The need for a German colonial policy], in *Das Buch der deutschen Kolonien*.

42. Karl Haushofer, Erich Obst, and Hermann Lautensach, *Bausteine zur Geopolitik* [Building blocks for geo-politics] (1928), 286.

43. Murphy, *The Heroic Earth*, 191.

44. Ibid., 192.

45. Nathanael Kuck, "Anti-Colonialism in a Post-Imperial Environment—The Case of Berlin, 1914–33," *Journal of Contemporary History* (2014), 155.

46. Gerhard Ritter, *Europa und die Deutsche Frage: Betrachtungen über die geschichtliche Eigenart des deutschen Staatsdenkens* [Europe and the German question: Reflections on the historical characteristics of German state thought] (1948).

47. Russell Berman, *Enlightenment or Empire: Colonial Discourse in German Culture* (1998), chapter 6.

Chapter 12: Nazi Anti-Colonialism and the War on Europe

1. Gerhard Wolf, *Ideologie und Herrschaftsrationalität: Nationalsozialistische Germanisierungspolitik in Westpolen* [Ideology and rational rationality: National Socialist Germanization policy in Western Poland] (2012), 11.

2. Klaus Hildebrand, *Vom Reich Zum Weltreich: Hitler, NSDAP und koloniale Frage 1919–1945* [From Reich to world empire: Hitler, Nazi Party and colonial question 1919–1945] (1969).

3. Heinrich Schnee, *Als letzter Gouverneur in Deutsch-Ostafrika: Erinnerungen* [Memoirs of the last governor of East Africa] (1964), 181.

4. Adolf Hitler; Christian Hartmann et al., eds., *Hitler, Mein Kampf. Eine kritische Edition* [Hitler, Mein Kampf: A critical edition], vol.1, (2016), 398.

5. Chunjie Zhang, *Transculturality and German Discourse in the Age of European Colonialism* (2017).

6. Birthe Kundrus, "Colonialism, Imperialism, National Socialism: How Imperial was the Third Reich?" in *German Colonialism in a Golden Age*, ed. Bradley Naranch and Geoff Eley (2014), 337.

7. Christian Davis, *Colonialism, Antisemitism, and Germans of Jewish Descent in Imperial Germany* (2012), 4.

8. David Thomas Murphy, *The Heroic Earth: Geopolitical Thought in Weimar Germany, 1918–1933* (1997), 211.

9. Lavoslav Glesinger, "Robert Koch and the Jews," *Hebrew Medical Journal* (1963).

10. Davis, *Colonialism, Antisemitism, and Germans of Jewish Descent*, 136, 247.

11. Ernst Count Reventlow, *Indien: Seine Bedeutung für Großbritannien, Deutschland und die Zukunft der Welt* [India: Its importance to Britain, Germany, and the future of the world] (1917).

12. Ernst Count Reventlow, *Völkisch-kommunistische Einigung?* [Ethno-communist unification?] (1924).

13. Wolfgang Schwanitz, "Photographic Evidence Shows Palestinian Leader Amin al-Husseini at a Nazi Concentration Camp," *Tablet*, April 6, 2021.

14. Yannick Lengkeek, "Staged Glory: The Impact of Fascism on 'Cooperative' Nationalist Circles in Late Colonial Indonesia, 1935–1942," *Fascism* (2018): 113.

15. Andrew Selth, "Race and Resistance in Burma, 1942–1945," *Modern Asian Studies* (1986).

16. Lengkeek, "Staged Glory."

17. Ibid.

18. Romain Hayes, *Subhas Chandra Bose in Nazi Germany: Politics, Intelligence and Propaganda 1941–43* (2011); Tilak Raj Sareen, *Subhas Chandra Bose and Nazi Germany* (1996).

19. Talat Ahmed, "Fascism, War, Independence and Partition: 1939–48," in *Mohandas Gandhi: Experiments in Civil Disobedience* (2019).

20. Łukasz Hirszowicz, *III Rzesza i arabski Wschód* [The Third Reich and the Arab East] (1963).

21. Jeffrey Herf, *Nazi Propaganda for the Arab World* (2009); Klaus-Michael Mallman and Martin Cüppers, *Nazi Palestine: The Plans for the Extermination of the Jews in Palestine* (2010).

22. David Motadel, "Review of *Arab Responses to Fascism and Nazism*," *Middle Eastern Studies* (2016): 377.

23. Israel Gershoni, introduction in *Arab Responses to Fascism and Nazism: Attraction and Repulsion*, ed. Israel Gershoni (2014), 3.

24. Thomas Kehoe and Elizabeth Greenhalgh, "Living Propaganda and Self-Serving Recruitment: The Nazi Rationale for the German-Arab Training Unit, May 1941 to May 1943," *War in History* (2017): 526.

25. Kundrus, "Colonialism, Imperialism, National Socialism."

26. Eliezer Be'eri, *Army Officers in Arab Politics and Society* (1970), 45.

27. Edwin Black, "When Iraq Expelled Its Jews to Israel," *Jerusalem Post*, June 7, 2016; see also Edwin Black, *The Farhud: Roots of the Arab-Nazi Alliance in the Holocaust* (2010).

28. Jeffrey Herf, "Haj Amin al-Husseini, the Nazis and the Holocaust: The Origins, Nature and Aftereffects of Collaboration," *Jewish Political Studies Review* (2014).

29. Great Britain, Foreign Office, Documents on German Foreign Policy 1918–1945, series D, vol. XIII (1964).

30. Philip Mattar, "The Mufti of Jerusalem and the Politics of Palestine," *Middle East Journal* (1988): 237.

31. Jeffrey Herf, "Nazi Germany's Propaganda Aimed at Arabs and Muslims during World War II and the Holocaust: Old Themes, New Archival Findings," *Central European History* (2009): 709, 721.

32. René Wildangel, "The Invention of 'Islamofascism': Nazi Propaganda to the Arab World and Perceptions from Palestine," *Die Welt des Islams* (2012): 539.

33. Joy Bernard, "Never-Before-Seen Document Penned by Nazi Leader Himmler Uncovered in Israel," *Jerusalem Post*, March 29, 2017.

34. Ofer Aderet, "Never-Before-Seen Photos of Palestinian Mufti with Hitler Ties Visiting Nazi Germany," *Haaretz*, June 15, 2017.

35. Joel Fishman, "The Recent Discovery of Heinrich Himmler's Telegram of November 2, 1943, the Anniversary of the Balfour Declaration, to Amin al-Husseini, Mufti of Jerusalem," *Jewish Political Studies Review* (2016): 84.

36. René Wildangel, "More than the Mufti: Other Arab-Palestinian Voices on Nazi Germany, 1933–1945, and Their Postwar Narrations," in *Arab Responses to Fascism and Nazism*.

37. Tendai Ruben Mbofana, "At Least Zimbabwe Regime Subtly Admitting Its Grand Failure!" *The Zimbabwean*, November 19, 2021.

38. Panayiotis Vatikiotis, *The History of Modern Egypt* (1969).

39. Ami Ayalon, "Egyptian Intellectuals versus Fascism and Nazism in the 1930s," in *The Great Powers in the Middle East, 1919–1939*, ed. Uriel Dann (1988), 402.

40. Gershoni, *Arab Responses to Fascism and Nazism*, 25.

41. Götz Nordbruch, "A Challenge to the Local Order: Reactions to Nazism in the Syrian and Lebanese Press," in *Arab Responses to Fascism and Nazism*, 53.

42. Haggai Erlich, "The Tiger and the Lion: Fascism and Ethiopia in Arab Eyes," in *Arab Responses to Fascism and Nazism*.

43. Andrew J. Crozier, *Appeasement and Germany's Last Bid for Colonies* (1988).

44. George Steer, *Judgement on German Africa* (1939); Ferdinand Joelson, *Germany's Claim to Colonies* (1939).

45. Sean Andrew Wempe, *Revenants of the German Empire: Colonial Germans, Imperialism, and the League of Nations* (2019), 219.

46. Karsten Linne, Deutschland jenseits des Äquators?: Die NS-Kolonialplanungen für Afrika [Germany beyond the equator? Nazi colonial planning for Africa] (2008).

47. Hitler; Hartmann et al., eds., *Hitler, Mein Kampf*, 432.

48. Willeke Sandler, *Empire in the Heimat: Colonialism and Public Culture in the Third Reich* (2018), 183.

49. Heinrich Schnee, *Die deutschen Kolonien vor, in und nach dem Weltkrieg* [The German colonies before, during and after the Great War] (1935), chapter 3.

50. Wempe, *Revenants of the German Empire*, 211.

51. Matthew Fitzpatrick, "The Pre-History of the Holocaust? The *Sonderweg* and *Historikerstreit* Debates and the Abject Colonial Past," *Central European History* (2008): 489.

52. Wempe, *Revenants of the German Empire*, 223.

53. Louise Diel, *Die Kolonien warten!* [The colonies are waiting!] (1939)

54. Louise Diel, *Mädels im Tropenhelm* [Girls in pith helmets] (1941).

55. Louise Diel, *Sieh unser neues Land mit offenen Augen: Italienisch-Ostafrika* [See our new country with open eyes: Italian East Africa] (1938).

56. Eric Roubinek, *Re-Imagined Communities: Racial, National, and Colonial Visions in National Socialist Germany and Fascist Italy, 1933–1943* (2014), 79–91.

57. Willeke Sandler, "Colonial Education in the Third Reich: The Witzenhausen Colonial School and the Rendsburg Colonial School for Women," *Central European History* (2016): 187, 193, 201.

58. Martin Kitchen, "Review of *Vom Reich zum Weltreich: Hitler, NSDAP und Koloniale Frage 1919–1945,*" *American Historical Review* (1970): 1743.

59. Arne Perras, *Carl Peters and German Imperialism 1856–1918: A Political Biography* (2004), 247

60. Hannah Arendt, *The Origins of Totalitarianism* (1951), 206.

61. Russell Berman, "Colonialism, and No End: The Other Continuity Theses," in *German Colonialism: Race, the Holocaust, and Postwar Germany,* ed. Voker Langbehn and Mohammad Salama (2011), 179.

62. Shelley Baranowski, *Nazi Empire: German Colonialism and Imperialism from Bismarck to Hitler* (2011), 49.

63. Thomas Kehoe and Elizabeth Greenhalgh, "Living Propaganda and Self-Serving Recruitment: The Nazi Rationale for the German-Arab Training Unit, May 1941 to May 1943," *War in History* (2017): 535.

64. Sarah Ehlers, *Europa und die Schlafkrankheit: koloniale Seuchenbekämpfung, europäische Identitäten und moderne Medizin 1890–1950* [Europe and sleeping sickness: Colonial disease control, European identities and modern medicine 1890–1950] (2019).

65. Annette Hinz-Wessels and Marion Hulverscheidt, "Die Tropenmedizinische Abteilung des Robert Koch-Instituts im 'Dritten Reich': Forschungsfelder, Personen und Beiträge zur nationalsozialistischen Eroberungspolitik" [The department for tropical medicine of the Robert Koch-Institute during the "Third Reich": Research areas, actors, and contributions to Nazi expansionist politics], *Medizinhistorisches Journal* (2009).

66. Christian Davis, *Colonialism, Antisemitism, and Germans of Jewish Descent in Imperial Germany* (2012), 26.

67. Erik Grimmer-Solem, *Learning Empire: Globalization and the German Quest for World Status, 1875–1919* (2019).

68. Henry Cord Meyer, "Review of *Dream of Empire: German Colonialism, 1919–1945,*" *American Historical Review* (1965): 236.

69. Wolfe Schmokel, *Dream of Empire: German Colonialism, 1919–1945* (1964), 22.

70. Daniel Brückenhaus, *Policing Transnational Protest: Liberal Imperialism and the Surveillance of Anticolonialists in Europe, 1905–1945* (2017), 194.

71. Lewis Gann, "Heinrich Schnee (1871–1949)," in *African Proconsuls: European Governors in Africa*, ed. Lewis Gann and Peter Duignan (1978), 519.

72. Schnee, *Als letzter Gouverneur in Deutsch-Ostafrika*, 179, 181.

73. Ernst Rodenwaldt, *Die Mestizen auf Kisar* [The mestizos of Kisar] (1927); Hans Pols and Warwick Anderson, "The Mestizos of Kisar: An Insular Racial Laboratory in the Malay Archipelago," *Journal of Southeast Asian Studies* (2018).

74. Wempe, *Revenants of the German Empire*, 20.

75. Helmut Walser Smith, *The Continuities of German History: Nation, Religion, and Race across the Long Nineteenth Century* (2008).

76. Horst Drechsler, *Südwestafrika unter deutscher Kolonialherrschaft: Der Kampf der Herero und Nama gegen den deutschen Imperialismus (1884–1915)* [Southwest Africa under German colonial rule: The struggle of the Herero and Nama against German imperialism (1884–1915)] (1966).

77. Horst Kühne, *Faschistische Kolonialideologie und zweiter Weltkrieg* [Fascist colonial ideology and World War II] (1962); Peter Schmitt-Egner, *Kolonialismus und Faschismus: Eine Studie zur historischen und begrifflichen Genesis faschistischer Bewusstseinsformen an deutschen Beispiel* [Colonialism and fascism: A study of the historical and conceptual Genesis of fascist forms of consciousness using German examples] (1975).

78. Jürgen Zimmerer and Joachim Zeller, *Völkermord in Deutsch-Südwestafrika: der Kolonialkrieg (1904–1908) in Namibia und seine Folgen* [Genocide in German Southwest Africa: The Colonial War (1904–1908) in Namibia and its consequences] (2003); Jürgen Zimmerer, "Colonialism and the Holocaust. Towards an Archeology of Genocide," in *Genocide and Settler Society*, ed. Dirk Moses (2004).

79. Jürgen Zimmerer, *Von Windhuk nach Auschwitz?: Beiträge zum Verhältnis von Kolonialismus und Holocaust* [From Windhoek to Auschwitz?: Contributions to the relationship between colonialism and the Holocaust] (2011); *From Windhoek to Auschwitz: On the Relationship Between Colonialism and the Holocaust* (2015).

80. Jürgen Zimmerer, "Holocaust und Kolonialismus—Beitrag zu einer Archaologie des genozidalen Gedankens" [Holocaust and colonialism: Contribution to an archeology of genocidal thought], *Zeitschrift für Geschichtswissenschaft* (2003): 1118.

81. Elizabeth Baer, *The Genocidal Gaze: From German Southwest Africa to the Third Reich* (2017); Klaus Bachmann, *Genocidal Empires: German Colonialism in Africa and the Third Reich* (2018); Carroll Kakel, *The Holocaust as Colonial Genocide: Hitler's 'Indian Wars' in the 'Wild East'* (2013); David Olusoga and Casper Erichsen, *Kaiser's Holocaust: Germany's Forgotten Genocide and the Colonial Roots of Nazism* (2010); Benjamin Madley, "From Africa to Auschwitz: How German South West Africa Incubated Ideas and Methods

Adopted and Developed by the Nazis in Eastern Europe," *European History Quarterly* (2005).

82. Baer, *Genocidal Gaze*, 132, 134.
83. Reinhart Kossler, *Namibia and Germany: Negotiating the Past* (2015), 120–21.
84. Bachmann, *Genocidal Empires*.
85. Marie Muschalek, "Review of *Genocidal Empires*," *American Historical Review* (2020): 1533.
86. Roberta Pergher and Mark Roseman, "The Holocaust: An Imperial Genocide?," *Dapim: Studies on the Holocaust* (2013): 44, 43.
87. Michael Mann, *The Dark Side of Democracy: Explaining Ethnic Cleansing* (2005), 225–78.
88. Robert Gerwarth and Stephan Malinowski, "Hannah Arendt's Ghosts: Reflections on the Disputable Path from Windhoek to Auschwitz," *Central European History* (2009): 285, 300.

Chapter 13: Communist Anti-Colonialism and the Division of Europe

1. Robert Cornevin, *Histoire de la colonisation allemande* [A history of German colonialism] (1969), 122.
2. Heinrich Schnee, *Als letzter Gouverneur in Deutsch-Ostafrika: Erinnerungen* [Memoirs of the last governor of East Africa] (1964).
3. Marco Sennholz, *Johann von Leers: ein Propagandist des Nationalsozialismus* [Johann von Leers: Nazi Propagandist] (2013).
4. Joel Fishman, "The Postwar Career of Nazi Ideologue, Johann von Leers, aka Omar Amin, the 'First Ranking German' in Nasser's Egypt," *Jewish Political Studies Review* (2014): 64, 68.
5. Alain de Benoist, *Racismes, Antiracismes* (1986).
6. Egon Flaig, "Faschistoider Antikolonialismus: Frantz Fanon" [The fascist anti-colonialism of Frantz Fanon], in *Die Niederlage der politischen Vernunft: Wie wir die Errungenschaften der Aufklärung verspielen* [The defeat of political reason: How we have gambled away the achievements of the Enlightenment] (2017).
7. Fratz Fanon, *The Wretched of the Earth* (1961), 34, 8.
8. Mathilde Von Bülow, *West Germany, Cold War Europe and the Algerian War* (2016), 117–19.
9. Ingo Cornils, "Denkmalsturz : The German Student Movement and German Colonialism," in *German Colonialism and National Identity*, ed. Juergen Zimmerer and Michael Perraudin (2011), 200–201.
10. Zhiguo Yang, "'This Beer Tastes Really Good': Nationalism, Consumer Culture and Development of the Beer Industry in Qingdao, 1903–1993," *Chinese Historical Review* (2007).

11. Edgar Winans, "The Head of the King: Museums and the Path to Resistance," *Comparative Studies in Society and History* (1994): 235.

12. Alison Redmayne, "Mkwawa and the Hehe Wars," *Journal of African History* (1968): 436.

13. Michael Gleave, "The Dar es Salaam Transport Corridor: An Appraisal," *African Affairs* (1992).

14. Arthur Knoll and Hermann Hiery, eds., *The German Colonial Experience: Select Documents on German Rule in Africa, China, and the Pacific 1884–1914* (2010), 495.

15. Sean Andrew Wempe, *Revenants of the German Empire: Colonial Germans, Imperialism, and the League of Nations* (2019), 229.

16. Dennis Laumann, "A Historiography of German Togoland, or the Rise and Fall of a 'Model Colony,'" *History in Africa* (2003): 205–6.

17. Horst Drechsler, *Südwestafrika unter deutscher Kolonialherrschaft: Der Kampf der Herero und Nama gegen den deutschen Imperialismus (1884–1915)* [Southwest Africa under German colonial rule: The struggle of the Herero and Nama against German imperialism (1884–1915)] (1966).

18. Ulrich van der Heyden, "Die Afrika—Geschichtsschreibung in der ehemaligen DDR: Versuch einer kritischen Aufarbeitung" [Africa historiography in the former GDR: Attempting a critical reappraisal], *Africa Spectrum* (1992): 207, 210–11.

19. Helmuth Stoecker, *Kamerun unter deutscher Kolonialherrschaft*, vol. 1 [Cameroon under German colonial rule] (1960, 1968).

20. Charlotte Leubuscher, "Review of *Kamerun unter Deutscher Kolonialherrschaft*," *Journal of African History* (1961): 353.

21. Lewis Gann, "Review of *South-West Africa Under German Rule 1894–1914*," *International Journal of African Historical Studies* (1973): 123.

22. Volker Langbehn, "Ferdinand Oyono's *Flüchtige Spur Tundi Ondua* and Germany's Cameroon," *Publications of the Modern Language Association of America* (2013): 143.

23. Joachim Zeller, "Review of *Deutsche Kolonialgeschichte(n). Der Genozid in Namibia und die Geschichtsschreibung der DDR und BRD*," *Monatshefte* (2018): 479.

24. Miriam Müller, *A Spectre is Haunting Arabia: How the Germans Brought Their Communism to Yemen* (2015), 277, 292.

25. Fred Halliday, "Catastrophe in South Yemen: A Preliminary Assessment," *MERIP Middle East Report* (1986): 37–38.

26. Noel Brehony, "From Chaos to Chaos: South Yemen 50 Years After the British Departure," *Asian Affairs* (2017).

27. Sascha Wisotzki, *Die Unterstützung der SWAPO von Namibia durch die DDR in den Jahren 1975 bis 1989* [The GDR's support for SWAPO in Namibia, 1975–1989] (2008).

28. Jens Gerlach, *Der Herero-Aufstand und die anderen* Deutschen [The Herero Uprising and the other Germans] (2005).

29. Roland Wingert, *Schwarzer Mohn: das Leben und Denken eines Aufklärers der DDR in Südwest-Afrika* [Black Poppy: The life and thinking of an enlightener of the GDR in Southwest Africa] (2006).

30. John Saul and Colin Leys, "Lubango and After: 'Forgotten History' as Politics in Contemporary Namibia," *Journal of Southern African Studies* (2003).

31. Henning Melber, "Germany and Namibia: Negotiating Genocide," *Journal of Genocide Research* (2020): 505, 512.

32. Thomas Falk et. al., "The Profits of Excludability and Transferability in Redistributive Land Reform in Central Namibia," *Development Southern Africa* (2017).

33. Henning Melber, "Colonialism, Land, Ethnicity, and Class: Namibia after the Second National Land Conference," *Africa Spectrum* (2019): 76.

34. Ibid.

35. Wolfgang Geiger and Henning Melber, *Kritik des deutschen Kolonialismus: Postkoloniale Sicht auf Erinnerung und Geschichtsvermittlung Broschiert* [A critique of German colonialism: Postcolonial views of remembrance and the transmission of history] (2021).

36. Tanja Müller, "'Memories of Paradise'—Legacies of Socialist Education in Mozambique," *African Affairs* (2010): 470.

37. Toni Weis, "The Politics Machine: On the Concept of 'Solidarity' in East German Support for SWAPO," *Journal of Southern African Studies* (2011): 363, 366.

38. Peter Katjavivi, "The Establishment of a Documentation and Research Centre on the History of the Anti-Colonial Resistance and the Liberation Struggle of the Namibian people," in *MBEC/GTZ Draft Report on the Preservation of a Namibian Heritage* (2000).

39. Siegfried Groth, *Namibische Passion: Tragik und Grösse der namibischen Befreiungsbewegung* [Namibian passion: The tragedy and magnitude of the Namibian Liberation Movement] (1995). The English translation was given a more frank title: *Namibia, The Wall of Silence: The Dark Days of the Liberation Struggle.*

40. Luís Madureira, "'Kalashnikovs, Not Coca-Cola, Bring Self-Determination to Angola': The Two Germanys, Lusophone Africa, and the Rhetoric of Colonial Difference," in *German Colonialism: Race, the Holocaust, and Postwar Germany,* ed. Voker Langbehn and Mohammad Salama (2011).

41. Gareth Winrow, *The Foreign Policy of the GDR in Africa* (1990), 196.

42. Jeff Haynes, "Review of *The Foreign Policy of the GDR in Africa,*" *Journal of Modern African Studies* (1992): 713.

43. Matthias Voß, *Wir haben Spuren hinterlassen!: Die DDR in Mosambik; Erlebnisse, Erfahrungen und Erkenntnisse aus drei Jahrzehnten* [We left our

mark! The GDR in Mozambique; experiences and knowledge from three decades] (2005).

44. Paul Friedländer, *Der Neokolonialismus der westdeutschen Bundesrepublik: Eine Dokumentation* [The neocolonialism of West Germany: Documentation] (1965).

45. Rui Lopes, *West Germany and the Portuguese Dictatorship: Between Cold War and Colonialism* (2014).

46. George Gretton, "Review of *Westdeutscher Neokolonialismus: Untersuchungen uber die wirtschaftliche und politische Expansion des westdeutschen Imperialismus in Afrika und Asien*," *International Affairs* (1964): 530.

47. Young-sun Hong, *Cold War Germany, the Third World, and the Global Humanitarian Regime* (2015).

48. Melvin Croan, *DDR-Neokolonialismus in Afrika* [GDR neo-colonialism in Africa] (1981).

Chapter 14: Woke Anti-Colonialism and the Hollowing of Europe

1. Joschka Fischer, "Speech at the World Conference against Racism, Racial Discrimination, Xenophobia and Related Intolerance," Durban, September 1, 2001.

2. Joachim Zeller, "Review of *Deutsche Kolonialgeschichte(n). Der Genozid in Namibia und die Geschichtsschreibung der DDR und BRD*," *Monatshefte* (2018): 479.

3. German Museums Association, *Guidelines for German Museums Care of Collections from Colonial Contexts* (2021), 12, 23.

4. Egon Flaig, "Faschistoider Antikolonialismus: Frantz Fanon" [The fascist anti-colonialism of Frantz Fanon], in *Die Niederlage der politischen Vernunft: Wie wir die Errungenschaften der Aufklärung verspielen* [The defeat of political reason: How we have gambled away the achievements of the Enlightenment] (2017).

5. Egon Flaig, "Memorialgesetze und historisches Unrecht. Wie Gedächtnispolitik die historische Wissenschaft bedroht" [Memorial laws and historical injustice: How memory politics threatens historical science], *Historische Zeitschrift* (2016).

6. Reinhart Kössler, *Namibia and Germany: Negotiating the Past* (2015), 71.

7. Bartholomäus Grill, *"Wir Herrenmenschen": Unser rassistisches Erbe; Eine Reise in die deutsche Kolonialgeschichte* ["We gentlemen": Our racist legacy: A journey into German colonial history] (2019).

8. Andreas Kilb, "Review of *"Wir Herrenmenschen",*" *Frankfurter Allgemeine Zeitung*, April 17, 2019.

9. Olaf Zimmermann and Theo Geißler, eds., *Kolonialismus-Debatte: Bestandsaufnahme und Konsequenzen* [The colonialism debate: Assessment and consequences] (2019).

10. Dirk Göttsche, "Postcolonial Concerns in Contemporary German Literature," in *German in the World: The Transnational and Global Contexts of German Studies*, ed. James Hodkinson and Benedict Schofield (2020), 126.

11. Uwe Klußmann and Dietmar Pieper, "'Konzept des rassistischen Terrors: Ist die koloniale Vergangenheit wirklich vergangen? Ein Interview mit dem Historiker Jürgen Zimmerer" [The concept of racist terror: Has the colonial past really passed? An interview with the historian Jürgen Zimmerer], *Der Spiegel*, March 6, 2016.

12. Gunnar Schupelius, "Die Betrachtung der Kolonialzeit ist einseitig und nicht mehr frei" [The debate on the colonial era is one-sided and no longer free], *B.Z. Freitag*, January 17, 2020.

13. European Center for Constitutional and Human Rights and Akademie der Künste, *Colonial Repercussions: Namibia; 115 years after the Genocide of the Ovaherero and Nama* (2019).

14. Christian Kopp, "Entschädigungen für den Völkermord? Nachfahren von Opfern des Genozids an den Ovaherero, Namas und San sprachen in Berlin auf dem Symposium 'Koloniales Erbe V—Das Beispiel Namibia'" [Compensation for the genocide? Descendants of victims of the genocide of the Ovaherero, Namas and San spoke in Berlin at the symposium 'Colonial Heritage V—The example of Namibia'], *Berliner-Zeitung*, December 1, 2019.

15. Akademie der Künste, "Colonial Repercussions Panel: Crimes Committed by Colonial Germany against the Herero and Nama," YouTube, January 27, 2018, https://www.youtube.com/watch?v=ynyiqkdORx8.

16. Steffen Eicker, *Der Deutsch-Herero-Krieg und das Völkerrecht* [The German-Herero War and international law] (2009).

17. Henning Melber, "Germany and Namibia: Negotiating Genocide," *Journal of Genocide Research* (2020): 503.

18. "Germany Apologises for Colonial-Era Genocide in Namibia," *Reuters*, May 28, 2021.

19. Ulrich van der Heyden, "Die Geschichte der deutschen Kolonialherrschaft [The history of German colonial rule]," *Archivführer zur deutschen Kolonialgeschichte* (2018).

20. "Coming to Terms with Compensation and Cultural Education on German Colonial Rule and Violent Crimes of the Colonial Era," Bundestag, 19th parliamentary term, Printed item #7109, 2019, https://kleineanfragen.de/bundestag/19.

21. Michelle Müntefering, "Ohne Erinnerung keine Zukunft" [No future without memory], speech on the 150th Anniversary of the Congo Conference, November 15, 2019.

22. Brigitte Lau, *History and Historiography* (1995).

23. Hinrich Schneider-Waterberg, *Der Wahrheit eine Gasse: Anmerkungen zum Kolonialkrieg in Deutsch-Südwestafrika, 1904* [An alley of truth: On the history of the Herero War in German Southwest Africa, 1904] (2011).

24. Werner Hillebrecht, "'Certain Uncertainties' or Venturing Progressively into Colonial Apologetics?" *Journal of Namibian Studies* (2007): 90, 91 (italics mine).

25. Melber, "Germany and Namibia," 509.

Index

A

AfD (Alternative for Germany), viii–ix, 254, 261
al-Husseini, Amin (Mufti of Jerusalem), 209–10
Allies, 5, 171, 173–74, 181–82, 214
Amin, Idi, 212, 216
anti-colonial resistance, 14, 44, 130, 153, 162, 244
anti-colonialism, German, 189, 230, 237, 241, 251
anti-Semitism, 180, 203, 212–13, 223, 232
anti-slavery, 68, 89
Arab nationalists, 207–8, 214
Arab-Nazi connection, 207–216
arms trade, 30, 43, 48
artificial boundaries, myth of, 34–35, 74
askari, 60, 76–78
Auschwitz, 226–30, 238, 251

B

Baleng, Johny, 93–94
Bebel, August, 63–64, 95–96, 173
Belgium, 4, 39, 131, 173
Bell, Chief Ndumbe, 86, 92, 95, 239
Bismarck, Otto von, 25–26, 28–33, 38–40, 60–63, 109, 129, 157, 197, 201, 218,
blood feuds, 132–34, 136, 146
Boer War, 82
Bose, Subhas Chandra, 206–7
Boxer Rebellion, 51, 158, 162, 171,
British Empire, x, 12–13, 97, 211, 218, 232
Bundestag, viii, 58, 257

C

Cameroon, 1–3, 6, 15, 33–34, 38, 55, 85–96, 104, 124, 168–69, 175, 187, 195, 201–2, 218, 235–38
cannibalism, 78, 133–36

effective occupation principle,
31–32, 61, 90, 131
Enlightenment, the, 8, 10, 12, 233,
251
epidemic, 46, 126, 150. *See also*
diseases
ethnicity, 21, 34–35, 45, 73–74, 111,
153, 188, 208, 212, 221, 231

F
Fanon, Frantz, 233, 251–52
fascism, 138, 179–83, 189, 191–92,
195, 197–98, 204–18, 221–25, 230,
232–33, 244, 251
First World War. *See* World War I
floggings, 16, 72, 77–78, 107, 113, 142,
149, 155
Foucault, Michel, 70, 128, 160
Frankfurter Allgemeine Zeitung, ix,
113–16, 252

G
Gandhi, Mohandas, 188, 204, 206–7
Ganisya, Martin, 69, 75
genocide, 8, 41–42, 50, 52–58, 221,
226–29, 242, 244, 255–57
German Cameroon. *See* Cameroon
German Democratic Republic
(GDR), 237–245, 250, 255, 260.
See also East Germany
German East Africa. *See* East
Africa
German military, 19–20, 44–46, 48,
53–54, 56, 61–62, 68, 76–79, 93,
101, 140, 153, 170, 228, 235
German settlers, 15, 41–48, 50, 52,
66, 68, 131, 152, 167, 181, 186, 228

German Southwest Africa. *See*
Southwest Africa
Göring, Heinrich, 44, 194
Göring, Hermann, 194, 220, 233
Great War. *See* World War I
Gruner, Hans, 112–13, 115–18

H
Hahl, Albert, 140–44, 148
head-hunting, 134–36, 139
Herero people, 9, 30, 41–58, 79–80,
120, 167, 176, 194, 220, 222, 227,
229–30, 241–42, 255–58
Hiery, Herman, 24, 129, 131–33, 136,
142–46 149–52
Hitler, Adolf, 6, 181, 191–94, 197–98,
201–2, 204, 206–13, 215–16,
218–21, 225, 230, 232
Holocaust, 10, 55, 151, 226–30, 254,
259–60
Honecker, Erich, 240–44
Hottentots. *See* Nama
human sacrifice, 15, 134

I
Islam, 81, 88–89, 210–11, 213, 216,
232
insurgency. *See* rebellion

J
Jews, 109, 197, 201–4, 208, 210–12,
218, 220, 223, 230,

K
Kirchner, Ernst Ludwig, 218–19
Koch, Robert, 46, 119–28, 203, 223,
247

Q

Qingdao, 157–63, 171–73, 186, 191, 235

R

racism, ix, 4, 14–15, 36, 111, 114, 126, 130, 142–43, 189, 204, 222, 228, 251–52

rebellions, 48, 50–52, 55, 62, 79–82, 152, 154–55, 158, 162, 168–69, 188, 229, 232–34, 242, 245

Reichstag, viii, 1, 5, 15–17, 30, 63, 65, 75, 103, 107, 110, 114, 142, 163, 184, 224

reparations, 57, 180, 255, 257–59

repatriation, 175, 184, 254

Reventlow, Count Ernst, 183, 202–4

Rohrbach, Paul, 42, 55

rubber, 39, 60, 92, 121, 129

S

Said, Edward, 27–28, 125, 252

Samoa, 32, 103, 129, 131, 144–47, 153, 185–86, 222, 225

Schnee, Heinrich, 6, 54, 62, 81, 89, 92, 135, 169–70, 176, 181, 183, 186, 190–195, 217, 224–25, 231

Seitz, Theodor, 55, 89, 195, 197, 218

sex trafficking, 80, 88, 137

slavery, 5, 8, 15, 17, 31, 38–39, 42–43, 59–60, 68–70, 74, 80–81, 88–89, 92–93, 103–4, 106, 112, 115, 117, 122, 148, 194, 222, 233, 235, 253, 255

sleeping sickness, 106, 119–22, 124–28, 223

Southwest Africa, 41–42, 45, 47, 53, 55–57, 109, 131, 167, 176, 194–95, 220, 227–28, 241–42

South West Africa People's Organization (SWAPO), 241–42, 244, 257

Soviet anti-colonialism, 166, 187

Spirit of Berlin, 25–40, 61, 70, 90, 97, 100, 131, 166, 177, 191, 194, 198, 203–4, 218, 221

Stalinism, 6, 116, 189, 196, 259

starvation, 46, 52, 240–41

T

taxes, 19, 21, 38–39, 79–80, 90, 95, 102–5, 113, 142, 144, 153–54, 163, 175

Third Reich, 180, 216–17, 222, 226

Third World, 4–5, 8, 124, 188, 197, 211–12, 215, 226, 231–33, 235, 248, 252

Togo, 8, 73, 90, 99–118, 120, 144, 148, 159–60, 167, 171, 174–75, 187, 218, 225, 235–36

Treaty of Versailles. *See* Versailles, Treaty of

tribal conflicts, 15, 41–44, 86, 106, 132–33, 138–39, 233

Trotha, Lothar von, 51–57, 62, 120, 158, 227–30, 241, 257

V

Versailles, Treaty of, 1, 3, 5–6, 95, 124, 165–77, 179–80, 182, 184–186, 190, 192, 194–96, 198, 202, 224, 236, 245, 247–48

W

Wahehe people, 61–62, 184, 213,
    235–36
Weimar Republic, 2, 40, 179,
    184–85, 196, 198, 224
West Africa, vii, 7, 16, 25, 29–30, 99,
    103, 117, 122, 127
West Germany, 243, 245, 247, 249
Western civilization, x, 11, 35–36,
    151
Windhoek, 220, 230, 256–57
Windhoek to Auschwitz thesis,
    227–30, 238, 251
Witbooi, Hendrik, 43–45, 47–48,
    51–52, 230
Woke ideology, viii–x, 6, 16, 22–24,
    36, 55–56, 166, 197, 219, 226, 245,
    247–61
World War I, vii, 5, 112, 119, 146,
    160, 180, 203, 229
World War II, 6, 182, 206, 237, 247

Z

Zech, Julius Graf von, 108–10, 112
Zimmerer, Jürgen, 9–11, 57–58, 73,
    127, 226–27, 250, 254